ence I.
hivak I.
Paul I.
George I.
Unimak I.
I.
SHUMAGIN I.
OCEAN
ALASKA PEN.
Kodiak I.
Yukon R.
Kuskokwim R.
RUSSIAN
AMERICA
Yukon R.
L. Iliamna
Kenai Bay
KENAI PEN.
Pavlovsk Harbor
(Kodiak)
Chugach Bay
Nuchek I.
Montague I.
Resurrection Bay
Mt. St. Elias
Yakutat
Yakutat Bay
Sitka
(Novo-Arkhangel'sk)

I0891951

Materials for the Study of Alaska History, No. 10

TWO VOYAGES TO RUSSIAN AMERICA, 1802-1807

By
G. I. Davydov

Translated by Colin Bearne

Edited by Richard A. Pierce

THE LIMESTONE PRESS
P.O. BOX 1604
KINGSTON, ONTARIO, CANADA K7L 5C8

Published in 1977 by The Limestone Press.

International Standard Book Number 0-919642-75-6

Printed in Canada by: Brown & Martin, Limited
Kingston, Ontario

CONTENTS

page

Preface vi

Introduction by Admiral Shishkov 1

Chapter I: My entry into the service of the Russian-American Company. Departure from St. Petersburg [19 April, 1802]. Arrival in Iakutsk [9 July] 22

Chapter II: Departure from Iakutsk [10 July]. What happened on the journey. Arrival in Okhotsk [11 August] 47

Chapter III: Preparations for the voyage. Departure from Okhotsk [23 August]. The *Elisaveta* runs aground near the Kurile Islands. We enter the bay of Tanaga Island. We pass Unalaga and Unalashka. Stormy weather and a serious leak in the ship. We land on the island of Kad'iak [1 November], where we spend the winter 82

Chapter IV: Meeting with Mr. Baranov. The state of company affairs in America. My occupations. Departure for Okhotsk [25 June 1803] 104

Chapter V: The voyage. Arrival in Okhotsk [22 August] and our return to St. Petersburg [5 February 1804] 124

PART TWO

Prefatory Note 146

I The position of Kad'iak and adjacent islands. The number of inhabitants, known as Koniagas 147

II The appearance of the islanders. Their artifacts and adornments 148

III The islanders' dress and its manufacture . 150

IV Their dwelling 154

V The Koniaga character 155

VI The upbringing of children 163

		page
VII	More on the habits and customs of the Koniagas	165
VIII	More on the habits and customs of the Koniagas. Their superstitions. Some examples of the ideas of the savages of northwest America	168
IX	Life-style and diet of the islanders. Some new customs	173
X	Illnesses and methods of treatment	177
XI	Burial rites	179
XII	The spread of Christianity. The islanders' religion	180
XIII	Marriage customs	182
XIV	Sports	182
XV	Festivals, dances and songs	183
XVI	History, geography, arithmetic and astronomy	185
XVII	Handicrafts	186
XVIII	Forms of warfare. Treatment of prisoners	187
XIX	Methods of government	190
XX	How the Russian-American Company administers the Koniagas, Aliaksintsy, Kinais, Chugach and other peoples	191
XXI	Notes on the Kinai people, the Copper River and northwest America	197
XXII	The Koniaga baidaras, baidarkas and hunting implements	202
XXIII	The climate of Kad'iak. Topography. Products of the soil	204
XXIV	Animals, birds, fishes and crustaceans of northwest America	208

Dialects 235

Index 250

ILLUSTRATIONS

Gavriil Ivanovich Davydov (from A.I. Alekseev, *Sud'ba russkoi Ameriki*, Magadan, 1975)

Okhotsk in 1786 (from Martin Sauer, *An Account of a Geographical and Astronomical Expedition to the Northern Parts of Russia*, London, 1802)

Unalashka settlement, about 1804 (from G.H. von Langsdorff, *Bermerkungen auf einer Reise um die Welt*...

Pavlovsk Harbor, Kad'iak, about 1804 (Langsdorff)

Aleut man (by Levashov, about 1768)

Aleut woman (levashov)

Toion Nankok, baptised Nikita, of Kadiak (by Tikhanov, 1818)

Map, routes taken by Khvostov and Davydov

PREFACE

DVUKRATNOE PUTESHESTVIE V AMERIKU MORSKIKH OFITSEROV KHVOSTOVA I DAVYDOVA, PISANNOE SIM POSLEDNIM (An account of two voyages to America by the naval officers Khvostov and Davydov, written by the latter), Parts I-II, St. Petersburg, 1810-1812, presented here for the first time in a complete English translation, is one of several major contributions to Alaska ethnography compiled during the Russian period.

The author, Gavriil Ivanovich Davydov (1784-1809), as indicated in the introduction by Admiral Shishkov, was enrolled in the Naval Cadet Corps at the age of eleven and in 1798 was commissioned. After serving in naval operations in the Baltic and North Seas, in April 1802 he and a friend, Lieutenant N.A. Khvostov, entered the service of the Russian-American Company. The two travelled across Siberia to Okhotsk and sailed from there on 29 August, reaching the company settlement on Kad'iak (Kodiak) two months later. They wintered on Kad'iak, at which time Davydov studied the island and its native population, and in the summer of 1803 made the return voyage to Okhotsk, again crossed Siberia, and arrived in St. Petersburg in February 1804. A few months later they traversed the whole route again, arriving in Russian America in 1805. In 1806, they took N.P. Rezanov to Spanish California with the *Juno* (see a portion of Khvostov's log in *Rezanov Reconnoiters California, 1806*, The Book Club of California, San Francisco, 1972). After the return voyage to Sitka they sailed to Okhotsk. In 1807, Khvostov and Davydov, commanding the ship *Juno* and the tender *Avos'*, in an effort to follow Rezanov's ambiguous orders, raided Japanese trading installations on Sakhalin, the Kurile Islands and Hokkaido. Upon returning to Okhotsk they were arrested for this operation but escaped. They fled to Iakutsk and from there were sent to St. Petersburg, where they were freed. (See Davydov's report to the company concerning this, published in P.A. Tikhmenev, *History of the Russian American Company: Documents*.)

In 1808, Davydov took part in operations in Finland against the Swedes. By then only twenty-five years of age, he appeared to have a distinguished career in store, but on the night of 4 October 1809 he and Khvostov, returning home after a convivial party with the American shipmaster Wolf, the naturalist Langsdorff, and the company official Kyrill Khlebnikov, fell in the Neva River and drowned.

At the urging of a friend, Vice-Admiral A.S. Shishkov, Davydov had already started to set down his experiences. He had covered only the first journey (1802-1804) but Shishkov, realizing the value of his account, managed to put together a second part from letters written by Davydov. The first part of the book consists of Davydov's description of the trip across Siberia, and his and Khvostov's experiences in America and their return across Siberia to European Russia; the second consists of ethnographic observations, a description of the climate and fauna of Kad'iak, and appended vocabularies of Tlingit and Kenai terms.

Transliteration follows the Library of Congress system, slightly modified. Geographic and ethnic terms in the original have been retained, thus Kad'iak for Kodiak, Koliuzh for Tlingit, and Kinai for Kenai. Natives of the Alaska Peninsula, which was then known as Aliaska or Aliaksa, are referred to as Aliaskintsy.

Richard A. Pierce

Queen's University
Kingston, Canada

ACKNOWLEDGEMENTS

For their help in various phases of this work, thanks are extended to Colin Bearne, of the University of Sussex, and Denise Bearne, for the translation; to Sylvia Carriere, who typed the manuscript; and to Ross Hough, of the Cartographic Laboratory of the Department of Geography, Queen's University, who made the maps.

Ed.

TWO JOURNEYS TO AMERICA

BY THE

NAVAL OFFICERS KHVOSTOV AND DAVYDOV

WRITTEN BY THE LATTER

PART ONE

INTRODUCTION BY VICE-ADMIRAL SHISHKOV

The printing of this account was undertaken while the two officers concerned were still alive, but before the second chapter could be finished their lives were suddenly cut short by a tragic accident. I thus consider it necessary to inform the reader both about the lives of these two men whose memory is forever worth cherishing, and about the condition in which Lieutenant Davydov left the unfinished narrative of his travels.

Nikolai Aleksandrovich Khvostov, son of the State Councillor Aleksandr Ivanovich Khvostov and Katerina Alekseevna Khvostova, née Shelting, was born on 28th July 1776 and in 1783 was enrolled as a cadet in the Naval Academy. He first saw service at sea, serving in the Marine Guard against the Swedes. At fourteen years of age he had already been in two major naval engagements and received a gold medal for his bravery. When peace was concluded with Sweden in 1791 he was commissioned. After he had completed several tours of duty in the Baltic, in 1795 he was attached to a squadron under the command of Vice-Admiral Khanykov, which was detailed to guard the English coast. After a year this squadron was sent back to Russia, but when it arrived in Copenhagen part of it, under the command of Rear-Admiral Makarov, was again sent to England, and Khvostov went with it. This section spent a year there and then returned to Kronstadt. The following year, 1798, with the help of the English fleet, the squadron was newly fitted out for action against the common enemy, the French and their allies. Vice-Admiral Makarov was given the command. Khvostov did not miss this third opportunity for a journey to England and the commission lasted for about three years. When the English squadron, which was under the command of Vice-Admiral Mitchell, took over the Dutch fleet then lying at anchor off Texel under the command of Rear-Admiral Storey, they were joined by two of our vessels, the *Mstislav* and the *Retvizan*. Khvostov, now a lieutenant, was on the latter. The tragic and horrible events which at that time overtook some of the English ships and our *Retvizan* are well known (see a description of this in a collection of nautical journals which I have published, Part II, page 108). Khvostov was in no small way involved in saving his ship. Yet in those very hours when death stared him in the face he wrote to one of his friends--

> our situation was pretty desperate. All the other vessels were sailing past us while we were stuck on a sand bar, serving as a buoy to the others! All hope we had of taking part in the fighting and the capture

> of the Dutch fleet had vanished. In our great frustration we began to grow angry with the pilot, to curse and reproach him, but he was already more dead than alive from shame. The English ship *America* also ran aground and this gave us some satisfaction. Although we should not be pleased at someone else's misfortunes, many factors make us do this: at least the Englishmen cannot say that only a Russian ship has run aground, and perhaps for want of two ships Mitchell will decide not to give battle and then if we do get off we shall be able to have a share in the honors.

And in fact, despite the terrible suffering that they had to go through that night, on the following morning they managed to get off the sand bar and take their place in the battle line next to the others, and though their ship was almost half destroyed they were still ready to fight the enemy. From this single example it can be seen with what firmness of spirit, amongst fear and confusion, this young man acted, and what fearlessness and love of fame burned in his soul!

On his return to Russia Khvostov had to remain at a shore station for about eighteen months because there were no other expeditions going anywhere. However much he loved his father, mother, brothers and sisters, however much he enjoyed the contentment of being with them, he felt he was not born to spend his life in peace, and tranquil idleness. He was dissatisfied with the normal shore duties, and awaited impatiently the opportunity which would open a path to him for some daring undertaking. An unusual devotion to his family and an unlimited love of fame were his two main qualities. We shall see to what heroic deeds these led him and what sacrifices they cost him.

His father, after twenty years of continuous bad luck, had been deprived of his modest estate and remained with his small family in a penniless condition. His son, without revealing his intention, found an opportunity to meet His Majesty the Emperor. He looked desperate and throwing himself on his knees besought the Emperor to look with favor on his impoverished parents. His Majesty was surprised to see before him an officer in such a condition, and thinking that out of poverty he was seeking a favor for himself, he ordered him to get up and calm himself. Several hours later Khvostov was brought a bounty from the Emperor of one thousand rubles. He would not accept the money and asked the man who brought it to return it, and to tell the Emperor that as he, Khvostov, was in receipt of a salary he did not need the money, and that he would not have troubled the Emperor on his own account, but that it was for the sake of his father and mother, who were in such need. This message was then conveyed to the Emperor who ordered him to accept the thousand rubles. In the meantime, he had made enquiries about the matter of the father's situation and had ordered that he be allotted an annual pension of one thousand rubles. The son was overjoyed and immediately sent off the thousand rubles he had been given to his mother, who was at that time living in the country, and soon thereafter he had the pleasure of informing his father of the pension he had been granted.

Thus one of his desires had been satisfied and another was fulfilled shortly afterwards. Chamberlain Nikolai Petrovich Rezanov, the prime mover and patron of the American Company (and who later became our plenipotentiary ambassador in Japan) who was personally acquainted with Khvostov and who had heard of his skill and daring, suggested to him that he travel overland to Okhotsk and from there to America on an American Company ship. There was no need to press the proposal with Khvostov. He agreed on the spot and asked only for five days' leave so that he might travel to the country and bid farewell to his father and mother. That same day he happened to be with some friends where he met Midshipman Davydov who, though still very young, was reckoned a good officer. He told his friends about the proposed journey to America, and this filled Davydov (who was not yet eighteen) with a burning desire to accompany him. Davydov's straightforwardness and boldness were much to Khvostov's liking so he took him to see Rezanov, and they both entered service with the American Company. A special edict then in effect allowed naval officers, without resigning their commission, to enter into service with a trading company. Khvostov immediately set off for the country. The surprise and sorrow of all his relatives may well be imagined, especially that of his mother. Their farewell was full of anguish and tears, and he, who loved his parents dearly, felt all the anguish that could tear at his soul. He joked about his mother's affection, and pretended to be cheerful, allowing no outward sign of his suppressed tears to appear. Then he tore himself from their embraces and farewells, leapt on his horse, gave it the whip, and galloped away. He had hardly travelled any distance when Nature took the upper hand and punished him for his transgressions. He fell into a faint and when he regained his senses he paid the debt in bitter sobs.

On his return to St. Petersburg there was little delay before he and Davydov and their companions set out for America. In this book the reader will find a description of their first journey.

After two years they returned from America. It seemed as though their wishes had been fulfilled: they had completed a long journey overland, sailed across rarely visited seas, and had seen a multitude of different towns, countries and peoples. They had performed no small service for the American Company, brought it profits and returned safely. Since they were never interested in making their own fortunes they came back much the same as they had departed, that is: the sum total of their worldly possessions was what they stood up in. Khvostov, however, had saved up eight hundred rubles which he wanted to give to his mother but she would not accept them. Thus all these circumstances gave one cause to expect that they would leave the American Company and return once more to the Fleet. Khvostov's mother and father both wished for this but, since they did not want to choose his destiny for him, they did not dare advise him. In the meantime the American Company, which was very pleased with the two officers, invited them to travel once more to America, offering them twice the salary they had received before; in other words each would receive four thousand rubles a year. Two or three months passed in doubt and uncertainty but finally it became obvious that a decision must be made as to whether to go or to stay. Although Khvostov made ready to go with the same cheerfulness that he had shown before, not revealing the slightest sign of unwillingness, yet regardless of how careful he was in front of his mother and father, it was sometimes noticeable that he was forcing himself to remain calm, and that this second journey weighed heavily upon him. Such presentiments could not be hidden from the searching gaze of his mother and close relatives. When they tried to dissuade him from making the decision, however, which had not even hardened in his own mind, he at once put on a cheerful face and showed himself to be unmovably firm, so that his behavior began to seem something of an enigma. He could not be motivated by curiosity to see distant lands since he had already been there and any prospect of making his name famous was vague and unreliable. The sum offered him as a salary by the American Company, although no small amount with regard to his position, was nevertheless not likely to be a motivating factor because of his complete selflessness and lack of preoccupation with amassing wealth, and also because of his experiences on the first voyage. Thus the clash of emotions which was evident in him and his inner struggle concealed some kind of secret, which no one could guess at, and which was not revealed until the conditions of the undertaking with the American Company were definitely confirmed. Then some two or three days before his departure Khvostov went to his mother and father and took them the money which, as we have already mentioned, his mother refused to take. In addition he asked them to read a certain paper. It contained an undertaking by the American Company which stated that as long as Khvostov was in America half of the four thousand rubles due to him should be paid in St. Petersburg to his mother and father. When his mother read the paper her first impulse was to tear it up, and weeping bitterly, she exclaimed, "What a sacrifice you are making for us!" But without giving her a chance to finish, he threw himself on his knees before her, kissed her hands and told her to hear him out. The matter, he said, was already settled, he could remain no longer, that was why he begged her at least not to deprive him of this comfort, which would give him pleasure during the long separation from her and which would remind him to take care of himself for their sakes. With these and similar arguments he eventually persuaded his mother and father to accept the aid he was offering them. And thus was revealed his secret reason for wanting to go to America. This was a rare and striking example of filial love! What was it he was undertaking to make life easier for his parents? Not only had he thrown himself at the feet of the Emperor and with the favors thus so graciously received managed to ease their lot somewhat, but he was devoting his life to patient sufferings, dangers, hard work and, in order to keep his own parents in a comfortable condition, would endure a long exile in distant lands among savage peoples. It is difficult at first to give credence to such an heroic deed but, to humanity's credit, it is all true, a living fairy tale.

When everything was subsequently settled and he and his colleague, Davydov (for the latter would not part company with Khvostov) were preparing for the journey, then Khvostov seemed to have within him the flame of a new ardor for the expedition. The reason for this was that one day he had called on the Minister of Commerce, who had asked him if he would still take it on if the expedition demanded of him even greater efforts and risks. To this Khvostov answered with his habitual fervor, that the more dangerous it was the better he would like it. At the same time the question had awakened within him the hope that an opportunity might arise whereby he might show more than the usual amount of good service. Thus they set off (14th May, 1804) on their journey.

Here we must inform the reader that some time before their return to St. Petersburg, Actual State Councilor and Chamberlain Rezanov had been dispatched as ambassador to Japan on the vessels *Nadezhda* and *Neva*, under the command of Captain Lieutenant (now Captain) Kruzenshtern. The Japanese Government, as is well known, refused to accept him as a representative, would not embark upon friendly trade talks and forbade our ships to enter their ports. All this may be examined in more detail in the account of the voyage published by Captain Kruzenshtern.

In the meantime Khvostov and Davydov arrived in Okhotsk towards the end of August, and left there for America on the ship *Mariia*. Their vessel sprang a very serious leak and, in order to save the ship, they were forced to put into the port of Petropavlovsk. Because the autumn was drawing on they spent the winter there. In the following year (1805) in May, the frigate *Nadezhda* arrived with the Ambassador Rezanov on board after its abortive journey to Japan. So Khvostov and Davydov joined forces with Rezanov and came directly under his disposition and command. Soon afterwards Kruzenshtern set off on the return journey to Russia with his two vessels, while Rezanov stayed in the area to direct the affairs of the American Company, setting off for America with Khvostov and Davydov.

They visited the islands of St. Paul, Unalashka and Kad'iak, finally arriving at the island of Sitka at the harbor known as Novo-Arkhangel'sk. Here Rezanov, feeling that he had been insulted by the Japanese as Ambassador of Russia, searched his mind for some way to revive their fading respect for our flag and remind them that by adopting a hostile and difficult posture they would be putting themselves in danger from our armed might; but that peaceful and friendly relations would be both advantageous and useful for them. This alone, he believed, would compel them to begin peaceful trading relations with us. His hopes in this were more than ever confirmed by the fact that during his stay in Japan he discovered by secret means that a great split had opened up between the two authorities ruling the country, the spiritual and the civil. The civil authority and the people were willing to accept our ambassador and to trade with us, but the spiritual authority opposed this and held the upper hand. Consequently, the slightest reinforcement we could give to the civil authority would force the spiritual authority into the background. Basing his hopes on these factors he made the following proposals. Near Japan is the fertile island of Sakhalin whose inhabitants form a separate people from the Japanese. At one time (about sixty years ago) we had made attempts to land and settle there but it was not known what happened subsequently to the settlements established there. The Japanese had occupied the island and settled there, subduing the people of Sakhalin and treating them as slaves, very harshly. Rezanov proposed that an expedition should be sent to this island to drive the Japanese away. All of the latters' installations on the island should be destroyed, moveable objects should be taken away, the remainder should be given to the local inhabitants or burned. The people of Sakhalin should be taken under our protection, the village elders should be issued with silver medals, and they should all be declared to be Russian subjects. In addition several Japanese should be taken prisoner, and a special attempt should be made to capture one of their priests with a temple and all the idols and religious objects in it. This last he considered necessary because the captured Japanese were to be taken to Okhotsk, where they would be kept in as comfortable conditions as possible and their priest would be allowed to perform his various duties and rituals. When a year had passed they should all be taken back to Japan, so that they could bear witness to the way we had treated them and so create a favorable disposition towards us among their fellow countrymen.

Rezanov considered trade with Japan not only necessary for the discovery of new sources of wealth but as the only means of feeding our settlements in these breadless and hungry regions. Because of this he viewed the insulting actions and the refusal of the Japanese to accept our ambassador as a good opportunity to compel them to comply by force of arms, and he did not want to let opportunity go by. But though he had this plan in mind, it still remained for him to work out the details of such an important expedition. The difficulties were as follows: first, the passage to Japan was very little known; second, although he was assuming that the people of the island and the Japanese who ruled them were not warlike peoples, there was simply no comparison between their numbers and ours; third, he was in no position to send more than two ships, and insufficiently armed ones at that; with sixty or seventy men, no good fighters, although chosen from hunters of all nationalities. We shall presently discover on what, in spite of all the difficulties, he placed his hopes.

Since he was persuaded both of the advantage and necessity of such an expedition, he ordered two ships to be specially built and wrote to Khvostov and Davydov the following letter:

> My dear Nikolai Aleksandrovich and Gavrilo Ivanovich,
>
> Your first voyage to America showed me your firm resourcefulness, and your safe return to Europe demonstrated your experience and skill. Your second voyage to these regions has shown the depth of your patriotism. Now, finally, after I myself have gone on several cruises with you I have been left with a very favorable impression as to your magnanimity in placing the common good above all else. In the manager of these regions we have another example of enthusiasm and hard work who will some day be appreciated, more likely by posterity than ourselves. Taking advantage of such a happy meeting of like minds all agreed on a single aim, I have endeavored to organize for next year an expedition which may open a new avenue of trade and give the support needed to this region and fill many of its requirements. For our purposes we shall need two warships--a brig and a tender. They may be built here, and I have already forwarded to the manager my proposals on this matter. It now remains

for me, my dear sirs, to inform you that the first vessels in this first expedition should also be crewed by the first officers. Since I am not an Admiralty official I can only bear witness to your efforts, activities and achievements. Being unable to expound in depth in this area about which I know nothing I can only judge superficially by means of simple comparisons based on my observations while working with you, but I am convinced in advance that your efforts will justify my opinions, and I shall not cease to feel sincere respect for those great and noble actions which have given you, in the eyes of all those who love their Country, the right to be considered first class officers. I ask you now, as my friends, ready to sacrifice yourselves for the general good, to which cause we have so readily devoted ourselves, to be ready to assume command over the vessels I have mentioned, dividing them between yourselves according to seniority, and to this end now to set about looking over the drawings with which we have been supplied by the gentlemen shipwrights. If you approve of the drawings, you will please take part in the supervision of their construction, so that it should be successfully completed by the end of April, and that we might already be under sail in the first week of May. I am aware that many items will be lacking, but when was a heroic deed achieved without overcoming obstacles? They do not frighten us, and will only serve to enhance our reputations. I do not deem it yet necessary to expand upon the purpose of this expedition and you will receive from me a more detailed exposition of this at an appropriate time. In the building of sound ships the efforts give fair promise of success. I must admit that, for my part, I await with impatience the results of your bravery, and so with a common effort we shall undertake this great adventure, and we shall show the world that in this happy century a handful of Russians is putting all its effort into those great matters in which millions of foreign peoples have taken part for centuries.

With absolute respect I have the honor to be, my dear sirs, your most obedient servant

(On the original signed: Nikolai Rezanov)

No. 475, August 29th, 1805, Baranov Island, Novo-Arkhangel'sk harbor. To the gentlemen officers of the Fleet Lieutenant Khvostov and Midshipman Davydov.

When such arrangements as were necessary for the proposed expedition had thus been made, Rezanov dispatched, in the presence of Khvostov and Davydov, a report on the matter to the Court, and to the Minister of Commerce, His Excellency Count Nikolai Petrovich Rumiantsov. To the latter, in his description of the benefits to be derived from such an expedition, he wrote that he would never have decided on such a daring undertaking if he had not been lucky enough to have under his command Lieutenant Khvostov, an officer filled with ardor, enthusiasm, skill and exemplary fearlessness.

While construction of one of the two vessels intended for the expedition was still proceeding, an opportunity presented itself for the purchase of yet another, from the shipmaster Wolf, who had put into the port by chance on his way from the United States of America. This vessel was placed under the command of Khvostov and given the name *Juno* [Iunona]; while the other, newly built one was given to Davydov, and given what in terms of this expedition was a very appropriate name *Avos'* [Forward!]. They remained at Sitka until 25 February 1806. At that time a desperate shortage of bread, which caused dreadful starvation, forced Rezanov to undertake a voyage to California on the *Juno*. This journey took several months. They were received very graciously by the Spaniards and returned to Novo-Arkhangel'sk (9 June) bringing with them a sizeable quantity of wheat, thus putting an end to the starvation which was by then widespread. The tender *Avos'* was finally completed and everything was ready for the expedition. On 25 July Rezanov himself put to sea with the two ships, with the intention of supervising the undertaking personally, but after several days at sea, to be precise on 8 August, he altered his arrangements. He now gave Khvostov a set of orders in which he recommended the policy on Sakhalin to which we have referred above, and gave him the task of successfully completing the brave venture which had been undertaken with such difficulty. He also gave him the task of compelling all his subordinates to sign an undertaking binding them to say nothing about the expedition outside their own company, and to keep the whole matter a complete secret. Of himself he added that although he had wished to be a witness and a participant in their adventures so that he might bear a report at first hand most humbly to His Imperial Majesty, the time was now late and he had to hurry back to St. Petersburg. In the circumstances he counselled the following change of plan: Midshipman Davydov should continue his course to the islands of Sakhalin and Matmai and there, in the bay known as Aniva, or in Laperouse Strait, he should await the return of the *Juno*. Khvostov, on the other hand should convey him, Rezanov, to Okhotsk, go to Aniva, join forces with Davydov and carry out their instructions in combination.

When the *Juno* arrived in Okhotsk Rezanov went ashore, and ordered Khvostov to stand ready to sail on the tide for the continuation of the planned and already begun expedition. But he also asked him to hand over the instructions he had been given on how to carry it out. When Khvostov was just ready to raise anchor, Rezanov returned the orders he had taken from him, with an addition at the end. When Khvostov read the added passage, he hurried to Rezanov for a personal explanation, but discovered that Rezanov had already left Okhotsk. The passage that had been added read as follows:

> On your arrival in Okhotsk I find it necessary to expound once more upon the task entrusted to you. The crack which has been discovered in the mainmast, the contrary winds which delayed us on our voyage here, and the late autumn season itself now compel you to hasten back to America. The time of your rendezvous with the tender in Aniva Bay has already passed. There can be no hope of any large catches of fish there now to sustain us, and, taking all these circumstances into account, I deem it necessary, in contrast to previous instructions, to dispatch you to America to support the population of Novo-Arkhangel'sk. According to plan, the tender *Avos'* will return, even if they receive no further orders. But if the winds allow you to make a speedy passage to Aniva Bay, then try to be generous to the people of Sakhalin, giving them presents and medallions, and try to discover how the Japanese in charge there are situated. The carry-out out of this commission alone will suffice to bring you honor and, more than anything, your return to America, which will bring a concrete advantage and should be the first and main aim of all your efforts. Should you rendezvous with the tender, convey the same injunctions to those on board her. Also any unforeseen circumstances which may arise on your voyage you will manage to the advantage of the company; your skill and experience will of course enable you to take the best possible advantage of this last injunction. I, for my part, am extremely sorry that the harbor we happen to be in is not suitable for replacing our mast, and that a combination of circumstances has forced me to change my plans.
>
> (24 September 1806. No. 609. The original is signed: Nikolai Rezanov.)

One can easily imagine in what a difficult position Khvostov was placed by this vague and ambiguous codicil. How should it be understood? How should he act, without fear of error? First Rezanov had said nothing to Khvostov about any change in the plan for the expedition, and had given him back the very same instructions which he had taken from him: consequently he had returned them with no other purpose in mind but that they should be carried out. Second, Rezanov could not himself postpone or alter such an important expedition which had taken so long to prepare, and an account of which had been passed to His Imperial Majesty, without the desire of the government, yet in his codicil he had mentioned none of this and nothing which would make it seem that he was acting as he did because he had received instructions from the government. On the contrary, he made it quite clear that these were instructions emanating from him personally, not abandoning the expedition, but simply postponing its execution for a while because of the reasons stated: the mast was not sound, the best time for fishing had already passed, and there was an urgent need to return to America. Yet at the same time he gave orders that if time allowed they were to call in at Aniva Bay to get on good terms with the people of Sakhalin and to observe the Japanese, adding as encouragement that the carrying out of this alone would bring Khvostov much honor, and then finishing with the words: "I, for my part, am extremely sorry that the harbor we happen to be in is not suitable for replacing our mast, and that a combination of circumstances has forced me to change my plans." Was not Khvostov bound to find such a codicil extremely confusing? An important, long prepared for, expensive State Expedition (for Khvostov could consider it as little else), was halted because of an unsound mast, while the tender which had been sent on ahead had been ordered to rendezvous, join forces and in concert act in accordance with the instructions. This tender would be deceived into thinking it was to be reinforced by the *Juno*, and might perish there, or be captured by the Japanese. The very piece added to the instructions was ambiguous--it instructed him to go to America, but to call in at Japan, did not demand of Khvostov that he carry out the instructions, but added at the same time that he might receive encouragement to do so from the fact that *this alone* would bring him much credit, and consequently assumed that he would demonstrate his enthusiasm even more in his further execution of the plans. Then the commander apologized for his commands, giving one to understand that he would not have given them if the port of Okhotsk had not been so unfavorable a place for replacing masts.

Khvostov had to take some kind of decision on all this by himself. It may be that another man in this situation, having regard to his own peace of mind and safety, would not have wished in such circumstances to expose his life to hard work and an uncertain fate, having the opportunity, in the event of government displeasure at the plan not having been carried out, to justify himself by referring to the codicil, but Khvostov saw the matter in a different light. He thought: "The expedition has not been abandoned, but simply postponed. Consequently if I do not carry it out now I shall have to carry it out in the coming Spring. In the meantime, this unexpected delay causes a great deal of chaos, and puts the tender which has been sent on ahead, in great danger. The reason for this delay, on the other hand, as was made clear in the addition to the instructions, was the belief that I would be unable to carry out successfully the task entrusted to me because it is so late in the year and because of the unsound mast on the ship. All the signs would seem to indicate that the commander would like to go ahead but feels that it is impossible. Duty compels me to exceed his expectations."

With this thought Khvostov raised anchor and set sail for Japan. On his arrival there he failed to discover the tender. A new obstacle! But it did not stop Khvostov. He went ashore and alone set about carrying out what they had been instrcted to do in concert; he carried out some of the orders, captured the Japanese warehouses and, taking on board a cargo of wheat, set off for the harbor of Petropavlovsk, in the hope of finding the tender there, and on his arrival he did in fact find it. Davydov had been forced to leave his post without waiting for the *Juno* because of illness amongst the crew and much damage caused to his ship. Their further activities were brought to a stop by the winter. They accompanied the *Juno* to Petropavlovsk.

The following year (1807), without waiting for the ice to clear completely from the sea, they broke through it, brought out their ships and immediately set off to complete the undertaking which they had begun. On their arrival in Aniva they carried out to the letter the instructions they had been given (as they describe in detail in the account of their voyage), they took on board sizeable quantities of wheat, and eventually set sail for Okhotsk with the intention of reporting there to the authorities, and of collecting there from the Company offices all that was necessary to transport to America, to Sitka Island, to the harbor of Novo-Arkhangel'sk, and thus fulfil the final instruction.

Thus, with the main part of their mission successfully completed, they returned well pleased with themselves to Okhotsk, where they expected to be greeted with praise and gratitude for the feats of valor they had performed. But a completely different fate awaited them there. Before Rezanov had reached St. Petersburg he had fallen ill in Krasnoiarsk, and had died there. The then commandant of the port of Okhotsk (soon to be replaced, as a result of widespread complaints in the region), Captain Second Rank Bukharin, his mind preoccupied with the notion that these ships had come back laden with gold and great riches, under the pretext of suspicions about the expedition, alleged that it had been carried out wilfully and, so that there should be no witnesses as to the cargo, placed both vessels under arrest. Without any orders from the government he put both Khvostov and Davydov in prison, as State Criminals, under armed guard. Everything was taken away from them, even their clothes and shoes. For a whole month they were treated in a most inhuman and bestial fashion. This savagery increased with each day. Khvostov and Davydov were confined separately, they were isolated and each knew nothing about the fate of the other. They could see that a most agonizing death had been marked out for them, that is for five or six months, until orders freeing them arrived from St. Petersburg, they would slowly die from the bad air, filth and hunger. In these extreme conditions they had no other means of saving themselves but to escape. But how could they wrest themselves out of such a strong prison and such strict surveillance? Where could they go without food, without clothes, and without money? The nearest town was Iakutsk, about one thousand versts away.

Yet even in the very depths of baseness there hides human kindness, and innocence will find its own protectors. Our two unfortunates, by their kindness, gained the general love of the people of Okhotsk, and even of the guards set with swords drawn to guard them who, when they observed such undeserved suffering, felt sorry for them. Khvostov communicated to Davydov through his guards that he intended to escape and he named the night, the time and the place where he would wait for Davydov. The latter, for his part, sent through his guards his agreement to the time and place mentioned. Thus while on the one hand in one of their peers they could observe only unbridled harshness, on the other they found that they had awoken sympathy in the hearts of the simple people around them who, without any thought for themselves, agreed to save them. They paid no heed to any danger to themselves, or the savage tortures which threatened them. It is impossible in such circumstances not to wonder at the infinite variety in human hearts, in which may be seen both the light of heaven and the murk of hell. Khvostov and Davydov had already grown weak in health and had begun to feel bouts of sickness which made them frightened lest they should end their lives on the difficult path they had chosen, yet the unavoidable fate which awaited them in Okhotsk forced them to choose the lesser of two evils.

The long awaited night came on. They quit the prison leaving as a defence for their guards handwritten notes in which they claimed to have made them sleep by giving them opium and met at the spot they had arranged. It is easy to imagine the joy at their reunion. They set out on their journey immediately. The generosity of several of the inhabitants, to whom they revealed themselves, saw them supplied with a rifle each and some dry biscuits. They were afraid of being pursued and they chose to travel through the forests, the swamps, and the rapids where no human foot had trod before them. To begin with they were exhausted, they grew weak and began to think that some cave or other would become a tomb for them; but the hand of the Lord strengthened them. The further they travelled, the more their strength was renewed. The fresh air and their energetic activities after their complete immobility and the stuffiness which they had had to bear for almost two months in prison, returned to them their former health and strength. The long journey, however, the hard physical effort and the lack of proper food exhausted them all over again, so that after suffering many deprivations and hardships, exhausted by starvation, and emaciated, they entered Iakutsk with their clothes in rags and hardly alive.

The civic authorities at Iakutsk had already received instructions from Okhotsk to apprehend the fugitives and to check whether they *had any gold with them.* This noteworthy phrase was actually contained in the letter to the constable. From this it may be concluded what an enormous influence was wielded by the word *gold* over the imagination of the person who wrote it: he even imagined them to have gold on their persons after they had gone through barren and hitherto unexplored wastes, at risk to their lives, so that a piece of biscuit had become a great treasure to them. The constable, as a consequence of receiving the order, apprehended them in Iakutsk. But soon after this the governor-general of Siberia, after hearing of the arrest, ordered them to be brought to Irkutsk. In the meantime when reports from them reached St. Petersburg the news was conveyed to His Majesty the Emperor, and an order came back from the Navy Ministry that they should not be detained anywhere.

Finally, after four years of wanderings, in 1808, they returned to St. Petersburg. They had hardly had more than two or three months' rest from their long labors when the commander-in-chief of the Army in Finland, His Excellency Count Buksgevden, found out about their return from America. When he heard of their exemplary skill and bravery he wrote to the Minister of the Navy, Chichagov, and demanded that precisely these two officers be seconded to him for use against the enemy. The Navy Minister asked if they were willing. The American Company was not very keen to release them. Without, however, paying any heed to their straitened circumstances, nor to all the insults and injuries to which they had been subjected, they answered that they were always ready to serve His Imperial Majesty and the Fatherland.

They set out straightway for Finland, and three days after their arrival there they put to sea in boats. This detachment, under the command of Captain Selivanov was sent, for a number of reasons, to one of the islands occupied by the enemy. It consisted of twenty long boats and one sailing vessel, of which fifteen of the boats in the van were placed under the special command of Khvostov, while Davydov was in command of the remaining five. The whole episode is described in Lieutenant Khvostov's account. In the battle which took place on 18 August between the islands of Sudtsal and Vortsella, Khvostov was mainly responsible for victory over the enemy, who came across them by chance and outnumbered them by three to one. This can be seen in the printed dispatch about the battle, in which amongst other things it is said:

> Captain First Rank Selivanov in his report to the commander-in-chief, made special reference to the bravery of the whole party, and mentioned Lieutenant Khvostov in glowing terms. The latter provided an example of amazing fearlessness, regardless of the constant hail of bullets, and heedless of the fact that four of the sloops under him had been sunk and that of six oarsmen only one was left, he advanced and defeated the enemy just the same. The commanders on land also mentioned his bravery to the commander-in-chief. All the lower ranks praised him and, in general, wherever he appeared, their courage was redoubled.

It is well known that when the commander-in-chief heard the noise of firing and thus learnt of the approach of superior enemy forces which had not been considered so close at hand, he did not expect even one of our boats to be saved, and when the detachment returned whole and Khvostov reported that they had won, then he was so pleased that as he happened at that time to be passing the watch, who saluted him, he pointed to Khvostov, saying, "It is not I who am the victor."

Similar descriptions, and accounts by other eyewitnesses to the fighting on land of this officer's valorous conduct, seemed to exceed all probability, so that the commander-in-chief wished to have the opinions of the lower ranks, and to do this he went ashore specially to the spot where the boats had been pulled up. He asked the soldiers and sailors--"Tell me, lads, who was responsible for our victory?" They all replied with one voice: "Khvostov!" This is underlined by the use in the report of the words: "All the lower ranks praised him." It could be said that the hand of Providence saved him in this battle, four times he had the boats under him smashed by enemy shells and bullets filling them with water, and four times he rose up again from the depths of the sea and his courage did not once flag. He was to be seen everywhere in the van, giving orders encouraging his men and shouting to them to follow him. When the first boat was blown up under him, and he had been dragged out of the water and was sitting in another one, his first words were--"Forward!", and when the shell which hit this second boat in the bows made a hole in it and killed several men, causing panic and confusion, when he saw water pouring into the boat, and because nothing could be found at that moment to stop up the hole and the men wanted to turn back, he ripped off his uniform, ordered them to use that and gave a shout of "Row on!" Deeds like this earned him universal respect.

Although he was not wounded Khvostov nevertheless

felt the effects of the adventures he had been through all over his body. In order that he should rest the commander-in-chief allowed him to spend some time on his yacht--but he did not rest there for long. Soon afterwards he and Davydov set off to see Vice-Admiral Miasoedov who was in another area in charge of the rowing and sailing ships allotted to him. There, in addition to several missions fraught with difficulty and danger, they were victors in two battles, one of which took place on 6 September near the island of Pal'vo, and the other on 19 September near the island Tevsalo. Khvostov was given a fairly sizeable force with which he everywhere showed extreme alertness, skill in tactics, and lack of fear; he defeated a superior enemy force, and Vice-Admiral Miasoedov bears this out in his reports where he praises Khvostov in glowing terms. Davydov was with Khvostov all the time and was slightly wounded in the leg; he also everywhere exhibited exemplary courage and was highly praised. When with the onset of winter the campaign came to an end the commander-in-chief wished to reward them for all they had done, and for their bravery. He ordered them assigned to his suite and transferred to St. Petersburg where at their own request they were to remain until their health was restored. But Fate everywhere placed barriers to their promotion and happiness ....
.... [two lines of dots in text] ....
....

Subsequently, on 4th October (1809) the above mentioned United States shipmaster Wolf arrived here, with whom they had been on the island of Sitka and with whom they had travelled together to California. Their relationship was most cordial. This explorer, together with Professor Langsdorff who was there, and was also a friend of theirs, had made an effort to contact them, and as he was going to Kronstadt the following day to join his ship and sail back to America they agreed to spend the evening at Langsdorff's, who lived on Vasil'ev Island. They spent some time there, and arrived at two in the morning at the Isakievskii Bridge, which by that time had already been raised. As they had some pressing reason to be home early in the morning they were very eager to cross to the other side. Then (as it emerged later from accounts of the incident) a barge passed under the bridge, and they must have tried to leap from one end of the bridge onto the barge and then from the barge onto the other bank. But something, we do not know what, went wrong and they both suddenly fell into the water and were drowned. The night was very dark, and the current very fast under the bridge, and the strong wind aided the Neva in dragging them down to its bosom.

Such was the end of these two such excellent, worthy, and unfortunate voyagers. Their bodies were never found. We will remain silent about the sorrow of their friends and the anguish of their poor parents--no pen could describe them.

After this brief sketch of their lives I must explain in what state the accounts which are here published were left. Davydov on his return from Finland lived for a while in my house. When I read some of the handwritten notes and jocular letters which at various times he had written to some of his friends about his stay in America, I found many good passages in them, and many an interesting curiosity. I advised him to tidy up the notes and put them into sequence--thus producing a description of his two voyages to America. But he declined, saying all the papers he needed, the descriptions for instance, notes, sketches and maps etc. had been taken from him in Okhotsk and, together with all his belongings, had doubtless perished. I was insistent, however, that he should, at least from those manuscripts remaining, recreate a narrative using memory to fill the gaps. He resisted this also by saying that he had no time; for he held a commission full time and had been ordered to report to Kronstadt. I sought permission for him to remain here and pursue his writing at leisure. When the account of the first voyage had been half-written, I looked through his notebooks and finding them worthy of publication, I made representations to the Minister concerning their publication by the Admiralty Department. The Minister agreed to this and proposed to the Department that they be read as a scientific work. The collection was accepted for publication and the Department ordered it to be printed. Meanwhile Davydov went on writing. He had completed the account of the first voyage, but had still not started on the second. When death put a stop to his efforts only eight signatures of the first voyage had been printed. The account of the second voyage by then was still in manuscript form and consisted of notes and letters to friends, to such an extent that putting them into a sequential narrative demanded no small amount of ingenuity, time and effort. I keep them amongst my own papers and hope (in so far as I am able to do so without the voyager himself) with time to collate them in such a way that they will be suitable for publication. The main body of the account consists of his diary; as far as the letters to friends are concerned they were not written with the object of publication in view. They are full of such detail and anecdote as is usual between close friends. There is also, however, much there that is both witty and amusing.

Finally I think the reader will not consider it an unnecessary addition if, in order to aid one's memory of these two voyagers, I present here, in all sincerity, a description of the nature and characters of the two.

Khvostov was a mixture of two opposites; the meekness of the lamb, and the fierceness of the lion. At home he was a most devoted son to his mother and father, and would not leave them for a minute when they were worried or ill, and he was ready to sacrifice everything for them. He was very deeply attached to his relatives and friends. He would have gladly died to save a friend. In conversation with his acquaintances he was fond of discussion and argument, but he would always remain very cool; although he sometimes suffered insults from those who had become heated in argument, he never took offence at it. Yet everyone knew that he feared nothing, and the strongest and boldest of his colleagues, who might frighten others, although they were stronger than he (for he was of medium height and average physique) did not dare annoy him if he was in any way angered by anything, for beneath his firmness of spirit and boldness, nothing could frighten him. To his commander and superior officers he was respectful and obedient, but when he had to he spoke out without being insolent, but nobly and boldly. To strangers he was extremely polite, he showed compassion for the poor and those in need, and often gave his last remaining money to such people. He was like this both at home and in society, but when he was at work or on the field of battle where the common good placed upon him a duty to sacrifice himself, or fame promised him a laurel crown, then his spirit flared up with such a flame that no one could extinguish it. The greater the obstacles that faced him the greater would be the drive within him to overcome them; and the more fearful the danger the more boldly he would advance to meet it. His bravery could only be equalled by his humility. No one ever heard him boasting or talking about his heroic deeds. He would often step in to praise others, but always stayed silent about himself. No disappointments in his naval career could dissuade him from going on with it or awaken envy within him. Daring ventures, journeys to the ends of the earth, military action--these were what fed his soul. There he would shine, like a kind of beacon, while in everyday life he seemed an ordinary person. But for all his quick temper and martial spirit he had a warm and sensitive heart. Eyewitnesses related the following incident in the sea battle off the island of Tevsalo. He was dispatched with a certain number of boats to meet the advancing enemy. They had already drawn close and were only two shot-lengths apart. With the enthusiasm which everyone had become accustomed to seeing he was issuing orders and preparing to give battle. At this very moment he was brought a letter from his mother, in which she begged him to remember her and take care of himself. He read the letter and wept. The men who were in his boat, seeing his thus distraught, were amazed and then frightened. But this triumph of Nature did not last long: the first enemy shell brought him back to his previous fiery state, his blood began to boil, his eyes shone, his voice rose, and during the whole battle he was always to be found where the fighting was fiercest.

Also one of those who served with him told me that in those areas captured by force of arms his main aim was to see that the local inhabitants were not offended or assaulted at the hands of the victors. If it happened that at night time, or from some distant parts a messenger would be sent to him to ask for protection, he was never too idle to go to the place to investigate the complaints and to see that justice was done. He died in his thirty-fourth year, long before reaching the age at which the Cooks and Nelsons earned themselves undying fame. What great expectations died with him!

Davydov (Gavrilo Ivanovich), the author of the account of the voyages, was educated in the Naval Cadet Corps, and was commissioned in 1798. Even as a very young man he had been marked out by his sharpness of wit and his extreme diligence. He gained a considerable knowledge of mathematics and literature, so that of the fifty or sixty men presented for commissions in his year he came top in distinction. He was quite tall, well built, good looking and pleasing in his manner. He was ingenuous, decisive and bold. His character tended to be more volatile and ardent than Khvostov's, but he was less firm and hardy. He was gifted with a powerful imagination and much common sense and had a quick and observant mind. He was widely read and fond of amusement, discourse, and social company, though he would willingly quit them to carry on his heroic labors in other fields. Yet a sense of fun was never far away from him, for he found the time to indulge himself and write businesslike, yet amusing, letters. The reader may judge from this narrative which was composed by him the extent of his knowledge and skill in the field of literature.

Davydov was four or five years younger than Khvostov. Their acquaintance and the close tie between them was formed at the time of their first journey to America. On that journey Davydov wrote to his friends as he left St. Petersburg,

> When, after our farewell dinner, we came to part, you returned home and we set off for God knows where, I must confess that when the two of us were left alone in the wagon I wept and was overcome with feelings of anguish. At that moment I glanced at Nikolai (this was how he always referred to Khvostov), and when I saw that he was trying to mask his feelings, perhaps in order to give me encouragement, I gripped him arm and said: 'The one hope we now have left is each other.' Then we swore eternal friendship. After this I became much calmer and we went on in silence to Izhora.

From that time on they became inseparable and even death they experienced together. Their sad end was bemoaned in the following verses:-

The autumn night has already
Let down its sombre veil upon the land,
The silent moon has hid
  its pale light behind the clouds,
Only the sadly moaning wind
  has stirred the depths of silence
  and driven up the black clouds,
  thickening the gloom of night.
All creatures into slumber sink
The voice of man no more is heard
  the mournful bell is tolling
  the tower clock strikes two.
In these very moments of peace
When nature is allotted rest,
  by an innocent stringent Fate
A savage abyss is opening up
Thunderclouds gather over the heads
Of these two true sons of Russia
They pass with hurried steps
  to the river, Davydov and Khvostov.
There fate that instant splits
The Neva bridge asunder for them.
Brave spirits know no obstacle:
Could they be aghast at this?
They feared not sea with boiling spume,
  nor shot, nor shell.
Despising danger, and despair,
With steps of fearless pride
They go..., and overcoming the obstacles
Chance has placed in their path,
Driven by the laws of boldness,
They forward strive.
Unafraid of lurking fate
  they wish to pass the hindrance by,
Firmly they grasp each other by the hand,
  and seek to leap the intervening space.
But alas, oh, Fate!
How may I depict it?
Their efforts were in vain.
They could not clear the distance,
Deceived by darkness,
  and the force of their own strength,
They go beneath the Neva's waves,
Alas! They are no longer with us.
Neva, O tomb of friends unfortunate,
Making an end so evil to their lives
  the cause of endless tears and anguish,
  of hearts that for them long.
Give back the remains that you have taken,
  now hidden in your watery depths,
Give back to parents the sacred
  objects of all their worldly cares.
Oh victims of an envious fate!
Brave heroes in battle!
Although senseless and dead,

they are alive in our hearts and
thoughts
you shared misfortunes,
At every moment
of this life you were inseparable,
Neither did Death separate you.

Anna Volkova

On the same occasion:-

Two bold warriors, two swift eagles,
Whose great deeds matured while they were
yet young,
Who were beating the enemies
amongst Finnish waters
At whose bravery the oceans were
amazed,
Met their end crossing a Neva's bridge...
O strange Fate! O mortal man!
That which neither steppes nor desert
could take
Nor steep mountainside nor fearful
ravine
Nor savage beasts nor the fierce enemy
himself,
Was taken by one careless step.

A. Sh.

CHAPTER I

MY ENTRY INTO THE SERVICE OF THE RUSSIAN-AMERICAN COMPANY. DEPARTURE FROM ST. PETERSBURG. ARRIVAL AT IAKUTSK.

Before describing my voyage I will enlighten the reader about my background, and the motives which prompted me to this undertaking. In 1795 I was enrolled in the Naval Cadet Corps where I spent three years, during which I was sent to England and had an opportunity to see something of Denmark and Sweden. In 1798 I was commissioned, but remained attached to the Corps. In 1799 I was seconded to the fleet transporting troops on their way to invade Holland and I spent the winter in Edinburgh. In 1801 I was transferred from the Corps to the fleet and took up residence in St. Petersburg.

1802 April One day, after I had just recovered from a month's illness, Lieutenant Khvostov came to me and told me that he was about to leave for America. To my question as to how this had all come about he replied that he had joined the Russian-American Company, of which His Imperial Majesty was patron, and had been instructed to cross the whole of Siberia to Okhotsk and there to board a company ship and sail to its American territories. He also informed me that if anyone else were willing to undertake this journey the company would readily accept them. This opportunity reawakened my lifelong passion for travel so that there and then I decided to go to America, and that very day I went to declare my intention to Mr. Rezanov, who was at that time in charge of the company's affairs. The matter was easily arranged. An order in the name of His Imperial Majesty released me from my commission without terminating my service with the fleet and, placing me on half pay, gave me permission to join the service of the Russian-American Company. Mr. Rezanov and the directors of the company, for their part, had no difficulty in coming to terms with this arrangement, for our main request was that we should be dispatched as quickly as possible. The desire to see such remote parts of the world, to be at sea, and to be in countries which were rarely visited, and about which little was known did not allow us long to ponder over any possible personal advantage to ourselves.

19th Having prepared in this fashion only those articles which were absolutely necessary for the journey, which promised to be a lengthy one, at eleven o'clock at night we left St. Petersburg accompanied by all our friends. At the fork in the road we bade them farewell, got into the postchaise, whipped up the horses, and galloped off--to America. In cannot describe the confused jumble of thoughts in my mind at that time. As long as the busy preparations for the voyage occupied me my positive visions of the journey were, it would seem, not marred by anything, but when the two of us found ourselves alone in the wagon, then the silence which set in allowed my mind to wander to various fields of speculation, while the rattle of the wheels reminded us that our journey had already begun. Then my heart contracted, my joy disappeared, and my spirit was great troubled. On the one hand I was grieved to be parting from my friends, parting, maybe, for a very long time. I was going to a place where I would be deprived of all the pleasures and comforts of life, I was going without telling my relatives, who would naturally be saddened by my joining this venture--thousands of similar ideas crowded my mind and weighed down my heart with sorrow. On the other hand the thought of completing such a long journey, of seeing such a large number of unusual things, of being in places I would not often have the chance to visit, of gaining new knowledge, and maybe of making a name for myself as an explorer, all this awoke my curiosity and flattered my amour-propre. I could already imagine to myself in advance the extreme pleasure I would have when such a difficult journey was over and I was returning and about to see my relatives and friends again, and would tell them of the adventures I had had, of how I had spent the time, of how I had crossed uncharted seas and islands, living with savage peoples and wild beasts. Labors performed are recalled with pleasure. I was sure that after all I would go through my pleasure would be greater and everything would replay before my eyes. In a word, I thought that after this voyage the days would stretch away before me into a golden age, and no sorrows would ever cloud my happiness. Such illusions as these came and went in my head, so that sometimes I would laugh, and sometimes cry, and with my spirit in this troubled state I travelled as far as Izhora.

It may seem strange to the reader that I have provided an introduction of this sort to my voyage, but I hope I will be forgiven when I say that I was eighteen, that I had only just begun to live in the world, and that the circle of my acquaintances was very limited. My love for my family and devotion to my friends were the only comfort for my soul, and parting thus with them I seemed to be parting from a whole world; for what do the millions of people we do not know mean to us? Such a strong emotional disturbance is not quickly pacified. Only time heals it gradually.

I left Tosna in the same frame of mind, that is, sunk in brooding silence, my thoughts far away, and my heart full of secret sorrows. My colleague seemed to be affected in the same way. His head was so full of America that once he suddenly leapt up and asked:

"What was that beautiful bird?"

"Wait a moment," I said, "we're not in America yet!"

The bird which had flown past was none other than the common Russian raven. This incident stimulated me for the first time to laugh out loud, and this caused us to break our silence for a while.

20th In Tosna the cart, which was carrying our scientific instruments and other articles, broke down. While it was being repaired I decided to write a few lines to my friends, but the feelings of the day before returned and I was once more said.

On the journey as far as Moscow we had to travel on post-carts full up to the top. For the whole of the three days and nights spent on the road as far as Tver we slept very badly and because of this we were obliged to spend several hours in this town.

On the 24th in the evening we arrived in Moscow where we bought some covered wagons and stayed for four days and nights. Here I bade farewell to my friend and we arranged to meet in Kazan. He took the direct route and I went into the country to say goodbye to my parents. This meant that I had to travel an extra five hundred and fifty versts as opposed to the direct route to Kazan.

My parents were extremely surprised at my unexpected visit and it may be judged that they were not overjoyed when they heard of the journey I had undertaken. There was nothing to be done, however, but to give me their blessing through their tears.

From there I travelled very quickly, without intending to stop anywhere, as though breaking my last contact with the world.

On 12 May I arrived at Kazan, where my colleague was already waiting for me. Kazan and Perm gubernias are very heavily forested. In some places many of them had been burnt down, and even as I passed through one place I came across a whole forest completely engulfed by fire, and in other places the fires had only just burnt out and were still smoldering. These fires are caused by travellers and settlers passing through and lighting fires on which to cook their food. These should always be extinguished when the people move on. But this is rather difficult to achieve when there is no water near at hand, and the great expanse of woods always stops people from believing that they have to be preserved; then, despite the fact that it is banned by the authorities, such fires which are left unextinguished often cause a great deal of destruction. It seems to me that the best method of avoiding such accidents would be to make it the job of wise priests to explain this evil in their preaching, an evil which is committed because the people concerned cannot imagine the serious and grave effects resulting from it upon their own good and that of the state.

The first town after Kazan is Okhansk, on the River Kama, which we crossed by raft. In this town there are no stone buildings except for one small official one, but the place is built cleanly and better planned than many uezd [district] centres.

On the morning of the 18th we arrived in the city of Perm. It is well-planned and soundly built, the streets are clean, there are few stone structures, but several are under construction, including a posthouse. Many of the local nobility are very rich, for they own iron works, thus it is to be hoped that with time this city will become incomparably better.

The first place beyond Perm is called Kungur and lies at the confluence of two reasonably large rivers, the Silla [Sylva] and the Iren. It contains several stone buildings and churches. The high mountains of the Ural chain are between Achitsk and Klenovsk post stations, but they are in no way as high as the mountains of the Stanovoi chain.

On the 21st in the evening we passed through Ekaterinburg, famous for its works, the quarrying of marble in the surrounding districts and the plentiful supply of different color rocks. It contains many stone buildings, and three or four stone churches of splendid architectural design. The marble from Ekaterinburg is brought by horse to the quays on the river Chiussovaia and from there it is floated to its destination.

As soon as you enter Ekaterinburg you are surrounded by a crowd of people selling various stone chips, rings, and other locally made trinkets. All this is sold very cheaply, but all the same none of it is of very high quality.

I have heard here that at the stone mill a hundred puds of gold ore will yield 4 to 6 zolotniks of pure gold.

Twenty-eight versts from Ekaterinburg the road to Irkutsk divides; one fork goes via the town of Ishim and the other via Tobol'sk. We took the first because it was two hundred and fifty versts shorter.

Two hundred versts from Ekaterinburg stands the town of Shadrynsk, situated on the river Iset which splits into many streams at this spot and makes a number of islands.

The further we travelled across Siberia the sparser became the habitations, although these areas could support many more. The soil is everywhere fine and fertile; when we had passed through the Ural Mountains the terrain became for the most part more flat, especially across the Barabinsk Steppes, which although it is called by this name is actually not steppe. Everything there is pleasantly varying scenery because of the great number of birch groves dotted on the large expanse of plain. Before you reach the Barabinsk Steppes and cross them there are the most splendid larch and pine forests everywhere, as well as several other kinds of trees.

The whole of Siberia, especially the Barabinsk Steppes, is rich in game, for across it there are many lakes and bogs. You can shoot duck without even getting out of the wagon. In addition geese, cranes, swans, quail and other species of birds all breed there. The inhabitants of the Barabinsk Steppes sew large blankets made from the skin flayed from the heads of drakes and sell them very cheaply.

The great amount of good quality grass on the Barabinsk Steppes means that horses can breed quickly there and are sold very cheaply. The lack of flowing water, however, often causes cattle sicknesses which prevents the local inhabitants from becoming very rich. This is the reason also, I believe, for the appearance of infectious diseases occasionally amongst the people there. The whole expanse of the Barabinsk Steppes has only one river, the Om, upon which is situated the town of Kamsk, which is in fact more like a large village.

On this steppe, in the summertime, there are at times so many gadflies that they sometimes bite horses to death. There are so many midges that the peasants always wear a net of hair over their face and plow only at night. They constantly have a smokey fire in their huts so that they do not become full of gnats.

In one village we were told of a sad occurrence which had happened shortly before our arrival. A merchant with his assistant was crossing the steppe by post horse. The assistant plied the driver and his master with drink. Then one night when he had got them drunk he carried out his evil plan. He struck down his master and the driver with an axe and left them for dead. Then he drove into the nearest station where he said that they had been attacked by bandits who had killed his two companions and he asked to be taken wherever they thought fit, either to St. Petersburg or to Irkutsk. What he said appeared suspicious and he was detained. Two days later the driver and the merchant recovered consciousness, but the former died before he could reach the station and the latter, when he arrived, said that they had been attacked by bandits. He was extremely surprised to see his wagon and his colleague whom he had thought dead. Then the assistant confessed to his evil deed, but the merchant died two days later.

1st June In the morning we arrived in Tomsk. The day was a holiday so that we could find no one to repair the sledges, and to our great displeasure we were forced to remain here for a whole week while we waited.

Tomsk is quite large. The streets are none too clean, and there are few decent buildings. There are three stone-built houses in the place. This town is one of the most important trading centres in Siberia and a large number of merchants live here. It is situated on the River Tom which abounds in fish and amongst the various species caught are some excellent sterlets. But the best and biggest specimens of these here are considered to come from the River Narym. I have seen some of these weighing more than a pud, and it is said that sometimes even bigger ones are caught in the Narym.

Through Tomsk flows the little river Ushaika. In the town there are 2,400 dwellings and a little over 5,000 inhabitants. Because of this imbalance between the number of people and houses many of the latter stand empty.

Once the wagon had been repaired we set off on our way from Tomsk. Near what used to be the town of Achinsk, we had to cross by ferry over the River Chulym, which flows into the Ob. From there on the countryside became high and mountainous and covered with larch and birch; the road also was extremely bad. Seven versts from the Chornaia River there is a high peak called Larch [*Listvenichnaia*] Mountain.

From the post station at Chornaia [Chernaia] River until Malyi Kemchug, a distance of 73 versts, the road goes through mountains and bogs where there are so many bridges, large and small, that you are practically always crossing them. On 7th June we passed through the town of Krasnoiarsk, which is 550 versts from Tomsk. On the site of this town prior to 1621 lived the Kacha Tatars. When Ermak opened the road to the conquest of Siberia then the cossacks on their wanderings through these unknown parts built a *zimov'ia* [winter quarters] here where they could shelter from the cold and from attack by the barbarian peoples who had previously controlled these territories. Then the authorities in

Tobol'sk, seeing that this was a favorable site, dispatched the Ataman Dubenskii with 300 cossacks. In 1628 they laid the foundations of the present town of Krasnoiarsk, so called because of the *Krasnaia Iara*, or river bank of red clay.

The situation of this town is splendid: it is laid out on a broad plain. On one side flows the swift Enisei River, which is about two versts wide at this point, and on the other the River Kacha; they converge at the edge of the town and form a very beautiful panorama. On the opposite banks of the river rise the mountains which virtually surround the town. In the ravines and on the peaks the snow lies practically all year round.

Krasnoiarsk uezd is very rich in wheat and many medicinal grasses and roots grow there; and they say the rhubarb is as good as that from China. But all these advantages and the beauty of the setting cannot, because of the severity of the climate, provide much satisfaction. In the winter the frosts are severe and in summer, from the month of June onwards, there is great heat bringing with it clouds of midges, which make it impossible to go outside without a net over your face. The local inhabitants speak well of the climate in those places about five hundred versts up the Enisei, where the Tatars now live.

Just under 500 versts from Krasnoiarsk on the high road is the town Nizhneudinsk on the banks of the River Uda. It contains some forty houses and about two hundred inhabitants and in the settlement belonging to it, on the other side of the river there are some five hundred souls.

Seventy versts short of Irkutsk, and a little off the high road, is a salt works built on the Angara River. The river divides into various channels at this spot, creating a large number of islands, on one of which are two salt works and two more on another, plus two on the banks of the Angara. The best salt deposits are on the islands; they can also be seen in the river itself from their white color, but salt is not extracted from all of them. Every twenty-four hours the salt mill produces between one hundred and one hundred and fifty puds of salt, but in a year the whole works produces no more than 100,000 puds, for the works cannot be constantly in production as time is needed to cool the salt that has been extracted, and to clean out the vats, the large rectangular buckets made of thick sheet iron, in which the salt is boiled leaving a crust or deposit which sticks firmly to the bottom. This normally takes some twenty days to remove and after that the vats themselves are repaired.

The labor force at the works consists of exiles who are billetted locally in houses. There are more than two hundred of them and they each receive ten kopeks a day, except for the salters and the woodcutters who are paid slightly more. All these people are noticeably unhealthy, perhaps from the constant heat in which they have to work, for the fires under the vats are kept burning round the clock, after which the salt is allowed to stand, and when it cools it is taken out. The salt is always black on the top.

At nine o'clock in the morning, on 17th June, we crossed the rivers Irkut and Angara by ferry, and arrived in the city of Irkutsk, which may be said to be the main center in Siberia. With the conclusion of trading agreements with the Chinese in Kiakhta the place has grown significantly. Tobol'sk, which has now ceased to be the center of trade between Russia, China and Siberia, is gradually declining. Irkutsk consists of about 3,000 houses and 25,000 inhabitants. This figure includes many merchants, some of whom are very rich with extensive trading operations. All the Chinese wares and soft goods are brought by them from Eastern Siberia, Kamchatka and America, and all the European and Russian wares for Kiakhta, Eastern Siberia, Kamchatka and America have to go through Irkutsk, and this brings the city considerable profit. The merchant class in Irkutsk is industrious, foremost in the trading relations it is engaged in, and more skillful in its dealings than Russian merchants in other towns. When you arrive you immediately notice the difference between Russian and Siberian merchants, for the latter never haggle. In general it can be said of the inhabitants of Siberia, that although they are for the most part descended from exiles or settlers, the peasants who have made their livelihood here are very little like their forefathers. The Siberian peasants, especially in Tobol'sk gubernia, are in general businesslike, honorable and hospitable--they are even more enlightened than the Russian ones.

The town of Irkutsk stands on the banks of the River Angara which flows out of Lake Baikal at a very rapid rate. Its waters are extremely cold. Opposite the town itself the River Irkut joins the Angara. The situation of Irkutsk, built on a plain, is fine enough, for the mountains surround the town and the two rivers provide constantly changing scenery. Many attractive buildings are beginning to embellish the city, and despite the great distance from the capital, the place will become of increasing importance to Russia.

Hurrying on our way, we spent as little time as possible in this city, and left early in the morning on 22nd June. The districts surrounding Irkutsk are heavily populated for the whole of Irkutsk gubernia is good wheat-growing country. Between the city and the River Lena lies the Buriat Steppe, named thus because it is inhabited by Buriats, or as they are called here,

Bratskie.

The Buriats are related to the Mongols and are similar in their language and customs. Some of them have been baptised but most have remained pagans. These latter fear devils more than they respect God, and thus try to placate the former by bringing them sacrifices. This consists of hanging up slaughtered dogs and sheep. The Buriat shamans, or magicians, command great respect amongst the people, who believe them to be on terms with the devil, and their advice is sought on all kinds of matters. A shaman normally, for purposes of his own gain, is the one who encourages sacrificial offerings, saying that in order to persuade the devil to leave he entertained him with meat and wine. Before moving into a new home a Buriat will usually be given a bag containing effigies of the good and bad spirit by the shaman.

The Buriats live in conditions of extreme filth: they are always salt- and grease-stained and black with soot from the smoke of their huts; they even eat out of the same platter as the dogs. They are all rich, however, for the breadth of the land they possess allows them to breed many horses, horned cattle and sheep. They do not engage in crop-growing as much as the Russian peasants.

The Buriat faces are unpleasant, their natural swarthy hue becomes even more so partly from their lack of hygiene; partly from the fact that they are almost constantly in the open air and frequently in front of a fire. Their hair is black and their cheeks hollow, their chin pointed at the bottom like the Hottentots' and there is in general in their faces something repulsive and bestial. The Buriats' clothing is quite normal, and in addition they all wear long plaits on the ends of which may hang amber or various colored bugle beads.

The Buriats are expert horsemen and they train their children to ride from an early age. Their babies generally suck a strip of fat instead of a pacifier. Either because of this or for some other reason their babies look quite comic, for they are so fat and shapeless that they look like balls of tallow.

Two hundred and thirty-six versts from Irkutsk on the River Lena is the Kachuga landing. From here normally all goods and cargoes bound for Iakutsk, Okhotsk and points beyond, are floated down the Lena on barges, *pavozkas* [a kind of half barge] and *doshcheniki* [river sail-barges]. Passengers may travel more easily by small boat.

A 28-foot *pavozka* had been prepared for us, covered over with fir bark. People travelling by post-horse normally take an order for a certain number of horses, and in return for them, as they go down the Lena, they receive at the stations an equal number of men who row them from one station to the next. In Siberia the stations are called *stanki* and long the River Lena *zaimki* [hiring stations].

The Lena in its upper reaches, and in the region of the river port at Kachugsk is quite a small river, so that the large barges are normally floated downstream when the ice first goes from the river and when the water level is very high from the melting snows. Boats coming upstream do not always reach this port and in autumn it is impossible to do so. The barges are usually sold in Iakutsk for firewood and other purposes, while the goods for destinations beyond there go by sailing barge.

The Irkutsk peasants are very different from the inhabitants of Tobol'sk gubernia, for the latter have been settled there for a long time and are what in Siberia are called *starozhily* [old-timers], who are all well-to-do. In Irkutsk gubernia, on the other hand, new settlers are constantly arriving, even from amongst the exiles. The greater part of these new settlers have no wives. Either from idleness or depravity they do no work at all, and they only serve as a burden for those villages in which they have been settled. In summer they plunder and indulge in banditry, and the measures against this adopted by the local police are not always effective enough.

In earlier days I had not been able to think of Siberia without feelings of horror, but before my departure for America I heard so many good reports of the place from people who had been there that I began to doubt the sincerity of their praise. True, in Tobol'sk gubernia, there was a noticeable abundance of everything, but in Irkutsk gubernia matters were completely different. The failure of the wheat harvest and the influx of a large number of the settlers (of whom many died on the way), and other factors have produced an unheard of price for bread this year in Irkutsk gubernia. A pud of rye flour has gone up by twenty to thirty kopeks from two and a half rubles to three. In other places, especially in the towns, it is impossible to get anything to eat. In Nizhneudinsk if the town constable, Mr. Alekseev (whom no one can praise too highly; the inhabitants because of his goodness and justness, and travellers because of his hospitality, so welcome in such a remote place) had not invited us to dine with him, we would not have found it easy to buy bread, and we might even have had to leave the town hungry.

On 28th June, at two in the afternoon, we transferred our goods to a barge and cast off from the quay at Kachuga. Sixteen versts away on the right-hand bank stands an extremely straight pillar of natural stone. The Buriats believed that this is where their god lived; for this reason they would often come here to perform their superstitious rituals. However, when the Russians began to settle near this place the Buriats decided that their god had left his dwelling and hid himself far away in the mountains.

There are settlements scattered all along both banks of the Lena, and they consist of two, three, or in general, a small number of huts.

From Kagus [Kachuga?] to Verkholensk volost the road runs straight for thirty versts, but by river the distance is about fifty. From there to Opushkin it is twenty-four versts.

In many gubernias certain peculiarities of language could be detected, and here this is more true than elsewhere. Many words and phrases have a changed meaning, some are slightly transformed, others it is impossible to recognize, as, for example instead of *Krichi!* [Gr. Russian, shout!] they say here *revi!* [Gr. Russ. roar!]. Instead of *tabaku poniukhat'* [Gr. Russ. take sniffing tobacco or snuff] they say: *kroshki shirknyt's nos* [shake the crumbs from one's nose]. Instead of *da!* they say *No!* Instead of *porokh* [Gr. Russ. powder] they say *chernaia krupa* [black dust]. Instead of *grebi druzhnei!* [Gr. Russ. row harder!] they say *vodom!* [more water]. Instead of *vet(e)r blagopoluchnyi* [Gr. Russ. favorable wind] they say *ponos est'* [we're being carried], and so on.

From Opushkin to Korkinsk -- 16 versts.
to Piragovsk [*] -------- 20 "
to Ponomarevsk or Davydov 26 "
to Zhigalovo ------------ 24 "

At fourteen versts between these zaimki [**] the River Lena is joined by the River Turuka [Tutura] near a village of the same name [Tuturskoe], in which there is a church. The Lena at this time of year was splendid; the changing scenery of its banks; the islands; the little villages dotted along the banks and the constantly varying panorama held my interest all the time. In addition our free and easy attire, frequent bathing, leisurely reading and other advantages as against travel by land decreased the boredom arising from the slowness of our journey.

[*] The distance indicated is from the station mentioned before in sequence.

[**] i.e. between the last two mentioned, and counting always from the first to the second.

to Ust'-Ilginsk --------- 30 versts.

This station is so called because it stands on the mouth of the River Ilga which joins the Lena on the left bank.

to Gruznovsk ------------ 24 versts.

Two small rivers flow into the Lena from the left bank; they are the Shulinga at 17 versts and the Fedorovka at 19 versts, both of them occasionally dry up. From the right bank the River Biga flows into the Lena.

to Botovskaia ----------- 24 versts.

Before we had even travelled two versts we came across the River Botovka, which joins the Lena from the left, thus giving its name to the nearby station.

to Golykh or Golovsk ---- 26 versts.

At the fifteen-verst mark the Lena is joined, again from the left, by the little River Shimana and near the station itself by the Golichovka, and a little further on, from the right, by the Chichiatka. In this area the banks of the river and the mountains become higher, with only occasional gaps.

to Diadinsk ------------- 31 versts.

At the twenty-sixth verst from the right and at the twenty-ninth from the left the Lena is joined by two little rivers known as the Sorofaniki.

The Lena at this point is shielded by high banks; between them a strong wind blew upstream straight in our faces. We moved very slowly against it and were sometimes driven towards the islands.

to Basov or Basovsk ----- 26 versts.

After three versts the Lena is joined from the right by the small River Domashniaia, and at the tenth verst by the Atylynga, flowing in from the left.

to Orlenga -------------- 21 versts.

Under a verst from the station the River Orlinga flows in from the right-hand side.

to Zekhin --------------- 30 versts.

After two versts the Kukhta flows into the Lena and after the eighteenth and nineteenth versts it is joined by two little rivers known as the Kytomy, all three rivers flow in from the left.

to Boiarsk ------------- 29 versts.

At ten versts the River Selenga flows in from the left, and at the station itself from the right the Icha.

to Omaloev [Omoloi] ----- 28 versts.

At a distance of some sixteen versts between these two stations there is a beautiful spot. Between steep meanders, for quite some distance the Lena flows absolutely straight. Between the upper and lower meander the banks of the river are so close together that it seems as though the straight course is surrounded on all sides by high mountains; above the river can be seen a line of mountain peaks, with one somewhat higher than the others, while at the foot of the nearest lies an island. The banks of the Lena consist of high, almost cliff-like mountains, sloping only slightly towards the water. In front of the mountain ridge the left bank bends away abruptly, so that the bend in the river is only visible when you come right up to it. The river at this point is dotted with fine-looking islands, which, together with the streams falling down the mountainsides, make an attractive picture. Further on the banks of the Lena become lower, but many high mountains rise up from them, one in the distance shaped like a dome.

to Riga [Rizhskaia] ----- 17 versts.

At three versts there is the Kakara, and, opposite Riga itself, the Shulaga; both these small rivers join the Lena from the left.

to Turuka -------------- 34 versts.

At the tenth verst the little River Shapkina enters the Lena from the right, and from the left at fifteen and twenty-two versts two small rivers called the Mokchonikhi.

to Ust'-Kut ------------ 15 versts.

After two versts the River Turuka flows in from the left.

to Iakurim ------------- 18 versts.

The name of this first station is derived from the fact that it stands at the mouth of the River Kuta, which flows into the Lena from the left; on it there is a salt works. After the eleventh verst the River Iakurim flows in from the same direction.

to Podymakhinsk --------- 28 versts.

The following rivers flow into the Lena from the left: at twelve versts the Polovinnaia, and at twenty-five the Koroleva.

to Kokui ---------------- 20 versts.

The Lena is joined from the left by at the seventh verst the Elovaia, and at the tenth verst the Sukhaia, two small rivers.

to Sukhovsk ------------- 22 versts.

From the left there flow in, at three versts the Ub'iunnaia, and at the eighth and twenty-first the Bachakty; all three are small streams. From the right-hand side at almost the half-way point the River Taiura flows in.

to Nazarovsk ------------ 23 versts.

After eight versts a small stream or half-river flowed in from the left.

The local inhabitants here seemed to me extremely uninformed. It you ask them if there are any rivers ahead they will tell you, no, yet afterwards you discover that there are three or four of them.

to Ul'kan --------------- 22 versts.

At the fifteenth verst the little River Tira flows in from the left.

to Potapov -------------- 32 versts.

Near the station itself, from the right, the river Ul'kan flows in and further on downstream the Elovoi and Medvezhii. From the left side at eight versts there is the Kazimirovka River.

to Makarovo ------------- 25 versts.

At the second and eleventh versts, from the left, the streams known as the Libavskie flowed in after the village of the same name which stands near the second of them. On the first stream there was a mill, part of which had just this year been washed away.

to Zaborsk -------------- 15 versts.

From the left at four versts the Makarova flowed in, and at eight versts the Olontseva, both small streams.

29th June to Polarot or Polarotov - 24 versts.

From the left-hand side at twenty versts the River Lazareva flows into the Lena, and at twenty-five the

Fedoseevskaia. Although the direct distance here is 24 versts, the meanderings of the river make it up to about 60, hence the area is known as *Krivye luki* [crooked bend].

to the town of Kiren'sk -- 7 versts.

From Ul'kan to this town the current was very slow, so that our barge had to be pulled downstream by horses.

The town of Kirensk lies at the confluence of the rivers Lena and Kirenga, whose headwaters are very close together. Both these rivers flow out of the mountains on the east side of Lake Baikal.

Kirensk is a very badly built place; there are five churches in the town, one of which is made of stone. Their unusual architecture attracts the attention of travellers.

to Alekseevka ---------- 24 versts.

At eight versts, on the left-hand side, the River Nikol'skaia flows in and at the twelfth, from the right, the Cherepanikha River.

You have only just passed the mouth of the Kirenga when the current becomes noticeably faster and the water colder. From Kirensk down the Lena to the next station the scenery is very beautiful.

to Gorbovsk ------------ 25 versts.

From the left side the Lena is joined at seven versts by the Saltykovskaia and at twenty versts by the Sukhaia; from the right it is joined after eighteen versts by the Kutalak.

to Veshniakovsk --------- 25 versts.

From the left side a small stream flows in whose name I could not discover. Eighteen versts from the station the mouths of the small rivers Emel'ianovskaia and Cholbanovaia meet at a rock known as the Cholbanov Rock.

30th to Sploshna or Sploshnago -- 20 versts.

From the left the Lena is joined at eleven versts by the Zakharovskaia, and a little above Sploshnago by the Kiliuda; both are small streams.

to Il'insk ------------- 25 versts.

From the left, at six versts, the Iamenichnaia River flowed in and at eleven versts the Nikonoshinskaia River, and near the station the Il'inskaia. From the right at twenty versts there is the River Chegui.

to Dorlinsk [Dar'inskaia?] --- 20 versts.

About half-way between these stations the little River Chaia flows in from the left.

to Igor or Igorsk ----------- 30 versts.

After ten versts the Lena is joined by the Mandra flowing in from the left.

to Modinsk [Mutinskaia?] ----- 22 versts.

After two versts the little River Ichora flows in from the left.

to Ivanovskaia -------------- 25 versts.

The Lena is joined from the left, near the station itself, by a stream at three and at fifteen versts by the two Froliki, and from the right at five versts it was joined by the Mezhevaia, and at nine versts by the Mel'nichnaia, both large streams.

to Chestinsk [Chistinskaia] -- 25 versts.

Almost at the station itself from the left side there flowed in the small River Stepakha.

to Dubrovsk ----------------- 37 versts.

1st July Not far from the station the Dubrovka joins the Lena from the right, and from the left at ten versts the Bobrovka flows in.

Between these stations there is a narrow place called the Shchoki [cheeks]; this consists of overhanging stone cliffs between which the Lena flows. There are three "cheeks" on each side of the river; the height of the lowest of them is about seventy sazhens; but the bank on the other side is lower for the whole of this stretch. Some people have assumed that this natural feature is the result of the river breaking through some mountain chain which stood in the path of its current. But to judge by its appearance I would not agree with this assumption, for the river at this spot, that is right in front of the "cheeks" themselves, turns at almost a right angle to the left, leaving a low-lying plain to its right. This latter would have been less of an obstacle to its flow than the mountain chain, and so some other explanation must be found for this natural phenomenon. The Lena as it flows between the "cheeks" turns and twists, whereas one would have expected a fast current on this stretch, but it is the same here as it was upstream. We fired several shots as we passed between the cheeks which produced loud echoes.

to Kureisk ------------------ 29 versts.

to Selianki [Solianskaia?] -- 21 versts.

Nine versts on, from the left, the little River Chaika enters the Lena through two mouths. From the right there flows in the Selianka, which comes in almost opposite the station, and slightly above it.

to Parshchinsk [Parshino] --- 19 versts.

About seventeen versts on the left-hand side the River Studenka flows in.

to Rys'ia ------------------- 23 versts.

One verst out on the right-hand side the River Parshchina joins the Lena; from the left there flows in at eight versts, and from the right at eighteen versts, the two small streams called the Iukhty.

to Chuia -------------------- 24 versts.

From the left at twenty versts there flows in the River Bobrovka, and from the right at seven versts the Iakutka, and, near the latter station, the River Chui.

to Vitim volost [district] -- 21 versts.

This volost is on the left bank of the Lena, and opposite it flows the large River Vitim, which has three river mouths. The first of these is just under one verst above the volost, the second opposite it and the third four versts downstream from it.

It is well known that Alekma and Vitim sables are considered to be the best. They are caught near the headwaters of these two rivers. They both flow out of the Stanovoi mountain chain, and the headwaters of the Vitim are near the village of Eravinskoe, not far from Nerchinsk.

The hunters set out in summer, following both rivers upstream. For the most part they drag their boats by rope and load them with food supplies and with everything they need for catching the animals and for spending the winter in these lonely and empty parts. These men are hired by merchants who give them credit for their equipment. In the winter they trap sables and other animals, and in the spring they return home. The merchant, whose guests we were in Vitim volost, had a sable business at the headwaters of the River Vitim. This man said that the banks of the Vitim were precipitous right up as far as Lake Aron, through which this river flows, and it falls into the Lena at a distance of about a thousand versts from this lake. Lake Aron is twenty-seven versts long and between five and eight versts wide. In the middle there is an island on which is good hay-growing and other prerequisites for a small settlement. Many trout and other fish may be caught in the lake.

About the Lena it should be noted that many valuable fur-bearing animals breed on its right bank, but on the left bank there are very few.

It is believed that there must recently have been heavy rains at the headwaters of the Vitim, because the level of the river has risen dramatically. For this reason the current in the Lena itself has become many times faster than normal, and it is to be hoped that the remaining part of our journey will be a little more speedy.

2nd July to Pelidui ----------------- 27 versts.

to Krestovaia -------------- 27 versts.

This latter station or hiring post was near a small river of the same name which entered the Lena from the left.

to Elovaia ----------------- 27 versts.

From the left, Twenty-two and twenty-six versts out, the Malaia [little] and Bol'shaia [great] Peskovka join the Lena. And halfway through this stretch the Studenka also joins from the right.

to Khamra ------------------ 50 versts.

From the left side, eighteen versts out, the Karym joins the Lena, at twenty-six versts the Ankochok, at forty-one the Podkamennaia, and, near the very station itself, the twin mouths of the Khamra. From the right side, at about forty versts out, the River Tura joins the Lena. Because of the high water level and the speed of the current from the Vitim, from midnight to mid-day we covered one hundred and thirty-one versts, which is the distance from Vitim volost to Khamra.

to Kon'ki ------------------ 27 versts.

From the left-hand side, at eleven versts, the Chiraroz flows in, and near the station the Lena is joined by the Kon'ki and the Kantia, two small streams.

to Mukhtinskaia or Chanchiki
[now Mukhtuia] ------------- 48 versts.

The first is the name given this station by the

Tungus, and the second by the Russians.

The following rivers flow into the Lena from the left: at thirteen versts the Bol'shaia, at seventeen versts the Seredniaia, at thirty-eight versts the Kamennaia, and near the station itself, the Mukhtui. From the right-hand side, at nineteen versts, the little river Khalamanda flows in.

3rd July to Muria or Mur'inskaia -- 20 versts.

At nineteen versts from the left, the River Mur'ia flows into the Lena.

to Saldykulia [now Sylty-Kiule] ------------------ 38 versts.

On the right-hand side, at sixteen versts, the Kulantaika flows in and from the left, at six versts, the Taryn, and at ten versts the Malaia Lamga, at eleven the Bol'shaia Lamga, at nineteen the Taban' and at twenty-eight the Sukhaia.

to Niui ----------------- 30 versts.

At the thirteenth verst, from the left side, the Chikiian flows in, and at the twenty-seventh, from the right hand, the Notora, and, two versts short of Niui, a small river of the same name.

to Zherba --------------- 30 versts.

This station has taken its name from the River Zherba, which flows into the Lena from the left, a little upstream from the station.

to Kamennyi Ostrov ------- 35 versts.

On the left side, after ten versts, the Lena is joined by the River Mastakh, and at sixteen versts by the Kamenka which has two mouths, on one side of which rise high mountain cliffs.

to Zhedai --------------- 23 versts.

About halfway between Kamennyi Island and Zhedai the small river Polovinnaia flows in from the left, and from the right the Patoma.

4th July to Machei --------------- 30 versts.

Flowing into the Lena from the right, there are at nine versts the Bol'shaia Patoma and at twenty versts the Malaia Patoma. From the left, at twenty versts, there is the Kamenka and at twenty-six versts the little river Terezits-Khomo. At the opening to the Malaia Patoma, a range called the Gusiny Mountains begins, which extends for a hundred versts along the bank.

to Kharatiubi or Berezovskii Ostrov [Island] ------ 50 versts.

From the left, flow into the Lena: at three versts the Macha, at nine versts the Daban, and at ten versts a small river with no name, halfway between Kamenka and Anokh-Takh. From the right, at ten versts, there is the Tul'tulakh, on whose banks there are animal salt licks. At forty versts there is another small river up which the Iakuts and Tungus travel to hunt animals, and this later joins the headwaters of the River Molva. On the right-hand side at the mouth of this latter river, on the bank of the Lena, is a mountain of red sand which has been washed so smooth by the rain that it looks man-made. There are three such mountains in a row, followed by several smaller ones, and they are all very beautiful.

to Gil'dei or Dil'gei [Del'chei] ---------------- 27 versts.

Six rivers join the Lena from the left, the fifth is called the Kamennaia, and the sixth, on which the last-mentioned station stands, has the same name; five small rivers join the Lena from the right.

to Nelen ------------------ 30 versts.

From the left, flow in the streams of the Malyi and Bol'shoi Sentakh, and at the station itself there is the small River Neleninskaia.

to Cheringei [Cherendei] -- 25 versts.

From the left side, at nineteen versts, the Bol'shoi Chiringei flows in.

to Berdianka -------------- 38 versts.

From the left side, at six versts, the Kukan flows in, and at seventeen the quite large Biriuk; at twenty-seven versts there is the Selianka which flows out of a lake one verst from the station last mentioned. On the right side, at seventeen versts, the Lena is joined by the Taryn-Uria.

to the town of Alekminsk [Olekminsk] --------------- 28 versts.

From the left, at eleven versts, the Iurokha flows in, at twenty-two the Bol'shaia Cherepanikha and at twenty-seven the Malaia Cherepanikha.

In the town, including Iakut yurtas, there are some

fifty houses and one wooden church. A yurta is built in a square made from wooden poles stuck into the ground and leaning slightly inwards--they are planed on the inside. Earth is placed against the outside, but dung is also used to a large extent. The roof is made flat, and there is rarely any floor. In the middle of the floor is a hearth with a pipe, made from thin poles and coated with clay, going up to the ceiling. Such a device is known here as a *chuval*. A fire is always kept going in the wintertime, and this keeps the yurta warm and dry, and is of great advantage to travellers in such a harsh climate, where fire is absolutely hecessary. Moreover in the yurtas fumes of the kind that bedevil the local *izby* are unknown. The width of the Lena at Alekminsk is five versts.

to Selianka or Solianka -- 25 versts.

At two versts from there the River Alalaika flows in, and at nine versts the Daban. From the right, at twelve versts, there is the large river Alekma up which the hunters go to trap splendid sable and snow-fox.

to Namana --------------- 44 versts.

From the left, the following rivers flowed into the Lena: near the first station the Selianka; at twenty-two versts the Khar'ialag; at twenty-six the Uoboidakh; at thirty-two the Namana; and at forty-three the Chemezova.

to Kharabalyk ----------- 44 versts.

Halfway along this stretch and from the right the river Atystakh flows in, and at thirty versts the Ambardakh, and at thirty-five versts a small river. From the left there are: at three versts the Khar'ia; at six the Tymny-Ulakh; at fourteen the Kamenka; at twenty-one the Bol'shaia Ruskaia; at twenty-four the Malaia Ruskaia; at twenty-nine the Malaia Elovaia; at thirty-two the Bol'shaia Elovaia; at thirty-four the Chortova; and at thirty-five the Talovaia.

It turned out to be a beautiful evening and the peaks of the savage high cliffs, past which we floated, turned golden in the last rays of the sun, still shining from behind the mountain range. The sky was growing darker: the stillness of the air was broken only by the noise of the oars. Finally the night became very dark; thick black clouds were piling up above our heads, in the distance we could hear the dull rumble of thunder and see far-off flashes of lightning. This majestic spectacle, which from golden splendor had been so quickly transformed into terrible darkness, seemed to produce a similar transformation in my soul. At the beginning I had been sunk in sweet pensiveness, I was glad to be left alone to my own thoughts. But soon, as the sky grew dark my thoughts grew blacker also. Life seemed to me like the Lena, which flows between pleasant and unpleasant surroundings irreversibly to the sea.

to Khatyn-Tumu --------- 40 versts.

From Kharabalyk down the Lena the following rivers flow in from the left-hand side; at five versts the Kamenka; at eleven versts the Chekura; at twenty-three versts the Ogin; at twenty-nine the Belaia; at thirty-three the Berezovka; and then the Bel'-Liakh; from the right side flows the Malaia Tolba.

6th July to Markha -------------- 22 versts.

From the left the Lena was joined at two versts by the Greznukha; at nine the Kamenka; at sixteen the Kuidelakh; and at the station itself by the little River Markha. It may also be that several rivers joined the Lena from the right-hand side, but as that is not the post route side, or the side along which the barges float regularly, the boatmen do not know. From Vitim, or even further up the river, to Iakutsk, all the post-stations are built on the left bank of the Lena. By then the river has become very wide and majestic.

to Sanyiakh-Takh [now Sangyiakhtakh] --------- 40 versts.

From the left side the little river Markhachan flows into the Lena.

to Malykan ------------- 37 versts.

The first of these stations stands on a small river of the same name which joins the Lena from the left. From this direction also flow in: at six versts, the Debikan; at sixteen, the Kabanushka; at the halfway point the Bol'shoi Khar'ialag and a little further on the Malyi Kharialag; and one verst short of the station at Malykan there is a river of the same name. From the right side, at thirteen versts, the Bol'shaia Tolba joins the Lena.

to Isik ---------------- 35 versts.

From the right side at eight versts a small unnamed river flows in, and at fourteen versts the Tiuga. At twelve versts the Tikriksia joins the Lena from the left, and at seventeen and eighteen two rivers called the Chury.

7th July to Zhura or Dzhura ----- 34 versts.

From the left at six versts the Nakhai flows; at twenty versts the Tastakh; and, near the station itself, the small river Zhura.

to Amuran -------------- 25 versts.

From the left at fifteen versts the Niurgun flows into the Lena; at seventeen the Mukhatta; and, near the Amuran station, the small river of the same name.

to Sinei --------------- 30 versts.

From the left side, at three versts, the Edei flows in and at eighteen the Khabyrma, and further on, another small river.

For the third day a strong contrary wind was blowing, and this meant that we travelled very slowly.

to Batamaiskii --------- 27 versts.

From the left side near the first station the river Siniaia flows in, and at eighteen versts the Gobzhova, and a little above the second station the little River Batamaiskaia.

Three versts before this latter station a beautiful panorama opens up on the right bank. On the mountain slopes there are isolated outcrops of rock, some of them like columns, some like pyramids, and yet others like ruined buildings. In places where the crumbling cliffs have left ravines the pillars look like gates or other man-made structures. Views such as this continue along the bank for twenty versts and the place is called Stolby [the columns]. All the small rivers or streams which flow into the Lena from between these cliffs or columns are called *stolbovki*. Further along there are stretches of sand which are known as the Tolokhniany Mountains. This comes to an end at the mouth of the River Batoma.

to Titar [Tit-Ary] ------ 22 versts.

From the right side, and a little downstream from the station, the Batamaika flows in, and at four versts the Kar'ia Ur'ia. From the left: at eight versts, the Kaiargas, at thirteen the Kutai, and at eighteen the Katyn.

The water in the Lena was very high, so that we sometimes went past places where normally there were hayfields but which were not under a sazhen of water.

to Toionar ------------- 42 versts.

From the right, at thirty-eight versts, the river Batoma; and from the left, at eight versts, the Bol'shaia Katema; at ten the Malaia Katema; at thirty versts the Malyi Khar'ialak; and at thirty-two versts the Bol'-shoi Khar'ialak.

to Bestiakha ----------- 27 versts.

This station stands not far from the river of the same name, which flows into the Lena from the left.

to Ulakhan ------------- 34 versts.

At nineteen versts from the first station, on the left bank of the Lena, stands the Pokrovsk Monastery.

to Tabaga -------------- 33 versts.

Our peaceful journey was coming to an end, and we were very glad of this: for it had begun to bore us. Because we could not move from the boat, we rarely got up before eleven in the morning, and often later still. We dined at six or seven and went to bed again at one or two in the morning. I had only reading to keep me occupied, or writing something, and I bathed at least three or four times a day. We were much troubled by gadflies and even more by mosquitos. In order to drive them away we had to have something burning all the time, and thus the cure was hardly any better than the disease.

9th July to the town of Iakutsk -- 23 versts.

Fifteen versts from Tabaga, on the left, the Lena was joined by the Zhestakovka or Barabanova.

Before talking about Iakutsk I shall say something about the people living along the Lena and on the boats plying this river.

The inhabitants settled along the lower reaches of the Lena, especially between Olekminsk and Iakutsk, are a pathetic-looking lot. The land is not suitable for cultivation, nor for seeds to germinate, and the general absence of any means of providing for themselves has made them all extremely poor. There does not seem to be a spark of cheerfulness amongst them, they are always glum-looking and appear unhealthy. When we passed through, a pud of flour cost between 1 ruble 70 kopeks and 2 rubles 50 kopeks, so that the majority of the inhabitants were using pine bark as a substitute for bread, mixing it with a little flour and milk. Some families have no sustenance but bark and water. All these misfortunes react upon the intelligence of these people, or so it would seem, for whatever it is you ask them about (except for the things which concern them most closely) you will always receive the answer: I don't know. It is almost as though they had nothing in the world but their miserable huts and themselves. Regardless of the extreme poverty of these inhabitants there are sometimes travellers who, thinking themselves to be in a remote enough area to escape the law, not only do not pay their passage but even rob the local inhabitants. In all fairness, it must be said that such people are more unscrupulous and savage than robbers who attack on the open road.

The Lena people make their boats or barges from willow, in the following manner: first they hollow out a treetrunk, and then steam it and measure out what width the boat is going to be. Sometimes they add planks at the top to make the boat larger. Sometimes when the frame has been fashioned it is planked round with the use of wooden nails. The Iakuts make small boats called *vetochki* from birch bark which they stitch together and then coat with pitch. From Irkutsk to Iakutsk is about 2,500 versts. We took seventeen days to cover this distance but we could have taken a day or two less if we had not had five days of contrary wind.

Iakutsk stands on the left bank of the Lena, which is seven versts wide at this point. It contains more than three hundred houses, including the Iakut yurtas, and about 3,000 inhabitants with six churches, three of which are built in stone. The town is not built to any particular plan, and there is no sign of any well constructed buildings. Near the town stands a wooden fort with towers, built one hundred and sixty years ago, but still strong regardless of its great age.

Iakutsk stands on what is already its third site. The first was twenty-six versts downstream from the present one, but that town was washed away. It was founded by Russian hunters and then subsequently the cossacks came. The second site was a little upstream from the present one but it was also washed away, so the cossack, Sen'ka Lazarev, came with a petition to the Tsar Aleksei Mikhailovich and asked him to allow the town to be moved. Three years later Sen'ka Lazarev and his companions returned and built the fort which still stands.

The name Iakutsk comes from the Iakuts who live in the areas round the town, and in the middle of whose lands it stands.

It must be admitted that the appearance of Iakutsk, neither from afar nor near, is not commensurate with its importance as a trading centre, for through this town pass all the fur goods from northeastern Siberia, Kamchatka and America, as do goods destined for those parts.

CHAPTER II

DEPARTURE FROM IAKUTSK. WHAT HAPPENED ON THE JOURNEY. ARRIVAL IN OKHOTSK.

10th July At about midnight we left Iakutsk by boat and crossed to the right-hand side of the Lena. We sailed into a small bay and came ashore near four Iakut yurtas. Here the post horses are kept, and the place is called *Iarmarka* or *Iarmonka* [fair, or market] as is every other place on the Okhotsk road where it is possible to pick up post horses, or where they can be foddered, although there may be no corral, or settlement, or anything remotely resembling what we would call a iarmonka.

11th July We stopped to wait for a cossack who was supposed to act as our Iakut interpreter, because very few of the Iakuts can speak Russian. This is because the Russian inhabitants of Iakutsk oblast have constant trading relations with the Iakuts and almost all speak their language. The term Siberian cossack does not mean cossacks in our sense, but a command of men under the leadership of the constables. They are descended from the cossacks, trappers and hunters who won Siberia. All these people called themselves cossacks, and this name was taken over by the descendants. Cossack children go into the same command, and so it still exists, although it has decreased considerably in size.

As is well-known the Stanovoi mountain range swings away from the Chinese border towards the northeast, and follows the strip of land dividing Iakutsk from Okhotsk, and is about four hundred versts wide. The mountains in this range are extremely high, rocky and barren. The path through them abounds in precipices and makes passage by wheeled transport absolutely impossible. Thus from Iakutsk to Okhotsk the normal means of travel is on horseback. Heavy loads go by packhorse. Instead of a saddle these packhorses carry a wooden frame with a plank fixed at either side sticking up vertically from the frame. To these are attached bales, which are here called *mesta*, of equal weight. They are between two to three puds, and in rare cases more. They are attached by ropes passing under the horse's belly and attached to the planks, and this constitutes a packhorse load. Sometimes if the bales are very light an additional load of some ten or twenty pounds is placed on top of them, and this is called a *prikladka*. The packhorses are roped together in fives or tens, and sometimes less, so that round the neck of the lead horse is a rope called a *kantes*. This goes under the tail of the horse and passes around the girth of those following. Several horses roped together in this fashion are called a *sviazka*, and they are usually led by a Iakut on a horse.

All articles which are between three and a half and twelve to fifteen puds can be delivered by pack horse in this fashion: two horses have strapped to their backs, one behind the other, a kind of litter to which these bundles are attached, and these two horses are led by a special Iakut; this is called "leading on a kachka [*vezti na kachke*]". This is also the way people travel who could not make such a long journey on horseback. But, because they are so uncomfortable, the kachki are hardly ever used. For this reason heavy metal objects such as anchors are normally broken down into parts and then welded together again in Okhotsk.

In the past heavy loads have been conveyed in the following way: by sledge from Iakutsk to the River Aldan (333 versts) and then in the spring by boat up the Aldan, the Maia and the Iudoma, as far as the Iudoma landing. From there they go overland, pulled by dogs, or some other means with great difficulty as far as the *Plotbishche* [boatyard] (so-called because this is where ferries and rafts were built) on the River Urak (seventy-five versts from the Iudoma Cross) and then they are floated down to the sea. But this form of transportation, involving great difficulty, expense of time, and normally large-scale loss of the goods carried, has now been completely abandoned.

As far as the mountains of the Stanovoi Chain (about three hundred versts from Iakutsk) there are everywhere good hay meadows, which is why the land is farmed by the Iakuts and why posting stations have been established at some distance from each other. For the next six hundred and seventy versts on the horses may be changed only once or twice, for there are no people living there at all.

At nine in the evening we mounted our horses and set off. We had with us two of our own men, a cossack and three Iakuts, who were in charge of eleven pack horses. Five versts from the *iarmonka* we crossed a bridge over the River Kumakhtakh, which goes dry in summer, and flows only in the spring or after heavy rains. Several years ago, however, the water in the Lena rose so much that the barges were able to come right up to Mount Kumakhtakh (at the foot of which the river flows) and they unloaded there. When we had cross the bridge we began to ascend the steep slope of Kumakhtakh, a Iakut word meaning sandy crossing. I must add that all the place-names that I am going to mention are in Iakut. From this steep slope the forest begins and extends almost without a break to the Sea of Okhotsk. It is mostly fir-forest and larch, sometimes intermingled with pine, birch and poplar. There are also various species of bushes. On Kumakhtakh we saw many hairs on the bushes from horses' manes and tails. This is called *bel'liakh*, or "gift", i.e. the sacrifice paid to the spirit of the place for letting the horses through safely. The Iakuts do this at every difficult or steep ascent, so that a horse which has travelled several times to Okhotsk and back has practically no tail or mane left. The Iakuts call their god *Boenaia*, and the Russian God *Tanara*. Halfway on our journey we forded the little River Sola, which flows into the Lena. At two in the morning we arrived at Tombyiakh-takh station, called after the lake on which shore it stands. From the iarmonka to this place it was twenty-two versts.

12th July Here we rested, and in the morning set off further despite the blistering heat.

From the Lena to the River Amga there is no flowing water, with the exception of the Sola [Suola], and so we were forced to drink the warm, foul-tasting water from the lake. I was assured that it was possible to get good water from the lake in the following way: a corked bottle must be lowered to the bottom of the lake. The cork has a string attached which is to be jerked when the bottle reaches the bottom; this will cause the bottle to fill. The water at the bottom is said to be always cold because in spring the ice covering the lake sinks to the bottom and does not melt. But I had no chance to put this to the test.

From Tolbyiakh-Takh to Temilia is fifteen versts.

All the posting stations from Iakutsk to the Aldan are named after the lake or river on which they stand, and they usually consist of only two or three yurtas.

When we asked for something to drink at the yurtas we were given *undana*, made from sour milk and water. This kind of beverage is quite acceptable, especially when the weather is very hot.

Most of the Iakut men and women smoke and take tobacco. Both sexes are equally filthy and take little care of their dress, especially those who are poor.

13th July To Chuchigiisk --------- 30 versts.

Here we saw, in addition to two winter yurtas, three summer ones. The former we have already described; but the summer ones were built as follows: several long stakes are bound together at the top, and covered with strips of birch bark sewn together, and then a further layer of stakes is added so that the wind does not carry away the bark. This yurta is cone-shaped; a fire is always kept burning in it, and at the top there is an opening for the smoke.

We spent the night at Chuchigiisk. Fortunately every station normally has a roof supported by several poles, and it was under here that we slept; for it would have been extremely unpleasant sleeping in a Iakut yurta.

The poor Iakuts wear only a shirt and daba breeches in summer (daba is a Chinese colored material which is thick but not very strong). When they are going horse-riding they put a short pair of leather breeches over the top.

A wasp stung me in the eye so badly that for half an hour I could see nothing. When your horse steps on a nest of these insects, or senses that one is there it begins to kick up its hindlegs, thrash with its tail, and gallop off. Subsequently I grew so used to this that I would cover my face when it happened and flail about myself with a kerchief or a horsehair switch.

To Porotov ------------ 33 versts.

The cossack Kolmakov, who was accompanying us, we found to be a very brave and energetic man. He was twenty-eight, but he could travel remarkable distances on horseback and at such a speed that sometimes for six or seven days he would cover two hundred versts every twenty-four hours. His father was a Iakut and his mother Russian, thus he was intimately familiar with the customs and habits of the Iakut people. I gathered much valuable information on these subjects from him, which I was later able to compare with what I saw myself or heard from trusted witnesses.

14th July To Churopchinsk ------- 22 versts.

Shortly before our arrival a Iakut came in who lived thirty versts away. He had stolen five horses and drove them off to his yurta, but he was caught on the road. I wanted to know what would happen to him after this crime, but I was told that he would be taken to the *kniazets*, for the authority here could only deal with minor matters, others had to be referred to Iakutsk and the criminals transferred there.

Something should be said in passing about the Iakut method of government. These people own and occupy a large tract of land stretching from the Stanovoi mountain chain to the west and northwest, as far as the mouth of the Lena, almost as far as the headwaters of the Viliui and other rivers which flow into the Lena, and even to the outskirts of the town of Turukhansk.

Their source of wealth is horned cattle and horses. This is why, so as not to exhaust the supply of fodder for the flocks and herds, the Iakuts never live in large settlements but only ones consisting of two or three yurtas. Several settlements like this form a *nochleg*, which is administered by a *knias'*, or *kniazets* as he is usually called. Several *nochlegs* form an *ulus*, which is ruled by a headman. The positions of headman and kniaz' are not hereditary but elective. The Iakuts of one *nochleg* call themselves *Chzhonnobut*, while the Russians call them *rodniki*, in other words people of one *rod* or tribe. The rodniki choose a *kniaz* for themselves and they respect him as long as he governs them well and does not demand too much of them. If he fails they choose another, but the old one is still marked off from the ordinary people. Not long ago the Iakuts replaced a kniazets who had received a gold medal and velvet coat as a gift from the Emperor Paul. Then he began to say that they should not treat him like the others, for he had signs of distinction from the Tsar. He was told: you may keep them because they were given you by the Tsar, but we do not need you as *kniaz*.

The kniazes of all the uluses choose one from among their number as headman. He has to rule for three years but, for the most part, he has the post for life. The process of choosing takes place as follows: a large box is made and surrounded by as many small boxes as there are candidates; each box is allocated to a candidate by name. Each kniazets has a ball which he places in one of the boxes; the one who receives the most balls is elected headman.

There are six *uluses* in the *Iakutsk okrug*, and there are up to forty thousand Iakuts in their fur-tax area.

All night there was such a thick mist that visibility was down to three sazhens.

In the morning we were approached by an old Iakut woman, who started to ask for alms for the love of Christ.

"Why are you poorer than the others?" we asked.

"I am no poorer than anyone else there," she replied.

"Then why are you asking alms for the love of Christ?"

"Because," she said, "I have been baptised and that is how I pray to God."

This is the kind of conception they have of religious faith!

We passed through a Iakut burial place. The graves

were scattered across the low valley, each one surrounded by a wooden fence, with a little flat, or pointed roof. On the nearby trees were hung the skins of horses and cows with the hooves and heads left on; there were also saddles, bridles, stirrups and other pieces of harness, so that the dead might ride their horses in the other world. The dead are buried in their best clothes. At the burial all the relatives gather together, a horse or a cow is slaughtered, and the meat is eaten and the skin hung up, as described, on a nearby tree. After this several other superstitious rites are performed.

About twenty-six versts from Churopchinsk we crossed a bridge made over the River Tattei, which gives its name to the *okrug* through which it flows. It comes out not far from the mountains and flows into the Amga, but at this time of year it was virtually dry and had disappeared altogether in some places.

To Arylakha ----------- 33 versts.

Because I was not used to riding on horseback, my legs and back ached so much that I was often forced to dismount and walk alongside.

Along the road on many occasions I saw Iakuts pulling hay and other loads on sledges harnessed to oxen even in summer.

On the shores of the lake past which we were riding, we saw many bowls hanging on the trees. They signified that Iakut shamans had been making magic here and they had made a wooden image of a devil, placed it in a bowl, and released it on the lake.

15th July To Lebegininsk --------- 27 versts.

In the morning it was raining heavily but about midday it eased off, and then ceased altogether. At this station there was one horse too few for us and in its place the Iakuts harnessed up an ox for us. They often ride on their backs also.

In every meadow there were great numbers of grasshoppers.

To Mel'zhegei ---------- 27 versts.

The postman whom we met here told us that a great many exiles (in Siberia they are called *varnaki*) were making their way in armed bands, pillaging along the road to Okhotsk. He had come across them at the River Aldan, but the bandits had let him go, probably because he had little of value with him.

To the Amga River ------ 26 versts.

At nine in the evening we forded the Amga, which flows into the Aldan. At this time of year it was only one hundred and fifty sazhens wide and the water in it was low, but earlier on when it had been wider and deeper there had usually been a ferry on it. On the other side of the river was a station: in other words a roofed-over enclosure in which travellers stop. We were overjoyed to get some fresh water. The bed of the river consisted of sand and small pebbles. Near the station there were a great many red currants which were already quite ripe.

On the Amga, a hundred versts upstream from this spot is a settlement called Amginsk, which was long ago settled by Russians for crop growing. I do not think that it is in a very good state now, for the settlers have adopted Iakut habits, talk their language, and live in Iakut yurtas, so that only four Russian *izbas* have remained, and the house in which the *voevoda* lived before the gubernia was established. During the term of the last *voevoda* the following incident took place not far from the settlement. Near the Iakut settlement there appeared some kind of animal which the inhabitants had never seen before, and which began to kill large numbers of their cattle. One Iakut who went out to look at the animal was also torn to shreds. When the others saw that their companion had not come back, they set out with their weapons, killed the animal and brought its skin to the *voevoda*. In view of descriptions still extant we must conclude that the animal was a snow leopard [*bars*] which had quite surprisingly made its way far to the north, for these animals do not usually come any further than the Chinese border.

16th July At midnight we left the station and at two o'clock we stopped at a lake in a small valley surrounded by forest. We pitched our tent under a tree, lit two fires near it, and began to cook our supper. The horses were wandering about nearby. The newness of all this comforted us, for this was our first camp yet.

About forty-three versts from Amga, we crossed a bridge made over the little River Nokha, which flows into the Aldan.

From Amga to Nokhinsk -- 47 versts.

The road between these two stations is very bad because of the many forest tracts on the way, the gnarled roots of the trees, and the potholes. In some places it was difficult to get one's horse through because of the tangled branches and thickets on either side of the road.

In addition to the currants we also came across bilberries [blueberries?] and strawberries.

We left the station at ten in the morning. My horse suddenly fell under me, but I succeeded in getting my feet out of the stirrups and therefore was not hurt badly. This was a good thing as it might have impeded our progress. An hour before midnight we stopped to camp.

17th July To the River Aldan ----- 33 versts.

At one o'clock mid-day we arrived there. The station has been built on the other side of the river, which is more than half a verst wide. We crossed by boat and made our horses swim across. The Aldan, which has many rivers flowing into it, that rise on the western slopes of the Stanovoi mountain chain, eventually flows into the Lena. There are quite large amounts of fish in the Aldan; some of which were sold to us by the cossacks which had been caught while we were there. These cossacks live here to take care of the post horses and the official storehouses, which contain flour and other cargos, which the Iakuts are unable to deliver to Okhotsk straight away.

Up until now we had been able to get milk and occasionally fish, but from now on, we were told, we would have to live on what we took with us, for as far as the River Alakh-Iun (two hundred and thirty-three versts) there was no settlement. The roof on each station had at least protected us from the rain, but from here, on our peregrinations to Okhotsk, its place would have to be taken by a torn canvas tent, with which the office of the Russian-American Company had provided us. The thought of bears and bandits also kept us on our guard and made us cautious.

At the Aldan we found six horses hired for us by the company at fifty rubles each, with one spare horse, or *zavodnaia*, as it is called here. There were also ten post horses in the absence of any others, capable of standing the journey, and in charge of them there were four Iakuts on special horses. The mail also travelled with us, for its own safety. The fastest time for the journey from Iakutsk to Okhotsk is ten to twelve days, but the Iakuts normally complete the trip in eighteen or twenty. The great part of the cargos dispatched from Iakutsk at the end of March or April, and the caravans cross the Aldan when it is still frozen. Then the horses are in their worst condition; they move very slowly, and stop for a month when they find good grazing. These convoys are called *plastovye* [spring ice] and the horses can be hired cheaply at this time. The goods coming into Iakutsk when the Lena is open are sent from the Iarmonka which is on the opposite bank of the river from Iakutsk (where the barges dock), and are thus called *iarmonochnye*; then each horse costs from fifteen to twenty-five rubles each and more. More expensive than this are the so-called light horses, which are used when it is necessary to reach Okhotsk in a hurry. In such cases the packs on the horses weigh no more than three and a half to four puds. So many cargos are carried from Iakutsk to Okhotsk and so few are brought back that most of the horses make the return journey unladen. Then the Iakuts usually fatten them up on the coast, where the grass is rather salty. They let them gorge themselves for fifteen or twenty days. Then the Iakuts hire them out cheaply so as not to travel for nothing, and they sometimes undertake to deliver goods from Okhotsk to the Aldan in eight days.

The day's rest helped me to recover so that the pain in my arms and legs was nothing like what it had been before. Like seafarers worn out by sickness we came into port after a long voyage, set our health to rights there, and then set out again, placing new hope in our strength. We were under way at ten in the morning.

The unfamiliarity of the road gave me the idea of keeping a record of all the names of features along it, and of describing it in great detail. These names are given by the Iakuts. The Russians call the distance between these features a *dnishcha*, and Iakuts call it a *kos* [spit]. The Russians always reckon a *kos* to be about ten versts. But naturally this method of measurement is not reliable because it is based upon how far the Iakuts will travel in a day, in spring, on the worst possible horses. And it does not take much insight to realize that such a method of measurement is not uniform. At the end of each *kos* the Iakuts pick out a natural feature, and give it a name.

Ten versts from the Aldan is a mountain ridge, very muddy during the rainy season, called Lipka-Yiabyst. It is some ten versts long. Then, after a further ten versts there is Berchzhiges' Ottu [pine grove], and ten versts beyond that a ford across the Belaia [Khanda] River, which flows into the Aldan. There is only a ford in the river when the water is low. But after the rains this river (like all those which flow out of the steep mountainsides not far away) floods its banks. This is why ferries are stationed on the Belaia and on many other rivers. The local agents, however, are often negligent in these matters, and cause enormous delays thereby. It is not unknown for convoys to wait ten to fifteen days on the banks of some rivers, and there have even been cases of delays of a month or more.

We had already forded several channels of the Belaia River and finally were a verst short of the main channel itself, when suddenly a Iakut came galloping up to tell us that there were more than ten well-armed *varnaks* on this side of the river, that they had captured him with the mail, held him for more than twenty-four hours, and that the postilion had run off and escaped. The Iakuts offered to guide us past the *varnaks* by another ford and we readily agreed to this proposal, for it was unpleasant enough to ride through seven hundred versts of desert on horseback, let alone to be wounded by bandits.

We crossed the Belaia by the other ford and went through some very thick woods and slimy bogs. We passed close by a bear which seemed just about as friendly as the bandits. In the end our horses were so tired that many of them were falling and we were forced to camp for the night in the middle of the bog. We had only just laid down to sleep, wrapping ourselves in our coats, when a violent downpour began and wet us through within a quarter of an hour. I ordered them to cover me with the straw palaisses which are used for the horses under the saddle, and are called *potniki*. This did not do much to warm me, and after half an hour the rain reached through to me again, and I could sleep no more. The biting cold and damp made me shiver uncontrollably and I was in agony. The night seemed endless. Finally dawn dawn broke, none of us had slept, but we had
19th July not spoken to each other because we did not want to raise our heads or move, for at each such change of position the cold made itself felt. I lay curled up in a ball until I heard that the horses had been saddled up and we were ready to ride off. Then I saw that none of my companions was in any better state, they were all standing round the dying embers of the fire and shivering. At ten in the morning we set off on our way. I held on to my horse by sheer force and envied those tucked up in warm rooms who did not have to think of the rain pouring down in rivers. I would have given all that I had just to be sheltering in some *shalash* [lean-to] which would keep out the rain. Such a weakness may appear comical to many, but they should only come to that conclusion when they have not slept for two days and have for more than half of that time been out in the rain, without a stitch of dry clothing on them.

The mud became very bad indeed; the ditches, which had been dry the day before, filled with water and became fast-flowing rivers, which we had to ford. To comfort ourselves, we thought that we had left the *varnaks* behind, and that they would not trouble us any more, specially at a time when all our rifles and pistols were thoroughly damp.

After we had travelled five versts along the road we stopped at one o'clock mid-day to feed the horses. We had hardly pitched our tent and lighted our fire, when we suddenly heard two gunshots very close at hand. Our Iakuts, on hearing them, threw themselves flat on the ground. At that moment seven men stepped out of the bushes around us, two of whom came straight up to us with their weapons at the ready.

Anticipating that nothing good was to come of this encounter we began to reach for our damp guns. Khvostov, who could not get his out quickly, with just a sabre in his hands, ran to meet them, and going up to their ataman said:

"What do you want? How dare you approach members of the armed forces like this? Lay down your arms or I shall order you to be shot!"

This bold act frightened the ataman. He ordered his companions to lay down their arms and he said, "We can see that you are military people, and we do not want anything from you!" The other bandits also shouted to us, "Don't shoot! Don't shoot!"

In the meantime, however, the ataman, still looking at Khvostov with some amazement, proposed that he should go with them to their camp which he said was only a hundred sazhens away from where we were. Khvostov, in order not to show himself afraid of such a suggestion, answered, "Let's go!" He went into the ataman's tent with him, where there were ten or so men gathered together. One of them began to speak coarsely to him, saying: "You're only a young skipper but you make a lot of noise," and he began tapping him on the shoulder. Khvostov realized that such cheeky behavior might encourage the others to deeds of violence, so he struck the bandit so hard on the cheek that he fell over. Then he grasped his saber and said, "If you try anything with me you won't get off lightly! I can deal with the lot of you and my companions are nearby."

The robbers were speechless. The ataman shouted at the man on the ground, "You are forgetting that you are a *varnak*, and that his honor is a government officer." After this he ordered him to kneel at Khvostov's feet and seek forgiveness. So peace was concluded with the bandits who afterwards, far from thinking of taking anything from us, offered us everything they could with the exception of sugar. They apologized for this, saying that they had so far failed to find a merchant who had any. We did not accept their favors and told them not to try any trickery if they wanted to part with us on peaceful terms. But they assured us that they would not dare do this, and that they were not really the robbers they were made out to be, but had run away to escape poverty and their hard way of life. They had taken from the merchants only as much as they needed, and would never kill anyone except in self-defence.

20th July In the morning we set off again without any interference from our neighbors. Ten versts from the ford across the Belaia the feeding station is called Ser'gakh Sibikhtia, then Siial'iakh Tumul [hanging mane] ten versts further, and then Siul'-liakh Tumul [muddy place], a mountain ridge so called because in rainy weather it is terribly muddy and full of *badarany*, or patches of slimy bog. Out of this latter the rain had made many streams which had to be forded like the many channels of the Belaia. They were all flowing very fast across the stony ground. We were unable to cross one stream in the usual place and we circled a swamp, looking for another way. We found one which looked suitable and began to cross, but many of the horses fell into the water and soaked their loads, which we then made even wetter dragging out of the water.

All the goods and articles transported along the Okhotsk road are put in sacks made of ox-hide, whose seams are so well coated with pitch that none of the contents will get wet even if the sack falls in the water, but as the company did not have the same need to worry about taking good care of our equipment as it did of its own goods and we, because we were inexperienced in the matter, did not know what to do, and had also deliberately been given rotted and torn sacks, so that most of the contents were completely ruined.

After this we rode through Bastyn Kharatit [the first black forest]. There are three of these woods in a row, each one about ten versts long and the last one a little longer. When we had passed through Bastyn-Kharatit we passed on the left a rocky mountain called Tyllakh-Niura [wind rocks] apparently because there are always strong winds blowing round it. When we passed by, however, it was completely calm. In the evening we crossed the River Mukhtula or Kondratova and stopped to feed the horses at *Orto Kharatit* [the second black forest]. In order to make our way to the iarmonka, where we intended to stay the night, we had first to ford some more streams.

To find out if they were deep we sent on ahead the Iakut armed with a bow, whose task was to guard the mail. Such men are called *batasta* [weapon bearer]*. Although the stream was only two and a half sazhens wide, and in a normal season would be completely dried up, at the time of our visit it was so deep that the batasta had to swim across it. So we unloaded the horses and drove them across and, carrying the stores and the saddles ourselves, we crossed on some logs we had placed across the river.

Instead of the word *brat*, used at home, when we

*This 'warrior' was so brave that earlier, when we had heard that the robbers were close by he had deliberately broken the string of his bow, so as to have an excuse for not using it.

wish to call someone, on the Lena they say *tovarishch*, and the Iakuts say *dagor*, which means friend.

21st July In the morning we broke camp. Around mid-day it began to rain, but it soon stopped and the sky cleared again. We were travelling between two mountain ridges, along the ravines where there flowed the little River Chegdalka which rises in the Chegdal'sk Mountains. We had already forded this river some fifteen times, and almost as many small streams made by the rain. The Chegdalka flows into the Belaia. The post horses were so bad that we were forced to leave one of them along the way with a Iakut. Those that we hired, on the other hand, were all good so that if all of them had been the same we would certainly have been able to cover sixty to seventy versts a day, which would have been a great deal on such a badly kept and stony road upon which unshod horses soon ruined their hooves.

Sometimes we picked many bilberries and red currants, which are known here as *kislitsa*. We also saw squirrels and *burunduks* (these latter are creatures a little smaller than squirrels. Their coat is reddish-grey and they have white stripes). Our dog would smell them out and chase them up the trees. This was our only interesting way of passing the time. We would occasionally shoot any game that came our way.

The mountains ahead of us were of various kinds. Some had pointed summits like sugarloaves, others were dome-shaped; some were wooded, but for the most part they were covered with small stones. Sometimes the ridges on either side changed their position so often that it seemed as though we were surrounded on all sides by mountains.

At seven in the evening we stopped between two ridges, on the River Chegdalka. The Iakuts usually let the horses stand and rest for two or three hours, and only then do they let them feed. But if they have plenty of meat on them they keep them tied up for a couple of days before they set out. And even after this, on the journey itself, they give them very little time to wander and graze.

Thunderclouds began to appear in the west and a storm was quickly gathering strength. The clouds were moving in various directions over the tops of the mountains, and the crackle of thunder echoed in the ravines. All these phenomena together made a splendid and terrifying spectacle. But the wind soon changed and drove away the storm clouds, while the rain continued until seven o'clock in the morning.

22nd July From the Belaia River we were travelling for almost all the time through mountains, and the track was very difficult to follow, in the most barren places it was only discernible by the different color of the grass. Today we forded the Chegdalka more than ten times and began to ascend the Chegdal'sk Range along the edge of the gorge where the river mentioned above, past whose headwaters we were now passing, rises. We reached the top of the mountain within the same hour and began to descend along a ravine along which flowed a large stream, flowing into the River Iunikanka, which rises in the Iunikansk Mountains and later joins the Belaia. We crossed this stream many times and drew near to the first ford across the Iunikanka, which is about one hundred and fifty-five versts from the Aldan. The distance between the Chegdal'sk Range and the above-mentioned river of the same name is called the "*Chekhonovo plachishche* [weeping]", so named because once a Iakut called Chekhonoe had all his horses killed by bears there, and this caused the Iakut to weep. This place is one of the three in which these animals breed in large numbers. The other two are the *bludnyi khrebet* and the *porozhnyi brod*.

When we had crossed the Iunikanka several times, we could see mountains on three sides of us. The peaks on the left were about a hundred and fifty sazhens high, composed of flagstone, and were completely overhanging. The ones on the right sloped more gently than the first and were higher and covered with small stones. We turned to the right where the peaks stood one after another only fifty sazhens away. Those on the left were of flagstone and looked like ruins. Many of them were so overhanging that it was dangerous to ride round them, but the Iunikanka flowing through their midst gave us no chance to find any other way round.

We crossed this stream more than twenty times that day by fording it, and at half-past ten in the evening we stopped at a place called *Pribylova Anbar*; the place got its name from a merchant called Pribylov who had once built a barn there to store his goods. Not a trace of it remains now. He also put up the cross which still stands to this day on a nearby mountainside which is completely conical in appearance.

Although our horses were very tired we pressed on to try and find some fodder for them, for there was virtually none in these mountainous regions. The road bed consisted of large, uneven stones, which made it extremely hard going for our unshod horses, so this often made their hooves raw and prevented them from going on.

At one spot along the Iunikanka there was ice which never melts, and we could see snow in the mountains and the ravines. At dawn it began to rain and at

23rd July seven in the morning we set off on our way. We forded the Iunikanka five times, and we began to climb up into the Iunikansk Mountains along the river on a road full of sharp stones, the ascent being very steep. The view from the top of the ridge was splendid. Looking at it I forgot about the rain which had soaked me to the bones. A terrifying abyss separated the two mountains. Along it noisily flowed the River Kunkui, which flows into the Belaia. Before me, gradually fading into the distance, there presented themselves to my gaze many ranges of mountains of increasing size, with pointed or dome-shaped summits reaching up into the clouds. All this formed a spectacle that would exceed that of the Alps if only it were described by as many travellers, but here there is no-one to appreciate such beauties. Dusk prevented me from looking more closely at the many mountains which showed blue in the distance. The peaks of the mountains were all bare, except that some ranges were covered half-way up with larch.

The descent from the Iunikansk Range is very steep. We went diagonally down the slope, with the River Kunkui on our left and then proceeded to ford it more than twenty times, and also several minor streams that flow into it. Sometimes I could not look enough at the awesome splendor of the views in these mountainous areas of the Stanovoi Range which is considered one of the highest on earth. What varied material, almost at every step an inspired artist or writer would find for his brush or pen!

The strong rain and fierce wind, the biting cold which are ever present, even in summer, in such altitudes finally exhausted our strength so much that it was with difficulty that we listened to the Iakuts who wanted us to go further to look for fodder. We once again came upon the Belaia and crossed it eight times. After the first ford we crossed the River Biukiakian which flows into the Belaia from the left. Between a fourth and fifth ford on the Belaia there are rapids almost a sazhen in height, and between the sixth and seventh there is a somewhat lower one, and many smaller rapids. The current in the headwaters of this river is extremely fast, and the recent heavy rains had contributed to its speed.

In other places the Belaia flows noisily between high, craggy banks, as though between gates and affords a very beautiful view.

At half past seven we stopped, immediately lit a fire and pitched our tent. Throwing off our damp clothes, we began to warm ourselves. We cooked some kasha made from black bread and ham and began to eat it. The reader will, of course, not envy our situation and will not think it a very good one but at that moment it seemed to us better than any luxury money could buy. The fire and the tent were to us better than the most sumptuous hearth, and the kasha made from dry bread better than any sweetmeat. This great value in our eyes was achieved because for fourteen hours we had been riding, hungry, in driving rain and a fierce, biting wind. Such experiences will be more finely felt by those who have gone through them than by those who simply relate them afterwards. Besides they train one for hardship and patient forebearance better than any finely phrased exhortations. A man who has the means of alleviating his own hardship does not bear it as firmly as he who suffers without any hope of improvement. The very impossibility of changing our lot gave us strength and forced us to say to each other: "Well, what can we do? Living one's life is not as easy as crossing a field." When you set out on a long journey, you have to consider every hardship a necessary temptation, which will lighten the burden of those labors which may be asked of you in the future. In addition, the man who has lived his whole life in undisturbed peace is deprived of the pleasure of recalling everything that has happened to him. Such were the thoughts that occupied us as we went on our way, and after them the tasty kasha seemed like a reward.

24th July We awoke early and were very glad to see that the rain had stopped and that the water level of the Belaia had fallen a great deal. A Iakut who was driving some cows to Okhotsk, and who had spent the night not far from us, brought us milk in the morning, for which we gave him some money and some tobacco, the latter he there and then crumbled up and mixed with some wood chips. The Iakuts are very fond of Circassian tobacco but because of its strength they always smoke it blended with chips. Each Iakut has a brass pipe which holds hardly more than a pinch of tobacco. The pipe is placed in a wooden stem consisting of two tubes bound round with a strap. When this latter is unwound the stem folds into two and can be more conveniently cleaned. The tobacco which has burnt up and the tar from the smoke are not thrown away, but again mixed with chips, and smoked for a second time. The Iakuts inhale the smoke and they take in so much sometimes that they fall over. In their belts, where they keep their pipes, the Iakuts also have a pair of tweezers with which they pluck their beard; there is also a little pouch containing tinder made from dried wormwood and a small knife with a wooden or bone handle.

At ten in the morning we went on our way, forded the Belaia another twenty times and began to ascend the first of seven mountain ridges. These are called the Seven Mountains, and they stand one behind the other. Sometimes we followed the banks of the river itself till the mountains on either side drew in so close that there was no other way between them but by the river. The summit of the first range of mountains is shaped like a semi-circle, and from this several others can be seen;

the farther away they were the higher they seemed to be, and the peaks of the most distant disappeared into the clouds. We began to descend at the place where the Akarskaia River rises, which flows into the Allakh-Iun. The first of these, like many of the large streams which flow into it, we crossed several times by fording. At each of the fords we could see small waterfalls. Some of the streams fell in cascades from the high, steep mountains, dashing with a roar against jutting rocks. Everywhere there were most wonderfully picturesque views.

At ten in the evening we arrived at the Allakh-Iun River which is two hundred and thirty-three versts from the Aldan. It flows into the Maia, which then flows into the Aldan. We stopped at a barn, which was nothing more than a crude roof on poles, constructed where the ferry crosses the river. In autumn, however, there is usually a ford. The Iakuts did not want to go on to the station because in that area many horses had recently gone down with disease. We had only just managed to get under the cover of the roof when it began to rain.

Allakh means 'bold' and this river is not so called without reason, because of the great speed at which it flows. Although the last rain shower had not been heavy the level of the river had risen a great deal.

Post horses are kept on the Allakh-Iun during the summer, but these are only for the couriers delivering mail and dispatches. For this reason, travellers, even with orders for horses, are forced to make the journey from the Aldan to Okhotsk on very bad horses, or to take fresh ones by force along the road from "returnees." This is the name given to the Iakuts who take goods by contract to Okhotsk, feed their horses there and return to their *uluses* with empty packs, unable to undertake to carry any goods from Okhotsk. These returnees normally seek, according to the judgment of the stationmasters, a high price from travellers for their horses, but the journey goes on for so long that no one makes a profit out of it, and so the returnees, in order to avoid any fuss and bother, return to their uluses by roundabout ways. If they are compelled to travel on the high road they always send two or three men to ride out several versts in front of them on their best horses. If these men meet anyone they would gallop back to warn their companions, and then they would all disappear off the side of the road.

In earlier times there used to be a cossack stationed on the Allakh-Iun, who would change peoples' horses and sell food supplies, and although he grew rich on this, the Iakuts and travellers also benefitted. Now there is no chance of this.

Sixty versts from the Aldan, the road starts with an uneven rock surface, and this continues as far as the

Allakh-Iun, and it caused many of our horses to injure their hooves. In addition, for the whole of this distance there is no decent fodder, and for these two reasons some of our horses were rendered completely useless for any further work. It was a good job that we had managed to obtain fresh ones by exchanging with an American Company caravan which we had come across.

25th July Since we could not discover a decent number of horses or a boat, of which there had been only one, and that had broken from its moorings and been carried away by the current, we were forced to remain on the Allakh-Iun. At about mid-day the rain stopped. During this enforced leisure we picked bilberry and arctic bramble.

In earlier days there had been a winter road here as well. But when the settlement on the Allakh-Iun was abolished it was realized that by passing further to the north the mail, the couriers and the dispatches could buy from the Tungus many squirrels and other fur goods, then they laid down a winter road along the Aimiakon, along which river it is two thousand versts from Iakutsk to Okhotsk, in other words, almost twice as far as by the summer route. In addition the going is more difficult for there are six-hundred and seven-hundred verst stretches of wilderness. There, when the frosts are hard, there are fierce blizzards called *burans*. In Okhotsk and on Kamchatka they call them *purgas*. I was assumed that the snowfalls on that road are not as deep as they are in places on this one, near the Seven Mountain ridges, for example, and in several other areas. The winter road takes the following route: from Iakutsk along the summer road, changing horses as far as Arylakh, where it turns off to the left. As far as the Aldan River there are frequent Iakut settlements; but from there on one must travel with the same horses as far as the river and the large Iakut settlement of *Aimiakon*, which is a thousand versts from Iakutsk and over six hundred from the Aldan; there are no habitations on this stretch. Here horses are changed and the road goes for more than four hundred versts through deserted country as far as the Tul'skii Range where, although there is also no settlement, deer can be bought from the wandering Tungus, if they should be encountered. Otherwise the road continues with the same horses for another two hundred versts as far as the Bargakhan River and mountain chain. Here, when Tungus nomads are encountered, deer can be bought and the journey may be continued for a hundred versts to the Lake and River Uiaga. "Foot Tungus" is the name given to those who have no permanent settlement. They wander summer and winter and change their camping ground, herding the deer with them and using them to transport all their possessions and yurtas. These consist of birch bark with which they cover several stakes bound at the top, so that the yurta always has a conical appearance, or they cover these stakes with the skins of deer or other animals. From the Tul'skii Mountain chain to Okhotsk the road follows the River Okhotsk. Dogs can be bought from the Tungus nomads on the Uiaga, and by these *narty* (a kind of sledge) one can travel the two hundred versts to Okhotsk itself. For the most part, however, the dogs are changed halfway at a place called Arka, where the Tungus nomads live, and then again with the Iakuts at Meta, fifty-five versts from Okhotsk.

The horses, even in winter, carry a four-pud pack. When a stop is made they are set free so that they warm up the snow with their hooves and faded grass may be found where they have trodden; or a small space is cleared of snow and they are allowed to graze there. Travelling on horseback is very boring in winter, because they are weak, thin and underfed, and move very slowly. Sometimes they become so tired that their rider has to make most of the journey on skis, carrying his own food and clothing. Reindeer are normally loaded with a pack weighing about three puds. If the journey is not very long the pack may be four or five puds. But for this burden they choose the two strongest deer and the load is swapped from one to the other. After two or three hours the deer have to stop and have something to eat. They dig away the snow with their hooves and eat a white moss which usually grows in the mountains; they are not made to stand for any length of time, but are allowed to graze straight away.

Finally, when we had managed to find some horses and a boat, we transferred our load to the far bank and drove the horses across, and at six-thirty in the evening we set off on our way. The water in the Allakh-Iun had become so high that it had washed away part of the road, and our horses walked flank-deep in water. Ten versts from the station we passed the Mountain Taskh-Tanara-Balagana on our left. *Taskh* means rock, *tanara*--god, and *balagana*--church, and this name has derived from a stone image which was once found on this mountainside. We went on for another half a verst and then stopped to camp for the night.

26th July Towards morning a very thick mist descended, but once we got under way the day became fine. We forded the river Mutinskii Krest [cross], so-called because a certain cossack captain Mutin, returning at one time with a company from Okhotsk, had erected a cross on the river bank. This river flows into the Allakh-Iun just like the eight or nine others which have no name because they only flow from the spring rain onward, and so these rivers, like all those that flow only intermittently, are called *sukhie*--dry rivers. After this we cross a high mountain, called Cape Anchinsk. Further on we passed the feeding-place called Dylga Asylyk [the feeding place on the hillocks] and Bagarakh Asylyk, and approached the Anch ford, where the water was so high that we had to stop and wait for it to fall. After we had been there for a little while we pushed a pole into the water and noticed that it had become lower, but at nine o'clock it began to rain and our hopes of crossing the river disappeared. There was supposed to be a ferry here, but as there was none travellers were often forced to stay around for some time.

On the road we shot a partridge and two squirrels, and on the lake we caught two large ducklings, which were still unable to fly. In addition a Iakut killed a partridge with a stick and made us a present of it. In return we gave him two squirrels, which he ate there and then, cooking them a little on the same stick. Squirrels' meat is very tender and white, but the local Russians will not eat it.

On the opposite bank of the Ancha, on the mountainside we could see snow in many places.

Although all the Iakuts are great lovers of tobacco and vodka, the one we had engaged liked neither the one nor the other--this was very rare indeed.

27th July When we saw that the water was not going to fall quickly we began to make a raft. By two o'clock in the afternoon it was finished and the rain had stopped. Then we lashed together all the traces and ropes and sent a man over to make one end of them fast on the other bank, so that we could in this way cross on the raft. When the man carrying the rope had got out into the stream the current began to pull so strongly at the rope that it began to drag his horse, and he had to come back. Thus all our plans for crossing this river had so far been frustrated. While we were waiting we went into the forest and picked berries and mushrooms, and I shot a woodchuck.

The most suitable time to travel the Okhotsk road is late autumn, when the rains have not completely begun and the water in the rivers is so low that there is no delay at any of the fords.

In the evening we again set about trying with the raft, but the Iakuts, afraid of being drowned on it, said that there was another ford ten versts upstream, but as it was already quite late we postponed our trip there until the morning.

28th July At eight we set off. The day was splendid. We crossed four dry river beds and drew near to the Ancha, but there was no chance of crossing it so we stopped on a small island. Nearby on a neighboring island there were many bilberries.

The Ancha splits into a great number of channels, forming many islands, and it was on one such that we had stopped, for this channel was small. Opposite here the River Anchakan flowed into the Ancha.

Towards evening we had only just had a chance to make ourselves some tea when one of our men rushed up to the tent shouting: "Robbers! Robbers!" We grabbed our guns and leapt outside. Seeing some people galloping up to us at quite close quarters we set our sights on them and shouted to them to stop.

There were eleven men in this bandit group. When they saw that we were ready to fire they stopped some -en sazhens away. We shouted to them to ride further off and when they had done this we took all necessary precautionary measures in case they should suddenly and unexpectedly attack us, and began to parlay with them. Their ataman said that they had thought we were merchants, and not military people, and that they would not dare undertake anything against us. He told us that they had all escaped from the wharves at Ust-Maisk and had come to the Aldan. He said that they had fled to escape their wretched lot and the arduous work. (The normal excuse for good-for-nothings). And so for a second time we had escaped great danger: for it must be admitted that the forces at their command vastly outnumbered ours. Afterwards when these robbers were caught and interrogated we discovered that it was the very same band that had lain in wait for us at the Belaia River, and who had heard from another band that had met us that we had gone past. They had then come after us with the intention of seizing an opportunity, while we were stopped, to rush into the camp and take us by surprise and strangle us all or strike us down.

29th July At four in the morning it began to rain; this went on for three hours, but the water had fallen a quarter arshin since the day before, and where we forded the Ancha the horses were touching the ground all the way. At almost the same time we forded the Anchakan. Soon afterwards we came across a Iakut, naturally one of the returnees, for he immediately galloped off in the direction whence he had come. We were very sorry that we had no chance to warn this man about the proximity of the robbers, who would of course not neglect to plunder him.

About fifty-five versts from Allakh-Iun we passed a sport called *Verbliuzh'ia pad'*, because a pack camel had once died there as it was being led to Okhotsk by some merchant. We were assured that this camel was four sazhens long, and that it had been loaded with two hundred puds--all the other tales told about it by the

Iakuts are equally improbable. About six versts from this spot is a glacier called Bus'Kiul [ice-lake]. It is more than a verst in length and about two hundred sazhens wide, and was said normally to be much more extensive. The ice here never melts completely. It is about one arshin thick, whitish on the surface, but deep blue inside and porous from the rains. The sun's rays, reflected from the surface of this lake, makes one's eyes ache. A little further on were two smaller glaciers the bases of which are fine gravel.

At a lake called Little Chzherga Talakh we shot three ducks. Between this lake and our night's camp we forded the Anchakan as many as twenty times, and more than that number of smaller streams. A little further on is the lake called Bol'shoi Chzhergatalakh. The streams which flow out of this lake join with others flowing from the mountains to form the River Akachan, which flows into the Iudoma. We forded it three times, and at nine o'clock came to a halt. Lake Chzhergatalakh is named after the many small fish found in these lakes which the Iakuts call Chzherga. As they pass through in the summer they catch them with nets.

30th July It rained the whole morning. Some sixteen versts from our camp of the night before we passed *Kapitan Taryn* [the captain's crossing], a glacier up to two versts in length and about two hundred sazhens wide, but this one too was said normally to be bigger. We had some difficulty in crossing, for the ice on its banks was high and steep and, washed along by the currents, the stream pushed between its banks with a roar like the noise from a cannon. To the south, over a high mountain, hung an ominous black cloud past which other clouds were blown on either side at great speed, but below it there was complete stillness. We anticipated rain or thunder, but a wind which sprang up blew all these clouds away.

Not far away from Kapitan taryn we passed a ruined *izba* [hut] two and a half sazhens square in size. Here a merchant travelling by had been forced to spend the winter because of a sudden heavy fall of snow which killed all his horses.

We continued to make our way along the left bank of the river Akachan so as to avoid the fords across this river, which would have halted us, although the road was much longer and extremely bad. With great difficulty we went round the mountain Sokolii kamen', on a road of sharp, uneven rocks, sometimes along the river itself and at others along the ridge of the very high bank. All this time it was raining very heavily.

Five versts from Sokolii kamen' we forded the Ognenaia [fiery] River, which has this name because of the extreme speed of the current there. The ford was so deep that when the rain was at its heaviest we were up to our waists in water, and it could well have been said that we made our way through water, suspended between heaven and earth. After this we went across two fields called the Kogon'ippyt [shot drake], and stopped to spend the night at the Kenchaisk ford.

Ken-chai means wide rocky field, and the ford is so called because the river here is wide and flows over a rocky bottom. Today we forded almost forty small rivers and streams. In the evening the rain stopped, but at

31st July four in the morning it started again and came down so heavily that the Iakuts did not even want to break camp, although they normally put up with bad weather with surprising patience. Even after the rain they rarely bother to dry their clothes and shoes.

Our company gathered in the tent in which only two or three of us could sleep. The rain, which had driven us into this crowded shelter, did not cease to bucket down. The Okhotsk road is difficult enough without this, but on this occasion there were plenty of extra obstacles. It must be confessed that wasps, gadflies, mosquitos, robbers, rain and fords were circumstances enough to try anyone's patience, or to reinforce anyone's impatience.

1st August The rain continued to come down. At six in the morning we dispatched someone to round up the horses, but the Iakuts were so unwilling to go on that we did not set off before eleven. On the day before everything around us had been dry, but today a fast-flowing river met our eyes. Doubtless the rains had caused many such rivers to appear and we should have to be fording them all the time. The Akachan had spread out very widely over its banks and presented a splendid spectacle; the little wooded hills had become islands. Down the river there floated many trees torn up by the roots and sometimes these got caught on the islands. One is not surprised by the height to which the waters rise if one travels near these rivers in the dry season and sees whole trees lying high up in the branches of others. Finally we drew near to a small river, and began to ford it. Our first Iakut was leading four horses. The three at the rear were torn away by the speed of the current, became entangled in the driftwood, and drowned, and only with great risk could their loads be salvaged. So we began to take one horse across at a time at another place where the fold was only a sazhen wide. Here we crossed safely and the only harm done was that all the bags got wet. It was good foresight that we had four horses in reserve and were not detained by the loss of the other three. Some forty versts from Kapitan taryn we crossed the glacier or ice-field Ken-chai which is about two versts long and about one wide -- but it is usually some ten versts long. At four o'clock we halted near Ken-chai on the little River Lamkova, because the water in it was very deep and the Iakuts were so frightened that they said, "If we cross this river, the rest of the horses will be washed away and we shall all be drowned ourselves." And so we were obliged to pitch our tent on the damp tundra or, to put it more accurately, on the bog. We arranged ourselves in it in the following manner: first we spread spruce branches on the ground, then our palliasses, then the saddles, as usual placed at the head. Our guns and pistols were placed between these two "beds," with our sabres at the other side. At the entrance to the tent were placed a box and the dry biscuits. After we had done all this we lay down on our damp blankets and awaited with some impatience for the end of the bad weather.

2nd August At four o'clock the sun appeared for a moment, but then the sky darkened again to such an extent that the hills which were half a verst away from us disappeared from view and the rain came on again heavier than ever. We were wet to the bone and shivering with the cold. Our misery was increased even more by the thought that it we were held up any more on the road by the rain, the ship might leave for America before we arrived in Okhotsk. Then we should be forced to spend a whole year in this town and lose a whole year's time.

Sometimes the Iakuts would not stop at good grazing places, asking us to go even further because this was where "drunken grass" grew. We asked what this drunken grass was. We were told that when a horse eats it it goes wild and throws itself all over the place, and then falls down as though poleaxed, and that the only way of saving it in these circumstances is to saddle it up and gallop it until it lathers and froths. Nobody, however, knows what this poisonous plant looks like. But once the Iakuts hear that a horse has gone berserk on a certain grazing-ground they will never stop there because they assume that that is where the "drunken grass" grows.

From Iakutsk to Allakh-Iun the forest for the most part consists of spruce and pine, and, much less frequently, birch, aspen, alder and cedar saplings, together with a great deal of willow and crowberry. The trees in the forest do not generally grow very tall. From Allakh-Iun onwards they are in places taller, especially the spruce. Then there are a great many poplars of which we had seen very few up to that point, but the firs become more sparse and finally disappear altogether. Along the sides of the road grow bilberries and red and black currents though the latter is rare; there is also a fair amount of crowberry and arctic bramble.

We stopped no further than three versts away from the river, where our horses had been drowned. So our heathen Iakuts took a pot and set off back to eat their fill of horsemeat. The Iakuts are renowned as gluttons and a fatty horse is a great luxury morsel for them, but those who have been baptized let it seem in the company of Russians as though they do not share this taste, although when they are at home in their uluses they live just like the others. The Iakuts eat not only horses which are killed for this purpose, but those that die of diseases, sometimes infectious ones, and they often contract these and die themselves. Three years ago the Iakuts from the Aldan went off haymaking, at which time there is usually feasting, in other words they eat as much as they can. They had with them a horse with plenty of fat on. It suddenly fell down, the Iakuts ran up and saw to their amazement that it was dead. With their usual superstitious turn of mind they thought that a devil had killed it. This, however, did not prevent them from eating the carrion. After several hours all those who had eaten had boils come up on their bodies and then open sores. After forty-eight hours many of them died and putrefaction set in on the wounds of those remaining alive. The same things happened at about that time on the Amga and the Allakh-Iun, where there was a sickness amongst the horses, which the Iakuts went on eating, though, until many of them died as well. Then they had recourse to their shamans; the latter besought the evil spirits not to kill any more of the horses, but notwithstanding this the epidemic went on until well into autumn. The cattle and the horses also suffered with boils and sores. These were so virulent that if anyone were to touch one of the swellings it immediately burst and a sore would appear. This incident taught the Iakuts a lesson and now they no longer eat horses which die of disease, although the epidemic, even so, wiped out many of them on the Allakh-Iun.

That night the ice on the Ken-chai ice-field often moved with a great noise. In the morning our Iakuts came back and brought with them the picked-over carcass of a horse, explaining that on the spot they had eaten only two buckets each, because it was very cold. They removed the manes from all three horses so that when they came back to camp they could show that the horses had been killed and not sold. By means of this ruse, however, when there is no owner of the horses with the convoy, the workers often eat the best of them and bring the mane back with them.

The water in the Lamkova River has fallen so we forded it and climbed up a steep mountain along a very muddy path. One horse lost its footing and tumbled head over hooves down the hill for a couple of sazhens, but when it regained its footing it walked very well. Some ten versts from where we had spent the night we came out onto a main road. We had to ford one channel of the River Akachan, but as it was deep and we did not want to wait we began to make our way along the bank. We rode along a steep and rocky slope or else in the water, where it was shallow, but it was full of wood carried by the floods. This detour was extremely hard going. The Iakuts had heard that there was a better path along the top of the mountain ridge, but they did not know where it was. We came out again onto the road and forded a small river, from where there began a series of "burnings," places where grasses had been burnt down so that better grazing could be obtained from what grew up afterwards. From this river as far as the Iudoma Cross the road is no longer rocky but quite reasonable, although the rains had damaged a lot of it. We forded several deep swamps and approached a small river in which the water was very high, but as it was no more than four sazhens wide we laid several tree-trunks from bank to bank and placed branches on top of them. On this bridge we carried all our load across and then made the horses swim over. The small rivers which flow across the road, and have no particular name, are generally referred to as "crossing rivers." Crossing this area took us three hours. After this we covered about three versts before being brought to a halt by another river. Here we came across several other people going to Okhotsk who were also waiting for the water to fall. Amongst them was the Iakutsk merchant Zakharov, for whom this was already the fortieth journey to Okhotsk. In all that time he had never seen the rivers so high. Along the road our Iakuts even ate horsemeat when it was rotting.

3rd August In the morning it was raining, but did not continue for more than a couple of hours. We had already started to construct a raft on which to make the crossing but our Iakuts were unwilling to try this and insisted that we look for another ford. Instead we found a ready-made bridge, similar to the one we had used earlier. After this river there is a second area of burnt grass. As we crossed it we had to ford several deep swamps and we eventually came up to the Griaznaia River, so named because of its extremely muddy bottom. It was flooded to such an extent that from the spot we stood on to the Iudoma there was hardly a dry patch of land (the river flows into the Iudoma), and this despite the fact that there is normally some two versts between the banks of the rivers. Not far from us there were several families of nomadic Tungus and we engaged one of them to go to Iudoma Cross and to bring back a large boat. We saw him set out in his "birch branch" [a kind of small river craft], like those used on the Lena, but these are smaller and appear to travel faster. The Tungus had stopped to catch fish. We rode on some of their deer. A very small saddle with no stirrups is used by the rider normally has in his right hand a stick which enables him to maintain his balance. The ride is uncomfortable, but fast, for the deer moves with large steps, and gallops very fast. A deer goes very easily up mountainsides because of its short front legs.

4th August In the morning a cossack arrived from Iudoma Cross; there are normally five or six of them living there to ferry travellers across the river. This man was in a wooden "birch branch," and told us that he had had to leave the large boat three versts back because the extremely strong adverse current had prevented him from rowing and it had not been possible to row or pull the boat by rope to where we were when the water was in flood in the forest. This cossack had lived for more than twenty years at Iudoma Cross and said that he could not remember when the water had been so high. All the cultivated land had been flooded, several yurtas and barns also had been washed away and also a bell-tower with a cross which had been constructed long before by Bering's expedition, and which had given its name to the place.

We had almost no food left, but as at two o'clock several goosanders [a kind of wild duck] appeared nearby, as though by design. I shot one, and the other which could not yet fly was caught by our dog. And so we dined in fine style.

Soon after this we bought a small ox for fifteen rubles from a Iakut who was driving his cattle to Okhotsk. Our Iakuts drank the fresh blood, and the guts, tail and offal that we threw away they gobbled up, after having first placed them in warm ashes for awhile.

In expectation of the continuation of our journey I asked the merchant Zakharov about the road ahead, and about the Iakuts and many other matters relating to this region. En passant, I shall copy down two notable incidents about which I heard from him, and later heard from others.

The merchant Tropin, who was travelling to Okhotsk with some of his companions, fell behind them a little and stumbled across a bear of enormous size which leapt at him to tear him to pieces. Tropin had no chance of escape but was forced to grapple with the bear. He seized it by its ears and shouted to his colleagues for help. When they and the Iakuts ran up to see what he was shouting about, they saw that the bear was standing on its hind legs, and towering over its opponent, although the latter was quite tall, and so they took to their heels in fright. And thus the two combatants fought without interruption for more than an hour. The bear tore several wounds in the merchant's shoulder, but it could not get to work with its teeth because it was in such a tight grip. Eventually it began to tire and when Tropin noticed this he managed to grab his knife from behind his belt and to plunge it into the bear's belly. The merchant was so angry with his brave companions that when he caught up with them he gave them all something to remember with a stick.

A similar incident took place a little later, when some of the merchant Lebedev's hunters were going to Okhotsk. With the party were to Zyrians, who were driving a black bull. One day they lost the bull and went into the forest to look for it, but instead of finding the bull one of them came upon a bear, which immediately attacked him. The Zyrian, apparently quite without fear, took one of the bear's arms under his, and with his other hand gripped the bear's ear, and in this way saved himself from being bitten. He shouted to his comrade, who had come up on hearing cries for help, to take out the axe from behind his belt. As this had already disappeared the other Zyrian took a large club and hit the animal so hard that it fell over. The hunters then skinned the bear and sold the pelt on the Aldan for ten rubles; later they also found the black bull and the axe. They never stopped boasting about their victory.

5th August The day was fine and the water level had dropped a great deal. The boat arrived from Iudoma Cross, and we set off across the River Griaznukha. We ferried our packs over on the boat, and made the horses swim across. Then we put their packs on again and sent them on to the Iudoma, while we ourselves set off in the boat to Iudoma Cross, which is on the left bank of the Iudoma. This river is as much as two hundred and fifty sazhens wide. Although the water level here and in the Griaznukha had fallen four arshins in thirty-six hours, the current was still so strong that the horses were carried almost a verst downstream. When they had dried off they were saddled and loaded up with their packs again. We forded the mouth of the River Krestovka, which flows into the Iudoma, where the cross and the bell-tower had stood. Then we crossed several swamps and forded the Krestovka six or seven times. This river flows out of Lake Sis'-Kiul, or Ridge Lake, which is thirty-five versts from Iudoma Cross. At twelve at night we stopped at Ala-ogus'-asylyk [the feeding ground of the White Bull]. The weather was very cold, and there was even a slight frost so that the fire which we quickly got going comforted us in no small measure.

6th August The day was fine, but cold. We forded the Krestovka about fifteen times and rode past Lake Sis'-Kiul, leaving it behind us on the right. We were told that it contained a great many fish. I believe that Sis'-Kiul is on a very elevated strip of land for out of it flow on the one side the Krestovka which flows into the Iudoma, which in turn flows into the Maia, which in its own turn joins the Aldan; on the other side there flows out the River Urak, which goes into the Sea of Okhotsk twenty versts south of Okhotsk itself. We forded this river seven or eight times and then halted at Kel'tegei-Kurum [empty grove].

7th August That night and during the morning a light drizzle fell, but it did not last long. The gadflies and mosquitos had disappeared, but in their place flies appeared.

We forded the Urak and arrived at a clearing where three yurtas had been built. In these there lived three cossacks and a soldier to guard any official property, which was occasionally stored in the four barns built specially for the purpose. At midday there was an hour and a half of heavy rain, but we could see the sun all the time it was pouring down. On the right we passed Kononov's pillar, erected by a certain Kononov in 1769. We forded the Urak and then a small river flowing into it from the left, and halted not far from Kislyi Ford, on the Urak. The Iakuts said that on all the rivers here there were many bears, which wandered there to catch the fish, which were now coming up-river from the sea in great quantities. So we fired our pistols several times to frighten these animals away.

We set off on our way, crossing the Urak at Kislyi Ford, and then the Porozhnyi [Rapids] Ford, so called because of its being situated between two small sets of rapids, and we began to ascend the *bludnoi* range, about ten versts from Porozhnyi Ford and about fifty from the yurtas. The ascent and descent were extremely steep. Down the first there flows a small nameless river, and on the descent there is the Bludnaia which joins the Urak from the left. Then we crossed two small rivers flowing into the Urak from the same direction, then forded the Bludnaia four times and stopped to camp for the night. On the way there I shot a duck and a quail. The Iakuts were very displeased that we had not shot any squirrels.

Some twenty sazhens from our tent was a steep rock-face on one side, and a little nearer to the other side was the Bludnaia River. The narrow strip on which we were camped was covered with sparse larch trees. The blackness of the night, the clear weather, the wind whistling sadly in the cracks of the overhanging rock-face, and the burning campfires, all produced a certain desolation of the soul.

9th August At seven o'clock we struck camp, and crossed the Bludnaia River and left the Grebenchatoi Kamen' Mountain behind us on our left. The mountain was so called because it was said to look like a comb, but it did not appear so to me. Some seven versts away from it is Bolbukta Otutta [thick cedar grove]; and some three versts away we forded the Bol'shoi Luktur, at the spot where it flows into the Urak from the right. It rises in the mountains thirty versts to the south of Okhotsk. Then we crossed two small streams and the Malyi Luktur, all of which flow into the Urak from the right. On the latter river there were two yurtas of nomadic Tungus, who were there catching the fish as they went upstream. Not far from here we crossed the Bobrovo Pole [Field] (a name derived from a certain Bobrov who once lived there), through which flows the River Bobrovka, flowing into the Urak from the right. Then we arrived at the Uratsk Ferry, where there are two cossacks stationed to ferry goods over in a boat. But, as the water was very low, we forded the river. Further on we came to a place called Kupetskoi anbar [merchant barn] and to At-kyayata [horse mountain] where we stopped to spend the night.

10th August We set off, crossed the Konnyi Range River and began to ascend the mountain of that name. When we had descended from it again we forded two small rivers; a cross-channel and the Chel'chikan, which flow into the Okhota, and arrived at Meta, where the Iakuts live. We went into one of their summer yurtas, made from cut logs. It was about one and a half sazhens square with a birch-bark roof, with a hole in the center to let the smoke out, for beneath it on the floor of the yurta is a hearth. On the fire stood a pot for cooking fish. It was quite dirty in the yurta, but less so than in the yurtas of the Iakuts living in Iakutsk *okrug*. The latter were said by the local residents here to live like dogs.

Further on we forded the Namova River which flows into the Okhota, passed through Kiokho-tiriakh [green poplar grove] and cross a side channel of the River Chzholokona, then we crossed the main river itself by boat. This river flows into the Okhota. Beyond it there are two mountain ridges, Chzholokon and Mal'chikan, with a river of the same name which flows into the Okhota from the right. Then we crossed the Ese-basa [Bear's Head] and at eleven we stopped to feed the horses. In these places we found more berries than we had before and also much honeysuckle, which is here called *Aleuktoia*.

Before I finish my description of the road to Okhotsk and our arrival there I consider it not out of place to tell everything that I myself saw, and could reliably discover from others, concerning the Iakuts.

The Iakuts, as is well known, come from the Tatar race. There is a great similarity between their language and Tatar and also a similarity of customs, so that this may serve as sufficient proof. I have already described their winter yurtas. In the summer most Iakuts live in the place where they store their hay. All the hay fields are normally enclosed. The princelings, who have many cattle and horses, do not feed them all on hay but keep the greater part of them in the steppes, where they scrape away the snow and feed on the grass remaining under it, because it is impossible to keep sufficient stocks of hay in, when some princelings have as many as a thousand or more horses and cattle.

Many Iakuts wear their hair in long plaits, those of the women being longer, starting at the very base of the neck. In summer the Iakuts wear short kaftans made of cloth, cotton, or velveteen, caught round with a belt two or three fingers width wide, in a color contrasting with that of the kaftan. Their shoes are sewn from ox-hide, with soft soles, or they are made from horsehide and these are called *saris*. *Saris* are made sturdily and strongly and because they are so good in wet weather the majority of inhabitants of Iakutsk wear them for walking, and even wear them in the town. Leather breeches, mittens and a hat complete the Iakut's vestments. In summer the women wear the same apparel as the men. The Iakut's winter wear consists of warm jersey, breeches, half-length coats and long boots, which are worn with the wool outside and are called *torbasy*. On top of this when travelling they also wear a *sanaiakh*, a kind of *tulup* made from deerskin, also with the fur on the outside. In addition when the frost is very severe they cover (with specially made strips of fur) their forehead, cheeks, ears, nose, and chin, so that only their eyes remain uncovered; on their knees they wear above their *torbasy* the so-called *sutury*. The Russians do this also when they journey across the wastes of Eastern Siberia where the frosts are unimaginably severe. In the winter the Iakuts wear *parkas*, trimmed with fox-fur or sable. A parka is sewn up from deerskin, and looks like a long shirt, which for the most part has a tall collar sewn onto it. The winter clothing of the rich Iakuts, especially their hats, is very expensive.

The Iakuts are a good-natured people, hospitable, generally very cowardly, idle and, when they get the chance, gluttonous beyond all bounds, and they can equally well exist for long periods without food when need or poverty forces them to do so. The staple diet of many Iakuts is *undana* and *soroia*, a kind of sour butter; but these same people can consume amazing amounts of food. I had it from an extremely reliable eyewitness that four Iakuts had eaten a good fat horse in two days. Their gluttony is the reason why, as I have already said, they never throw away dead horses or other kinds of carrion. The meat when eaten is either raw, fried, or boiled; it is all the same to them. They even eat the skins from the bulls, simply rolling it in hot ashes to singe off the fur and they do not all do this, simply because they are hungry. The Iakuts are very fond of moles, but most of all of pork fat, of which some of them can eat upwards of a pud at one sitting. Gluttony amongst them is rated a virtue and they talk about gluttons with respect: *Utío asatchi khise*--which means: "he is a good eater." They laugh at those who eat little, saying, "what kind of man are you?"

But in order to give a clearer idea of the Iakuts' gluttony, I shall describe the rituals conducted at wedding feasts.

When someone is courting he agrees beforehand to pay the bride's father *kolym*, consisting of several bulls and horses, half of which are later given back to the groom as a dowry. The wedding and the feast take place in the father-in-law's house, but at the groom's expense. The festivities usually last two days, and relatives and friends from both sides gather together. A rich man will entertain his guests with wine, but those who are not so rich, with *kumiss*. After this, several horses are eaten, or bulls, and sometimes a great many moles which are considered a delicacy; wine is drunk again, or kumiss, and small amounts of fat are eaten. For the festivities all kinds of fat are gathered, mixed together and placed in a tub. When the *kurum* [banquet or wedding breakfast] comes, all the fat is heated up, and everyone sits round the tub. A huge spoon, or it might be better described as a ladle, called a *khamyiak*, is passed round until someone refuses. Fanatical devotees can be found who will drink a hundred and twenty spoons of heated fat, and it must be remembered that this is at the end of the main meal, a fatty meal, a meal during which, naturally, no Iakut had spared his stomach.

Kumiss is made from mare's milk which is mixed in half measure with water, poured into a leather bag and left hanging up in the yurta until it goes sour. Then they take a whisk made from wood carved out like a cup, with four or five slots drilled in it, and with a stick set in the bottom. This whisk is used to beat the sour milk until there is a kind of cheesecake on the bottom--the liquid remaining is called kumiss and is equivalent to beer in strength.

When Iakuts are married there are no religious rituals at all. If the *kolym* is all paid, then the young girl, attended by many women, comes to the groom's house. If the *kolym* has not been cleared she remains in her father's house, and the husband goes off to his. Each time that he drives over some of the *kolym* animals, he stays for several days with his wife, and when he leaves he receives half the *kolym* back. A father-in-law will never release his daughter until all the *kolym* has been paid, even though this may take several years. When it is paid the wife, as has been said, goes to the husband's house accompanied by many women, and at that time there are another two days of feasting. The *kolym* can sometimes be as much as eighty cows.

Many Iakuts also celebrate the birth of a son, or daughter, with the same kind of feasting.

The Iakuts, especially the poor, are very dirty. In winter they keep the cattle in their yurtas, and this will give some impression of the smell in their homes. In the summer they make mortar from cowdung and in winter they pour in water and allow it to freeze there. In the dish formed by this they crush fir bark, which they use as food.

These people have preserved some of their stranger customs, as for example: If a Iakut has been away for some time when he comes back to the yurta he greets no one, but sits to one side like a stranger, his wife cooks for him and entertains him as a guest. Only when he has eaten well does he become master of the house again.

When the bride is present the brother-in-law must wear a hat, otherwise both she and he are dishonored. If he has been sitting in the yurta bareheaded, then he puts on a hat when the bride comes in.

The Iakuts believe in their magicians or shamans, who carry out superstitious rituals in secrecy, for if the local priests discover them they have them brought to trial. But even to this day the Iakuts still place faith in them and fear them. Sometimes the shaman, a year or more after a Iakut has died, brings to his house a decorated image, and says that this is the dead man and that he demands a cow or some animal furs, or something else of this kind. And he threatens that the dead man will devour them all if they refuse. These cowardly people give everything that is demanded of them and the shaman carries it all off with the statue. The Iakuts tell remarkable tales about their magicians, and especially about a certain kachikat who used to stick several knives through himself, and that he had cut off peoples' arms and hung them up on the trees without causing them any pain. Also it was said of him that if food ran out on a journey he would ask his companions if they would like something to eat. Then he would intone a few words and spread his arms, into which there usually dropped some tasty morsel, for example, part of a fat mare, or a *simir'* with butter (*simir'* is the name given to the leather bags in which they carry undan and butter which forms of itself or, as it is called in Iakut *khaiak*. Cow's, or heated, butter is, on the other hand, called *ary*). This kachikat, so it is said, always knew what was going to happen two or three days in advance. They also assured us that he had made a wooden cuckoo and placed it in a tree, and that it called for three years, that is, until the Russians burnt it together with the tree; also that when kachikat died the Iakuts dug a hole next to his grave and placed in it his shaman's dress, and for three years afterwards they could hear the sound of it jingling in the evening. In short, this kachikat had performed so many miracles that the Iakuts feared him more than *Boenaia*, and it must also be admitted that many of the Russians believe in him no less than the Iakuts.

When one of their princes has a horse which he loves but which has grown old, it is set free, but if it lives long enough afterwards for its teeth to begin to fall out then the prince kills it and it is eaten at a gathering of all the relatives. But it more often happens that other cattle are killed for a prince's feast, and that his favorite horse is buried, and in another hole nearby are placed all the items of harness such as: saddile, bit, packbags, a bow and arrow, and the *pal'ma*. Almost every horse on the road has saddle packs, they are thrown across the saddle and hang in such a way that they do not get in the rider's way at all. A *pal'ma* is the name given to a knife larger than a kitchen knife which is placed in a wooden scabbard about one arshin long. It is usually used for cutting wood.

When the Iakuts see a bear on the road, they remove their hats and bow to it; they ennoble it by calling it *toion* [chief], old man, uncle, and other terms of endearment. They beseech most humbly to be allowed to pass; they assure him that they will not hurt him, and they will not even speak ill of him. If the bear remains unconvinced by these assurances and throws itself upon their horses then they begin, as though against their will, to fire at him. If he is killed they eat him with great ceremony. At the same time they fashion a statue depicting *Boenaia* and bow down to it. The senior Iakut present goes behind a tree and twists about. When the meat is cooked they eat it with a great cawing noise, like crows, and they chant: "We are not eating you but the Tungus or the Russians; they make the powder, they sell the guns; but you know that we do not know how to do these things." All the time they talk in Russian, in Tungus, and they do not break any of the bones. When they have eaten the bear, they gather the bones together and wrap them, together with the image of Boenaia, in birth bark or anything else to hand, and hang them on a tree saying: "Grandad! The Russians (or Tungus) have eaten you, but we have found and gathered up your bones." From this ritual it may be concluded to what degree the Iakuts are afraid of the bears' vengeance, or of their spirit, even after they have been killed.

Some Iakuts, even to this day, when they cook a meal on a journey, raise it up in their hands and make a speech to the spirit of the place, then they place the food back on the ground and each of them throws his first spoonful into the fire and only then begins to eat. The Iakuts believe that every place has a spirit, which is neither a god nor a devil, but a special kind of spirit.

11th August That night it rained. At seven we set off and travelled past the *charcoal pits*, that is the place where the exiles burn charcoal for special government smithy works. The nearer we came to the sea, the lower the trees in the forest became, finally bushes began, and on the coast itself there was no growth at all. We came to the place called *Amunki*, on the coast itself; then we turned to the left and went along the coast. In Amunki there were a great many crowberries.

The sight of a perfectly calm sea, and of a fish playing in it, the snorting of the sea animals, and the sound of the waves eternally breaking on the beach produced an indescribable sensation of pleasure in me. I felt that all our troubles were behind us and I had come to my own element. The limitless ocean, which I was soon to sail across, scorning the anger of the waves, gave me a sense of satisfaction, and I was ready to put to sea at that very moment.

Ten versts from Amunki is the town of Okhotsk. As you approach it you can see its church and bell tower from a distance, and then the whole town, which we reached at six in the evening.

CHAPTER III

PREPARATIONS FOR THE VOYAGE. DEPARTURE FROM OKHOTSK. THE *ELISAVETA* RUNS AGROUND NEAR THE KURILE ISLANDS. WE ENTER THE BAY OF TANAGA ISLAND. WE PASS UNALGA AND UNALASHKA. STORMY WEATHER AND A SERIOUS LEAK IN THE SHIP. WE LAND ON THE ISLAND OF KAD'IAK WHERE WE SPEND THE WINTER.

1802
August

12th We quickly made the acquaintance of Mr. Polevoi, the company's agent living in Okhotsk, a kind and able man. The ship *Elisaveta* on which we were to sail for America had already been fitted out, but it had been done so badly that everything had to be done again. This work had little prospect of success because the crew consisted of only one reliable man, bosun Semchin; the remainder were hunters in company employ, in other words men hired in various parts of Siberia for dispatch to America. Many of them had never seen the sea before. To this it should be added that the ship had been built of wood felled in winter, and that all the rigging, the blocks and other mechanical equipment seemed to have been manufactured specially to increase our troubles and not to lessen them. I honestly could not imagine that with the art of navigation at the stage of development it is at present, such bad ships as those in Okhotsk could exist.

Here I also met my friend Baron Shteingeil, whom I had last seen in Portsmouth. We were together for the whole of our stay in Okhotsk.

I shall not devote space to a description of Okhotsk, for this has already been done by other travellers. I shall say only that the town is built on the end of a lot spit of land consisting of small, round pebbles. This promontory, called a *koshka* [cat], is in places no wider than twenty-five sazhens. On the one side it faces the Sea of Okhotsk and on the other the River Okhota which ceaselessly washes against it with the result that the inhabitants often have to dismantle their houses and move them somewhere else. For this and several other reasons, over the course of several years the number of houses has been cut by half. When there is a strong wind from the sea and the tide is coming in, it sometimes washes across the spit. The town is then under water and is in danger of being washed away to its foundations.

There are an extremely large number of dogs in the town, as they are used in winter to pull the sledges.

At about midnight one dog would begin howling, then others would join in, and then all the dogs in the town would be howling together in different keys; they made such a loud and awful concert that while it was in progress it made one wish to be deprived of hearing.

It is well known that the dogs here, and the ones in Kamchatka, never bark, but only howl. They are very well behaved and never attack people; but if they were to do so it would be difficult to save oneself. When two of the dogs are fighting the others gather at the noise and pace around, watching to see what the outcome of the struggle will be. The dogs owned by one man quickly become accustomed to one another and always live together. If a stranger enters the pack it runs the risk of being badly mauled unless it manages to escape. The dogs here and those in Kamchatka have pricked ears, those with hanging ears are very rare.

At this time of year the dogs were very fat, for there were many fish washed up all along the river banks. Like bears they chew the fish heads and eat only the brains. Also at this time they are shedding and some look very peculiar. On many all the fur had gone from their head and torso, but as it was a tight fur much of it had caught on the tail and was dragging along behind. In winter they are kept tied up, used for travelling and fed small amounts of dried fish, known as *iukola*, by which name it is known both here, on Kamchatka, and in America. At the end of autumn when the rivers freeze over and the snow begins to fall, everyone sets out to round up his dogs, some come in of their own accord because they can find nothing to eat.

The inhabitants of the eastern coast of Siberia, the whole of Kamchatka, and Northwest America would not be able to live in such wild and impoverished places at all, were it not for the fact that nature has provided them with special methods of acquiring food. During the summer, in all the rivers which flow into the sea, there are great numbers of fish going upstream, the great majority of them salmon, which the inhabitants catch and lay in stocks of for the winter by various means. In Okhotsk they salt it, but as there is very little salt, the greater part of the fish is dried. It is first cut up the middle to the tail, gutted, filleted, and hung on poles where it dries and is then called *iukola*. This is normally given to the dogs, but if needs be people eat it too. Sometimes in winter the price of one iukola goes as high as fifty kopeks. In the autumn when the weather is not so hot and the flies which might spoil the fish as it is drying disappear, then they begin to hang it out, gutting it, but not filleting it, and this is called *kachemas*. Kachemas must not be as dry as iukola and is prepared as food for human consumption.

Then, when the frosts begin and the fish are still

being caught, they are frozen and buried in the snow, where they remain fresh all winter as long as there are no large-scale thaws.

In the summer the simple people here wear mostly *kamleikas* made from *rovduga*; this is the name given to any kind of deerskin prepared without the fur. A kamleika is like a shirt, but with a hood at the back. Kamleikas are also made from cotton. In the winter they wear parkas and *kupliankas*. This latter garment is like a parka, but with a hood which is pulled over the head during a blizzard, and there is a cloth sewn onto the collar at the front, which can be lifted to cover the face. Kupliankas are usually made double, with fur lining inside and outside. Less well-off people are more likely to wear dog-skin parkas which are incomparably warmer than the others. Deerskin clothes and hides are brought in by the Russians from Gizhiginsk and Tigil, from the Chukchi and Koriak, while merchants take to the above-mentioned towns (as well as to Kamchatka) vodka, tobacco, tea, sugar, shot, *daba* [cheap cotton], *fanza* [foulard] (a Chinese silk material), and other articles necessary for the life of the community. All these goods are dispatched from Okhotsk on government ships which make the return journey carrying supplies for the small military contingent maintained there. A *poltina* per pud is levied for the cost of transportation, but the goods are sold locally at extraordinarily high prices.

Okhotsk is the centre for trade between Siberia and Russia's eastern possessions, America, Kamchatka and Gizhiginsk, but more will be said about that in another place.

21st Finally our ship was ready. In accordance with tradition we held a church service on board, followed by a meal. I do not think anyone will be sorry if I do not describe this splendid repast.

23rd The rivers Okhota and Kukhtui flow into the sea through one mouth, where the depth of the water at low tide is no greater than four and a half to five feet. Vessels putting in, therefore, have to do so at high tide, and the tide enters the river at great speed. When the water rises in the river mouth it can at various times of the year be between ten and fifteen feet deep and more; it is normally somewhere between nine and eleven. For this reason the beginning of the receding tide is usually chosen for putting to sea, when as they say, the water "trembles." The route is through the delta of the river, full of shallows, and across the river bar, or barrier. There should also be no fresh breeze from the sea because this causes a heavy surf on the bar, which makes access to the open sea absolutely impossible. Many ships have been wrecked because they paid no heed to this danger, amongst them the *Dobroe namerenie* [Good Intention] which was built for Captain Billings' expedition.

At about midday we approached the mouth of the Okhota; but a fresh wind suddenly sprang up from the southeast, and we had to wait for the next high tide.

24th From midnight on we began to use our kedge anchor. Our pilot did not know the *manikhi* (high water at unusual times which defy any calculations). The current changed much more quickly than we had anticipated. The kedges we had cast began to drag, though they had been holding, thus the boat was driven towards a sandbar, and the swell beating against her became quite strong. However, the water level soon began to drop. The vessel grounded and lay peacefully, for there was only one and a half feet of water underneath her. When the tide came in the boat came off the bank with the help of its sails and stood in four sazhens of water. At this time I went onto the quarter deck, banged against the wheelhouse, knocked into a davit, and was forced to go to my cabin and rest. But the cabin was full of smoke and no one seemed to know where it was coming from. Since I knew that there was more than fifty puds of gunpowder under the cabin, I went out to the deck to see if I could discover the source of the smoke. Up above many people had come to the ship from the town, and they were all shouting: "Smoke! Fire! Fire! We're finished!" and other things in this vein. Those who were standing on the shore some fifty sazhens from us began to run farther away; afraid naturally, of being killed if the powder exploded. But it was soon dragged out and placed in a rowing boat. Then two bales of warm thread were discovered and it was thought that they were the cause of the smoke, but it was later realized that smoke from the galley had been entering the cabin through cracks in the decking, and then been escaping through the door, because as soon as the fire in the galley was extinguished, all the smoke went from under the deck, and did not appear again.

After this incident we got under way, but the current of six to seven knots caused us to drift and pushed us in the direction of the shore. We managed to come off with great difficulty, and came to a stop again in four sazhens of water.

When the direction of the current began to change the anchors and the kedges began to drag, and the Kukhtui current caused us to drift towards a sandbar on the left bank of the Okhota.

25th All the expediencies we employed were in vain, and we had to wait for the next high tide yet again. We were brought a kedge anchor which also did not grip or take the strain.

26th At five in the morning the tide was high, but *manikha* was so great that the difference between high and low water was less than four and a half feet. When the tide came in in the evening we came off the sandbank and in addition to the anchor we cast three kedge anchors from the bows and the stern.

There were in all forty-nine people on board the *Elisaveta:* Lieutenant Khvostov, who was in command of her, myself, the steersman, the understeersman, bosun, three sailors and thirty-four promyshlenniks, two Aleuts from the Fox Islands, one American from the Aliaksa Peninsula, a company agent and his assistant, and our two men. Towards midnight there was a strong wind with squalls from the north-northeast, but in the morning the wind dropped. In the evening I met one of the company's older navigators; he had hardly any idea what a compass was, had never seen maps, yet he sailed the sea, albeit slowly, yet safely nevertheless. It was then that I recalled the proverb: *Schast'e luchshe bogatyrstva* [Luck is better than brave deeds]. An official sloop left the mouth of the river, but the water was still too low for our ship.

28th At seven in the evening we began to pull out of the river mouth against the incoming tide. At nine we had reached the bar, which is about two hundred sazhens wide. As the wind was light, but favorable, we raised the topsail and foresail, the jib, cross-sails and, with the aid of a tug, crossed the bar. There we stopped because the wind had dropped, and we dropped anchor in five sazhens of water. The sea bed was fine sand.

29th At four in the morning we raised anchor in a light favorable wind, and at ten we hove to and raised the baidaras which are normally on company ships instead of dinghies. Baidaras are rowing boats which are used in those parts of America where there is no wood for the building of dinghies, or where they do not know how to make them. The Russians took over such rowing boats from the savages. In constructing baidaras, at first a frame is built of a very light and sparse pattern and over this a sewn skin is stretched tightly, and this serves instead of planking. Sea-lion skins are mostly used for this purpose but, in Okhotsk, when need demands, rawhide is also used. A baidara is more often steered by an oar than by a wheel. The prow is steeply upright and slightly rounded, while the stern is very long and sloping, so that the baidara may ride the waves more easily. It may well be imagined how uncomfortable such rowing boats are.

The work on our ship had been carried out extremely badly and, indeed, we could not have expected anything else, when not one of the hunters or sailors knew what he was about. At about midday the wind freshened, causing the waves to whip up considerably. Most of the men felt nauseated and other symptoms of sea-sickness.

30th At night the wind dropped, but in the morning it freshened again and forced us to take in the top-gallants and the top-gallant yards. At around midday a hawk appeared over the ship, but was quickly lost to our sight again.

Until noon the weather was fine, but in the afternoon it rained and the wind blew from the north. Several small birds which could not go very far from the shore flew around the ship and they were, of course, finally blown away by the wind. One of them was so tired that it landed on the deck and was easily caught by hand. Although we carried it into the cabin straight away and fed it some seed, it soon died.

The rain continued until four in the afternoon. A small species of duck flew and swam round the ship. As we had a fair amount of free time we read about the terrible plight of the English ship *Centaur*, under the command of Captain Englefield[?]. With only thirteen or fifteen of its crew left alive, it was the only ship to survive from a great convoy of naval ships and merchantmen. Although a similar fate could easily befall us, the descriptions we read did not alarm us. Perhaps this was because it is difficult to think deeply about other people's misfortunes when you are near to them yourself.

5th Sept It was a splendid day with a light wind. At five in the afternoon we could see from the bridge the island of Alait, the rounded summit of which was covered with snow. One of the sailors sitting in the cross-trees in order to look at the shoreline said that he had sighted the island some time before but had been afraid to say so.

"Afraid of what?" we asked.

"I was once whipped for doing so," was the reply.

We finally succeeded in solving this mystery. It appeared that when they went for a long time without seeing land they would quite justifiably ascribe this to the ineptness of the ship's captain or navigator (as they are called here) and they would sometimes jokingly pretend to see land. For this they were beaten and consequently they now stayed silent even if they actually did see land.

It might not be out of place here to say something

at length about the sea journeys by Russian promyshlenniks and merchants across the Eastern Ocean. They were in the past and still are carried out under the very crudest of conditions and with crude equipment. The remoteness makes it difficult to attract people skilled in the art of navigation, and supplies are expensive, especially shells of any kind. The local private entrepreneurs are self-seeking, with ingrained habits. Instead of the government overseeing things, there is the harmful rule of always concealing what is bad. These, and other reasons, allow for only slow and gentle progress in bringing navigation up to the desired level. Concealing these conditions is the same as wishing for them never to be improved. Thus we shall describe these activities just as they really are. Up till now boats have been built in Okhotsk in the worst possible way; for it has either been carried out by one of the promyshlenniks with no knowledge of shipbuilding, or by some shipbuilder's apprentice, whose stock of knowledge is also not very great. A ship built under these conditions is then loaded and armed in exactly the same way, in other words, in complete ignorance of the rules for doing these things. Then a skipper or seafarer has to be found to sail the vessel. The harbormaster at Okhotsk lets them have, in return for several hundred rubles, an apprentice navigator who is half-drunk and knows nothing. More usually one of the promyshlenniks who has been to the islands several times is chosen. Such a man is known as a *starovoiazhnyi* [old voyageur], while novices are called *kazaras*. The skill of this seafarer will consist of his knowing the compass, having a fair idea of the course necessary to bring him from one place to another, and being familiar by sight with various coastlines. From Okhotsk he will first make for the Kamchatka Peninsula and there, if his vessel is not wrecked on the shore, he will cross to the First Kuril'e Strait. Seeing some familiar landmark is known as *perekhvatit' bereg* [steering by the shore]. From the Kuril'e Islands he will go farther and try to sight one of the Aleutian Islands. He will follow the Aleutian Chain and try to remain in sight of the shore, as far as Unalashka or Kad'iak, wherever the ship is bound for. Going along the Aleutian Islands is known as *probirat'sia po za ogorodu* [following the fence], for these islands lie so close to each other all the way to America that if you follow them it is virtually impossible to lose them from sight.

A vessel leaving Okhotsk will never reach Kad'iak in the same year. A seafarer is afraid of staying at sea after the beginning of September, so as soon as this month begins he will make for any land in sight and shelter in a suitable bay or in an enclosed strait. He will choose a sandy shore, that is, "a soft place," to drag his boat up, build huts for his men, and feed them with any animals and fish they catch until the following July. For it is only then that he reckons it safe to sail; then the boat will be refloated and make its way further on. Rigging a galley with a mizzen mast without a top-mast cannot take a great deal of time. There have been cases where a ship leaving Okhotsk has taken four years to reach Kad'iak. They sail for only a very short period and then only with a following wind. If there is a contrary wind they simply heave to, even if the wind is only a gentle one, for they have no conception of tacking. If during this time the boat is carried away from the shore by a current or by a strong wind, they try to keep the land in sight again wherever it may be, so that they can keep to the only course they have learned to take. If they are unable to do this they are in dire straits. It has happened that boats have been carried away from the shore for a month or two and no longer know in which direction there is land. Then the men have suffered greatly from the lack of food, and even more from the lack of water. They have even been reduced to eating their shoes and the leather wrappings of the rigging. As a result vessels have either perished altogether, or lost most of their crew, or arrived late at their destinations with all their cargo ruined. These misfortunes, which arise from ignorance, have been in the past ascribed to Fate, and no one has given any thought to trying to prevent them.

There is the well-known case of the vessel [the *Zosima i Savvatii* in 1792] which set off from Kamchatka and failed to make the Aleutian Islands. It was driven so far to the south, supposing the islands to be still in the same direction, that in November the pitch had already begun to melt. I met many of the men from this ship, and they told me that eventually, not knowing what to do or where to go, and suffering unbearably from a lack of fresh water, they had decided to give themselves over to the will of the Almighty. They brought an ikon of the Mother of God onto the deck and prayed to it saying that they would go with the wind, from whichever quarter it blew. An hour later it began to pour with rain, and a strong wind blew from the south which went on for eighteen days and nights. All this time they were simply running before the wind. They passed some land, and finally, after the eighteenth day, they sighted some more. The men were so overjoyed that they crossed themselves, hoisted all sails, and made towards the shore. It turned out to be the island of Afognak, north of Kad'iak, on which latter island there was at that time already a settlement left by Mr. Shelikhov, which was now in the charge of Mr. Baranov. The voyage made by these hunters confirms that there is land in the area of the fortieth parallel.

What happened to these voyagers in the Eastern Ocean seems absolutely improbable. One of them sailed three times in one summer from Unalashka looking for the Seal [Pribilof] Islands, about one hundred and sixty miles away, and each time he failed to find them.

Another voyager ran aground on the shore of Kamchatka in a fierce gale and so luckily that afterwards hardly a wave reached as far as the ship. The captain was awoken and told that they had run aground and were on dry land. Then there was great confusion as to where they were--in Japan or in America--but a soldier who happened upon them in the morning told them that they were near Bol'sheretsk.

A third company, as their ship was driven towards the shore during a storm, put down two anchors and all went ashore. Later the wind changed and the vessel was blown out to sea again, but Providence, which enables even the blind to see, carried the ship back again, several days later, to the same spot on the shore and the crew were able to board their ship again.

The coastline of Kamchatka, which these old-time navigators would usually try to follow, often bore witness to their ignorance. When one ship went ashore with every inch of canvas on her, various means were tried to get her off again. Several of the crew favored using kedge anchors, and others thought to get off with all sail, but the incoming tide lifted them off and saved them the bother.

The ship *Orel*, travelling from the Bering Straits to Kad'iak, was blown onto its side by a squall. The skipper was in his cabin and refused to come out because he was praying. To their entreaties he replied, "Now we are in God's hands." Finally one of the promyshlenniks who was a little bit braver than the others, and who had realized that neither the skipper nor anyone else was going to do anything to save them, took in the sails, and the vessel righted itself.

There are many similar examples. These latter-day Argonauts, also journeying for fleeces, but this time to America, are worthy of more amazement than those led by Jason. For thought they are equally ignorant and their equipment is just as primitive, yet the seas they have to cross are far greater in expanse, and are completely unfamiliar to them. To their complete ignorance of seamanship must also be added lack of leadership, for the promyshlenniks have absolutely no respect for their skippers, whom they often beat and lock into their cabins. When land is not sighted for a long while they then consult among themselves and replace the skipper; the old one is locked up, and under the new one they dash to any land, wherever it might be. I say "dash" advisedly, for there is no other way to describe how the ships are pulled up on any old beach. The ukaz of his Imperial Majesty, announced by Minister Mordvinov, which allows members of the Admiralty to keep their rank and at half-salary enter service with one of the merchant companies, established to develop trade, will provide a means of improving the state of navigation in the

Eastern Ocean. Khvostov and I were the first naval officers to enter service with the American Company. Thus it is easy to imagine with what difficulties, what shortages in everything conceivable, what ingrained prejudices, what hot-tempered and disobedient people, and finally what ignorance we had constantly to contend with and overcome.

6th The weather was foggy. At midday we sighted the shore and reckoned it to be the island of Paramushir but, as it was too overcast for us to make it out clearly, we turned away from it.

7th There was a thick fog all day, and for most of the time it was calm so that we only caught very brief glimpses of land.

8th When dawn broke and the fog lifted a little, we found ourselves between the island of Alait and the Kurile pan-handle (this is the name given to the southernmost tip of Kamchatka) and the first island in the Kurile chain. The current had, of course, carried us there during the night, for we had been more than two German miles away from this spot on the evening before. When the wind began to blow from the Kamchatka coast we sailed away from the Peninsula and passed a sleeping whale. Soon afterwards a squall blew up and then it was dead calm again.

The land hereabouts presents a very wild aspect, and in many places we could see snow. Mist covered the peaks of some of the mountains, and others were half-shrouded in it. In the distance we could see Mount Opal'sk, rising up to the same height, perhaps as Mount Teneriffe. The coastline seemed to consist entirely of high, jagged mountains. To complete this, for me, new spectacle, whales were playing round the ship and sending up waterspouts.

9th In the morning the Reaumur thermometer, which was our only means of recording heat and cold, showed plus five and a half degrees. The calm and the mist were with us until noon and then the wind suddenly sprang up from the east. The night was very dark, the waves breaking over the deck washed up many shiny insects, and the whole surface of the sea seemed to be covered with fiery sparks.

12th From noon onwards there was a light following wind. The sky cleared, we sighted the shore and entered the third Kurile Strait.

There was just a light breeze from the southwest and we moved forward very gradually. The wind had carried us about eight miles--so the ship had gone well! The dolphins, or orcas, played around the ship in large groups. At eleven the following morning

13th there was a fire in the galley, with smoke coming out from below the stove. The order was given to cut away the beams below it so that the fire could then be seen, and when it had been extinguished it was discovered that half the beam had already burnt away. Thus the stove had to be broken up to get at the smouldering wood. No one will be surprised that we might have met our ends as the result of such a trifling matter. Sidor Shelikhov, the manager of the company office in Okhotsk, because of his praiseworthy custom of saving every penny he could, had failed to pay 1 ruble 70 kopeks to the man building the stove. The latter had promised to get his revenge by building on the ship a stove on which no one would cook more than once. The promyshlenniks heard this threat but said nothing to anyone about it. The workman, the vandal, kept his word and by his stupid desire for revenge had almost taken the lives of a great many people who had never done him any harm.

At nine in the evening, when we had already passed through the straits separating Poramushir and Onnekotan, we heard a man's voice calling and we spotted a small baidara. We threw out a rope and it came alongside. One Kurile islander came aboard, and another three and a woman remained in the baidara. They all spoke Russian, and the one who came aboard gave us a fox-fur and asked us to sell him powder and shot. We told him that we could not sell him anything but we would give him some powder, even without the fox-fur. Then we gave him three pounds of powder, two pounds of tobacco, several biscuits and each of them a glass of vodka. Then he asked would we give him all these things for ten rubles, and he showed us a note for that amount. We asked him how he had come by our currency, and he told us that each year Russians from Kamchatka would come to his island to collect iasak [fur tax] and to barter for animal pelts. We wanted to make the man a present of a little vodka but the difficulty was in knowing what to pour it into, for we had virtually no glass vessels with us. Then the islander went back to his baidara and returned with a bladder containing seal fat. This he tipped out, then held up the bladder inside out, and we poured in the vodka.

The islanders who had come out to us lived on Poramushir. They were short of stature with small, rounded faces almost completely covered by short, but curly beards, black in color like their hair. The first man to come aboard told us that there were only some forty of them left on the island, and that the others had gone off hunting animals. In earlier times sea otters had bred off Poramushir. They are hereabouts generally referred to as sea beavers. But now they catch only sea lions (here called *nerpy*--hair seals) and foxes, the best species of which is considered the *Ognevka* [flame-red coated variety]. The Kurile islanders possess guns, but are often short of powder and shot. One of their customs is worthy of note: when a Kurile islander is entertaining guests he makes them dress in all his clothes, so that the poor guests can hardly move. Then the guests are given food and endless drinks of melted fat, though the sweat is by now pouring off the guest in streams and in spite of the fact that he himself may offer the most obvious evidence of his incapability of eating and drinking any more.

14th In the morning there was a calm and in the afternoon a wind from the east to south, which had strengthened to such a degree by the evening that we reefed our mainsail. At about midnight the wind became strong from the southeast. We did not reef any other sails, however, in case we were driven onto the shore of Kamchatka which was on the leeward side. Also the ship's movement would have become even worse, as it was already most unsteady, and rolled most disturbingly. It was constantly rising up on the windward side and shipping water on the leeward side.

15th At one o'clock at night we turned with the wind onto a port tack. In the morning the wind very quickly backed to south-southwest, and we consequently turned and headed east. The day became splendidly warm and fine. At noon the wind strengthened a great deal; the ship began to roll alarmingly but we moved forward tolerably well.

17th After a calm the wind came from the south and we lay on a course east-northeast. Today we saw petrels and skuas.

21st Again we saw gulls which flew around us in flocks.

25th During this period the wind was for the most part light and variable, but from midnight on it was quite fresh from the north-northwest, and we went north-northeast. We saw a great deal of seaweed or fucus floating in the sea. The hunters call it sea cabbage. Even when we were furthest away from land we saw this, though naturally in smaller amounts. At three in the afternoon we sighted the island of Attu, with great numbers of gulls and petrels flying round it. We approached the islands of Attu and Agattu, and that night lay hove to, for we had heard from many people that in the straits separating the two islands there was a rocky reef, barely covered by the sea.

26th At dawn we shipped anchor and passed between Attu and Agattu, passing another two islands on the starboard side. The wind was blowing freshly from the northwest and the weather was the whole time overcast with mist and drizzle.

27th At two in the morning there was a shout of land off the port bow. We had not expected this and so we hove to until dawn. We assumed that we had been carried off course by a current or that there was a large error to the east in the compass which we had not been able to correct for a long time because of the continuing overcast weather. When day broke we shipped anchor and set a course to the north so as to move away from the Aleutian Chain. Then we went north-northeast, but at nine we again sighted an island ahead of us. Then we went east-southeast to east and seemed to be entering the straits between two small islands, but when the fog lifted we saw that we had entered a large bay on the island of Tanaga, which was open to the west. We wanted to tack out of it, but in such a poor ship every turn brought us nearer to the shore. So we dropped anchor, and then a second one, in a depth of twenty-four sazhens. The sea bed consisted of small pebbles and coarse sand. After this we fired two shots with our guns to let the inhabitants know of our arrival, should the island be inhabited.

28th The wind continued to blow from the west, but in the morning the mist had thinned a little and we were able to examine the shore nearby. The north shore consisted of high mountains, three of which were towering peaks, especially the middle one which had a sharp cone-shaped peak. The easternmost one was volcanic and sending off smoke. The summits of all three mountains were covered with freshly fallen snow which, because of its whiteness, stood out from earlier falls which had begun to turn blue. There was also much snow lying in the crevasses. The south shore of this sound was considerably lower and ended in a low, rocky cape. At six in the morning we sent off one of our baidaras to the north shore. At four in the afternoon it came back bearing eight wild geese, of which there were a great many on the island. In the northeast sector they had found a small bay where it was suitable for rowing boats to come ashore. The water there was nine feet deep. A little further to the west there was a second inlet and both contained streams with fresh water. After this I set out for the island in the same baidara. The sea bed was virtually the same depth all the way in and only began to rise some short distance from the shore. The bed consisted of fine gravel or black sand. As we approached the island we noticed something black in the water. Some of the men said it was a seal, and others a piece of wood, but it turned out to be a sea otter, which had been sleeping on its back. When it heard the sound of our paddles it turned over and dived underwater. We dragged the baidara up onto the beach and camped under it for the night.

29th I arose with the first light and set off into the interior of the island. At first we crossed low foothills, covered with a sparse moss and, for the most part, overgrown with sedge. It was waist-high which made the going very hard, where the ground was boggy. Between these foothills were many lakes overgrown with sedge and small streams. Geese, ducks and partridges were present in abundance. I shot only one duck. When we had crossed these boggy areas we climbed a high ridge, but because of the mist and the high mountains on every side I could not see anything. We returned to the shore and on the way spotted in a mountain pass a lean-to [*shalash*] left by the Aleuts who come here from time to time to hunt animals. We filled a barrel with water and returned to the ship.

After midday a squall blew up from the east, and we raised our remaining anchor (one had been raised on the preceding night), set sail, and moved out of the bay. When the wind had dropped we used both baidaras to pull us but, as we were making no headway, we were forced to drop anchor again.

30th With our arrival off the island of Tanaga the weather had become quite warm and pleasant. Around midday, with a wind that had blown up from the east, we raised anchor, but we quickly had to drop it again when the wind shortly afterwards veered to a contrary quarter. At three in the afternoon we went ashore and tied up in a bay a little to the west of the one I had been in before. Here a small stream flowed into the sea and from it we could conveniently take fresh water. A little further to the west from here there was a rectangular cave in the cliff-face, about two sazhens long, three wide and three sazhens high. It was full of straight lines and seemed to have been fashioned deliberately. From here we split up and went in various directions: I went inland, clambering across numerous ridges each becoming higher the further away from the shore. When I reached the high smoking mountain it was already dusk, and so, fearing lest I lose my way in the dark, I returned to my companions.

The land around this bay is less boggy but is also overgrown with a tall, coarse grass. The shore is steep and consists of black, ashy sand which is constantly tumbling into the water, so that it is difficult to climb up it. It is very easy to come tumbling down together with the sand as there is nothing to hold on to. None of us shot anything, for the geese had become very wary and kept to the high ground so that they could see us from some distance away, and the ducks did not come near the shore very often. I forgot to add that as we approached the island we saw many cormorants (of the *baklan* type) sitting on the rocky shore and on isolated cliffs. We shot several of them but could not retrieve any of them because they are very strong birds and when wounded they dive under water for a long time.

Along the shore we found several pieces of wood that had been washed up, the only wood that could be used here. There are no trees growing on any of the Aleutian Islands and, on many, no shrubs or bushes. We did not notice the tracks of any land animals, as as far as sea animals were concerned we saw only sea lions and one sea otter. On the beach we found the bones of round sea crabs and shrimps--which had, of course, been eaten by the Aleuts. The Americans [Aleuts?] who were on our ship dug up a yellow root which tasted like beans and whose stalk produced pods. There was also another root which looked like a radish, but was white, and from this they prepared food for themselves. We caught several halibut with lines cast from the ship.

At nine at night we heard the cannon shot telling us that the wind had become favorable. So we began preparation to sail and awaited two further shots which would indicate that we were raising our anchor. But as they did not come we went back to sleep--some of us in the open air, and others under the cover of the baidara.

1st October In the morning we returned to the ship. After midday the wind blew from the southeast. We raised anchor and travelled about two English miles, before dropping anchor again in a depth of twenty-two sazhens, for the wind had become contrary, and there was no chance of rounding the western headland of Tanaga. In the evening the wind became easterly and with its help we put to sea.

Great numbers of porpoise [marsouins] swam round the ship and made little noises as they leapt out of the water. All this time the wind was from the east and the southeast.

5th In the morning there were great numbers of gulls about and the porpoises swam around the ship. The wind was from the northwest and we held a course to the east.

12th At three in the afternoon we sighted an island northwest of Unalashka, known as the Pillar because of its appearance. This island had suddenly burst out of the sea, naturally, as the result of a tremor on the sea-bed. Another similar island had appeared suddenly to the north of Unimak and, according to the evidence of the Aleuts and the hunters, this one was growing all the time. To start with this island had been so hot that the people who approached it had been unable to put ashore, but it was gradually becoming cooler with each year. Looking at the Aleutian Islands, each one of which consists of a great heap of mountains most of which have sharp pointed peaks, it is obviously most likely that this part of the globe suffered a severe tremor and changes in the earth's crust, and that the Aleutian Islands are a continuation of the mountains of Northwest America which run through the Aliaksa Peninsula, and which have remained after the swallowing up of all the earth between them and the Bering Straits. The following reasons cause me to come to this conclusion: (1) Soundings can be made all the way from Unalashka to the Bering Straits, and nowhere does there seem to be a depth of more than sixty-five or seventy sazhens; (2) When the Seal Islands were first discovered there was nothing growing on them except for very sparse grass, which has since grown a little. This is a sure sign that that is new land which has come up from the bottom of the sea; (3) The coast of America, especially between Bristol Bay and the Aliaksa Peninsula, is surrounded by shallow water, and from this it might be concluded that there was once land there; (4) There are many extinct volcanoes, and islands are still appearing now from the sea, and this is a clear sign that this land is still affected by the action of subterranean fire, and has perhaps in the past been affected even more; (5) The similarity between the language and customs of the Aleuts and Greenlanders goes to show that they have originally descended from the same stock, and that there had been contact between them at some time in the past; (6) The discovery of copper in pieces on Copper Island has shown clearly that subterranean fire has affected these places. In addition there may be still other reasons unknown to me.

13th At dawn we sighted the island of Unalashka, which consists of a multitude of sharp mountain peaks, some of which were covered with snow. We went through the straits separating Unalashka from the island of Unalga.

The Aleutian and Kurile Islands form a barrier to the incoming and outgoing tide which runs through the straits separating these islands. Such a large amount of water trying to pass through the narrow straits causes an extremely strong current in them, both on an incoming and an outgoing tide. When the flow changes the water rushes into the straits with a roar, producing lapping waves and eddying currents, sometimes whirlpools. This goes on until a new flow takes over from the other, then it becomes very fast, but gradually slackens off, and the waves and spray also become calmer. Such a fast current is called a *suloi* [rip tide] here. The local inhabitants always know when one will occur and will never venture to cross the straits then, as it seems to boil because of the great waves which are sometimes very high, and because of the opposing currents. When the wind is strong a *suloi* can be very dangerous for sailing ships, which are spun round and rocked violently, the waves break over the cabin and sometimes break the topmasts, and even the masts. A strong suloi can be a fearsome spectacle. It seemed awesome enough to us in the straits between Unalga and Unalashka but the Aleuts told us that this was a very normal one.

14th In the morning we sighted Unimak and its neighboring islands, and in the distance the Aliaska Peninsula. Around midday there was a shout that a sail had been sighted. To come close to we close-hauled on a port tack with a wind blowing from the north. But coming onto a cross tack we saw that instead of the supposed ship there was a stone pillar like the one north of Umnak. This one, as far as I know, had not yet been seen by anyone else.

15th Towards morning the wind freshened and after midday we had to take in another reef and the topsail. That night it turned into a real storm and we stayed under a mizzen and a reefed main topsail on the topgallant stays. The gusts of wind were terrifying, and the fierce waves broke upon the vessel with such great force that all of its timbers shook. The ship began to take in water so much that it soon filled the hold despite the fact that both pumps were working. It may easily be imagined what effect all this had on people who were not used to danger at sea; fear forced them to give their strength unsparingly and to work with great energy. The leak was in the galley, on the starboard side near the main hatch, and was very likely the result of bad caulking or because there were bolts and nails missing and the holes where they should have been had been patched with pitch, for after we sailed from Okhotsk and before we reached America many such holes were discovered. To add to the danger the cargo in the hold (which because of our short stay in Okhotsk and the many things we had to do we had had no time to pack properly) shifted, the ballast had also shifted from the bow to the leeward side. At midnight, however, the water in the hold began to go down.

16th At dawn the storm seemed to be at the height of its ferocity but because of the buffeting it was impossible to stand on deck without holding onto something. The men were exhausted by this dowsing and their work at the pumps, but there was no chance to do anything about it until morning, when they could be reduced to two watches.

17th At dawn the wind abated a little but soon went

round to east and became stronger again. We lay to the northeast under a foresail, a main topsail and a mizzen. At twelve o'clock the sun showed for a moment and then the damp mist closed over us again.

18th Towards nightfall the wind began to drop and finally it became completely calm. Apart from the leak no great harm seemed to have been done; after the storm we found that only a dinghy and the baidaras had been damaged.

19th By the morning repairs had been carried out on everything damaged in the storm. One baidara was repaired by being made 1½' shorter than it had been; and the chains which had been broken near the mainsail stays were replaced by a strap. In the afternoon the wind blew from the southeast, but soon went round to northeast.

20th That night the wind blew quite strongly from the northeast and fell towards morning and at about midnight there was a calm period. The lanyard broke on the flying mainsail shrouds and was straighway replaced.

21st From midnight the wind blew from the southwest. With all our troubles and cares we did sometimes have free time during which we read the voyage of the Dutch under Hemekerk and Barents across the Arctic Ocean. It seemed as though the misfortunes which these navigators suffered cheered us and made us forget our own unpleasant and dangerous situation.

22nd From midnight on the wind from the northwest became quite strong so that we stayed under a reefed foresail and main topsail and topgallant. The gusts of wind with hail and snow were very savage; we began to take in more water, but not so much as to be dangerous. In the morning the reef in the foresail was let loose and a reefed fore topsail was raised with mainsail and jib. At 11 o'clock a fierce squall blew up with snow, and while it was with us the wind was from west-northwest, then northwest. We lay northeast by north. The day was pleasant enough with occasional glimpses of sun and sometimes a little snow fell. That night the wind dropped.

23rd A slight breeze from the west blew all day, and sometimes it was completely calm.

24th The next morning was splendid, the sun shone and there was a favorable wind; we were delighted and thought soon to sight the island of Kad'iak, but suddenly the cloud began to thicken to port and the sea grew black. We began to take in sail. At eleven o'clock in the morning it was but little lighter than at night. Then a fierce squall with hail blew up from the north-northwest. After this there was a thick fall of wet snow. And so our hopes of reaching Kad'iak quickly were dashed. The reader will not be surprised that I am talking about Kad'iak as though it were the most beautiful place on earth, where thousands of pleasant things awaited us. It is unpleasant to be at sea in cold autumn weather and to have to do constant battle with the wind and the waves, and to toil away for so long, that the wildest and most barren island seems like paradise. At noon the snow stopped and for a while cleared up, but for some time afterwards there were stormy gusts of wind with thick snow.

25th At 11 o'clock a very savage squall with thick snow blew up, which brought snow to a depth of four arshins on the deck in a very short time. All the rigging and sails got wet, and iced up. While this was happening the wind reached its strongest in the gusts and we remained under a reefed main topsail with topgallant and mizzen. At noon it was one degree above freezing; after midday the sun appeared momentarily and there were occasional snow and sleet showers.

26th We had only 15 puds of biscuits left and 19 casks of water, and this made our situation most unpleasant.

Towards morning the wind began to drop and changed to the west. We lay to the north to east and gulls, guillemots and fulmars flew around the ship. At two o'clock in the morning there were seven degrees of frost, at four o'clock two degrees, and at eight o'clock one degree. At noon the mercury rose to three degrees above freezing. Taking advantage of the calm we managed to draw the topmast shrouds, help to strengthen the stays and set up a third pump. At six in the evening the wind began to blow from the south, and soon became so strong that as we lay to the north under reefed topsail and foresail, we were driven at 8 to 9 knots, which was fast for our heavy ship. At seven o'clock a fierce squall broke on us from the port side, and turned the sails but without doing any damage. Then the wind veered to west-southwest.

27th The swell was big, but because of the unbroken sunshine it was also very warm, although there were occasional showers of hail and snow. Many fulmars and albatrosses flew round the ship.

28th From midnight we lay north-northwest. The day turned out to be very fine and, by observing the sun at midday, we discovered that we were much further to the east than we had calculated ourselves to be, which caused us to set a course to the northwest. At three in the afternoon the day became overcast and there were strong squalls of sleet and snow. At four there was such a fierce one that the water on the deck reached almost to the main-hatch, so that the boat took on a list. Then we took down sail and remained under a reefed foresail and main topsail. The wind began to blow from the west.

29th At two at night, we sighted land on the port side and went towards it, close-hauling on the port tack. When it grew light we could see that it was the southeastern shore of Kad'iak, thickly covered in snow, so that the rising sun turned the tops of the mountains to gold and the whole scene presented a remarkable spectacle. The day was warm. At nine o'clock it grew calm and in the afternoon a fresh wind blew from the south-southeast, bringing rain and mist that obscured the shore completely. We passed the island of Ugak, and for the rest of the night we coasted under very little canvas, because all that remained before entering Chin'iatsk Bay, where there was the harbor of St. Paul and the main company settlement, was to round Cape Chin'iatsk.

30th We had no map at all of this harbor and no one could tell us how to navigate to it, so we therefore decided to inspect the entire bay, starting with its south shore. At eight in the morning with an east wind and slight mist we set a course to the southwest and, when we had passed Cape Chin'iatsk, we began to keep to the shore of the bay of the same name, firing our guns as a signal. There are three tides in Chin'iatsk Bay. We did not dare enter the south part of the bay, when we saw at the entrance to it many underwater rocks. At 10 o'clock it seemed as though a baidara were rowing out to the ship, but on closer inspection it proved to be a rock in the middle of the bay. Half a verst away, to the northeast, was another underwater rock. At twelve o'clock we came into a small bay, slightly open to the north; we dropped anchor at a depth of twelve sazhens. The bottom was rock with shells.

In the afternoon two Americans came out to us in a two-seater baidarka. Their clothes consisted of cotton trousers and jerseys and kamleikas sewn from sea animal skins; both were barefoot. One of them wore beads in his ears with silk tassels; they both wore hats of plaited straw or grass, which were very skilfully and attractively fashioned. When they came aboard the ship they hauled their baidarkas up after them. They drank some vodka, ate some biscuits and anything else that was given them. They knew a few words of Russian and told us that they lived on one of the islands near the harbor.

These Americans stayed the night with us.

The shore lay less than two miles astern*. There there was a birch wood and a stream in the form of a waterfall. The lee shore was scattered with underwater rocks which were revealed at low tide. This particular spot must look very pretty in summer, but now that snow had fallen and the trees were stripped bare of their leaves it presented a very mournful sight.

There was still a strong wind blowing with rain and gusts and, despite the fact that we were sheltered from it by the shore, at five we began to drift; so we dropped the large anchor and let down the top gallants and the lower yards. The vessel stopped in a depth of nine sazhens with a shoal of rocks one mile astern.

The weather conditions were the same. After midday a pawl on the capstan broke as a result of the swell.

31st At ten in the morning two three-man baidarkas came out to us, in one of them the hunter Slobodchikov, who had been sent by Baranov the same day as they had sighted our ship coming into the bay, but they had not been able to come out to us before because of the strong wind. In the first hour after midday a three-man baidarka brought out a present from Baranov, a fish-and-goose pie, which we were very glad to receive.

1st Nov During the night one cable broke, but after that the wind began to drop. At seven in the morning we raised anchor and with the help of the three baidarkas which had come out to us from the harbor we were towed from the bay. As we drew near a wooded islet we passed it on the starboard side and kept close to its shore because there is a line of rocks running on the left from the island. There are a great many of these chains on this side of Chin'iatsk Bay. Not having seen such a pleasant shoreline for so long I greatly admired the wooded islet. In the middle of it was a small valley surrounded by fir tree groves whose constant greenery gave a happy aspect to this part of the island. From the island came a multitude of baidarkas carrying two or three men each, and sometimes women and children came out to us. These savages stared at our ship and all about it with curiosity, and came with us as far as the anchorage. When we came in sight of the Russian settlement six or seven ragged shots were fired in salute from various places, which we answered with our three-pounder unicorn which had been specially lashed to the side of the ship for this purpose. This mutual greeting was worth of those distant parts in

*In all places where miles are mentioned these are, of course, Italian miles which are a verst and three quarters long.

which it echoed out.

The entrance into the New Harbor, or St. Paul as it is called, which is situated between the coast of Kad'-iak and a small island is no wider than fifty sazhens, the depth here and beyond is between seven and nine sazhens. On the headland at the entrance to the harbor is a kind of fortified structure. At three in the afternoon we dropped anchor at a depth of seven sazhens, the seabed being sandy with small shells. Lines were attached between the stern of the ship and the shore. The weather, which had for a long time been overcast, now turned clear and warm.

CHAPTER IV

MEETING WITH MR. BARANOV. THE STATE OF COMPANY AFFAIRS IN AMERICA. MY OCCUPATIONS. DEPARTURE FOR OKHOTSK.

And so here we are in America! So I have set foot on this wild and almost unknown shore, which I have so long desired to reach! I had already seen crowds of what for me were new tribes of people, called savages, in every way different from ourselves. But now I would have an even better chance of seeing them and of noting the difference between a man enlightened by science and one guided only by nature.

We had hardly managed to make fast the ship when Mr. Baranov arrived to greet us on our safe arrival in America. I could not but look with respect on a man like this who had devoted his life to the improvement of trade in its various forms. He had already been in America for twelve years, in the company of wild and primitive people, surrounded by constant danger. He had been struggling with the deep-rooted depravity of the Russians living here, working constantly, in need of many things, often hungry, and at the same time almost without anyone who could work with him with the same energy. He was deprived not only of means of spreading trade here, but even of resisting the vengeance of some peoples, alleviating the lot of others enslaved by the Russian-American Company. It seemed as though he had been left completely alone to find within himself the means to make his lot better, and to support the settlements in America. All this work, these obstacles, sorrows, deprivation and failures had not blighted the spirit of this rare man, although it had naturally had an influence on him and thereby made him rather somber in manner. Baranov was not very talkative and seemed like a dry stick until you come to know him, but on the other hand he always explained matters with enthusiasm, especially when he knew his subject well. He is not easy to get to know, but he will do anything for his friends and he likes to entertain foreigners with all that he has and is always ready to help the poor. His complete selflessness is not his only virtue. He is not interested merely in amassing wealth at other peoples' expense, but will willingly share his own just salary with absent friends who are in need. His firmness of spirit and constant presence of mind are the reason why the savages respect him without loving him, and the fame of the name of Baranov resounds amongst all the savage peoples who live on the northwest coast of America, even as far as the Strait of San Juan de Fuca. The savages who live in isolated areas sometimes come to see him and are amazed that such wide-ranging schemes can be undertaken by such a small man. Baranov is shorter than average, fair-haired, well-built with very prominent features erased neither by his labors nor by his age, although he is now fifty-six.

We set off with Baranov to his house. There we found everything simple and clean. A British ship had called at Kad'iak lately and Baranov had bought from them many goods and household utensils, and consequently he gave us a very decent meal, at least for local conditions.

Baranov expressed very sincere pleasure at the unexpected arrival of the *Sv. Elisaveta*. Not a single ship from Okhotsk had called there for five years, except that in the previous year the galiot *Aleksandr Nevskii* was dispatched; en route it lost 15 men with some kind of contagious fever which had broken out while they were still in Okhotsk. It wintered on the island of Atkha where it transmitted the disease to the inhabitants, who were decimated by it. All the food supplies were used up and it arrived in Kad'iak about a month before us with an empty hold and was manned by a few feeble or sick men. The master of this galiot told them that the *Sv. Elisaveta* was being built in Okhotsk and that it would come out the following year. From this Baranov did not expect us at all, the more so since the Company's ships do not stay at sea in November unless there is some special reason which keeps them there.

The *Sv. Elisaveta* carried a fair amount of various supplies--the men were healthy (one died on the voyage) and this reassured the people on Kad'iak, where the savages were inclined to follow the example of other native peoples who had that year destroyed the Russian settlement on the island of Sitkha, or Sitka, and killed all the people there. The savages also on Kad'iak, when they saw that no boat had called there from Okhotsk for five years, began to think that all the Russians had already come to them, and that they only had to kill these latter to free themselves forever from their authority. In order to teach them some kind of trade Shelikhov had taken some native boys to Irkutsk, who later came back home. These boys told their countrymen that there were a great many Russians, but they were not believed and they were told, "You are deceiving us," or "They have been showing you things that cannot and do not actually exist." In the preceding year several hunters had arrived from Unalashka and they had already been on Kad'iak some time before. When the savages saw these old men whom they already knew they thought that these must be the last Russians; it took the arrival of two of our ships to dissuade them of this belief. For all of these reasons our arrival in America was of the greatest importance to the company's affairs, the more so since there were some sixteen thousand sea otter pelts and other furs lying in the company storehouses on Kad'iak. Baranov was afraid of entrusting such a rich cargo to some inexperienced person to take to Okhotsk; on the other hand if it remained in the storehouses he was afraid of it falling into the hands of some sea pirate, if he got wind of it. Thus he was very glad to have the opportunity of sending off this cargo in the coming year, and he communicated this to us. We were also pleased to have the chance to indulge our curiosity by spending a whole winter on Kad'iak, and also by the fact that we should soon return to Russia, and third by the fact that we should be doing the company a valuable service by a speedy transit of goods worth about two million rubles. Thus at our first meeting it was agreed that we should set off on the return journey in May so as to be in Okhotsk not earlier than 20th June. For, any earlier it would not be possible to approach the shore because of the ice packs off it. This ice is carried from Iamsk and Gizhiginsk Bays by the northeast current which usually is off these shores.

7th When we had unloaded the cargo and anchored our ship in a safe place and made it secure by all means we could against the fierce storms which can come here in winter, there was nothing at all to prevent me from making several journeys of exploration round Kad'iak.

Whenever the company establishes a new settlement or a fort, it always takes hostages [*amanaty*] from the local natives and they serve as a guarantee of trust. The children of chiefs, or of people who are trusted by the natives either for their wit or their riches, are usually the ones chosen as hostages. These children are taken off to Kad'iak, which is the company's capital, and as the most secure place for the Russians, who have been there the longest and have trained the natives there to be patiently obedient. Hostages have also been taken from the Koliuzhes of the Bering Bay or *Yakutat*, as the natives call it. These hostages, amongst them some adults, sometimes entertained us with their dancing, of which there is a description below. The Koliuzh war-dance is such that it cannot be seen without inducing terror.

Koliuzhes is the name given to the inhabitants of the northwest coast of America between Bering Bay and Sitka Island, and further south. Their languages are similar, but each tribe has its own chief. These people are generally fierce and tend towards war and murder. They consider it a pleasure to torture enemy prisoners, and in almost everything they are similar to the inhabitants of northeast America, who are described in the writings of Reynal, Campe and others. I have related how that summer the Koliuzhes had destroyed the company's small fort on the island of Sitka. There were also in the fort more than 200 savages from Kad'iak who suffered the same fate as the Russians, but some managed to escape and make their way back to Kad'iak. And now six Aliaskans from amongst those who escaped from Sitka arrived.

16th In the morning it snowed, and towards evening there was an east wind with rain, which drove away all the snow which remained, leaving only some on the mountain tops.

19th The windows of the little house in which we lived looked out over a bay and we would often shoot from them at the seagulls and ducks which swam up to the cliff on which the house was built. Today I fired a gun which someone had loaded with a very large charge in my absence so that the explosion kicked me off my feet. No great harm was done, however.

20th During the night the wind was so fierce and came in such strong gusts that our whole house shook and seemed almost about to fall down.

The large huts built by the Kad'iak Americans for their festivals are called *kazhims* and at the harbor this is the name given to the round wooden building in which the *kaiurs*, or the company employees, live. In the middle of this kazhim an empty space is left so that various tasks may be carried out and around this space small huts are built for the American to live in. It is here that they conduct their festivities.

8th Dec. Today we were summoned to such a festival--and at eight in the evening we went into the *kazhim* where spectators were already assembled in one of the little side rooms. As we entered we were struck by the unbearable stuffiness and heat caused by the fact that in this confined space some sixty people of both sexes were sitting around on benches or on the floor. The men, so as to escape the heat, wore no top clothes, and many were completely naked. The action was supposed to represent hunters setting off to catch animals.

Near a large lighted torch in the middle of the hut sat two men with tambourines, or with animal bladders inflated and stretched round a hoop with a handle so that they are like a shuttlecock racket, only bigger. The tambourines are of different sizes and the biggest is in the hands of the actor who takes the part of a chief. On either side of the 'stage' stood two young girls wearing cloaks, and all bedecked in finery, such as a long bone through their nose and beads in their lower lip and ears, and on their heads they wore a great many eagle feathers. Near them stood two men carrying in one hand trinkets and in the other baidarka paddles. The trinkets consisted of two round hoops around which were hung a great number of bird beaks from a bird simply called a *toporka* [puffin], known to natural historians as the sea parrot [*perroquet de mer*]. The paddles are decorated with fish and sea animals or amphibians. The two actors have their faces daubed with red and their head and back were covered with eagle feathers. Instead of hats they had a sort of helmet made from bent twigs, one of which went into their mouth like a line into a fish's mouth. All sorts of feathers and rock ferns, also gree in the winter, almost hid the faces of these Americans. Those who sat with the trinkets wore hats decorated with feathers. From the ceiling above the scene of action were suspended various crossed darts and attached to them were: (1) a baidarka; (2) pelts, representing various animals; (3) some hunting weapons and decoys or *manchiki*, which help the Americans to lure seals. A man seated to one side on a bench swung all this paraphernalia in time to the actors' voices by a specially attached rope. This man was also one of the actors for he wore a kamleika or cape. To complete the description of this shameful place it should be added that the whole ceiling was festooned with dry grass.

The actor taking the part of the chief and those who were sitting by the torches beat with their fingers on the tambourines; the hunters, with little paddles in their hands, beat the trinket charms in time and all of them sang more or less in harmony, sometimes altering the refrain, which was led by the chief. If the beat of the tambourines quickened then everyone would suddenly shout out, for most of the spectators had joined in the singing too. The girls all the time held on to their capes and simply rocked from side to side. The chief was constantly shouting something like: "Here is the shore! Let us tie up to it! The animals will come to he who has not yet killed!"--and other similar things. Whenever he said, "Here are the animals!" then all would cry out in different voices, imitating the various animals; they blew into specially constructed whistles and, in a word, made a most fearful noise! Then the performance was interrupted for several minutes while the hunters rocked and swayed and beat the trinket charms, harmonizing with one another.

In the meantime various foods were brought to the actors, which consisted mostly of berries and fat. These dishes were placed around the circle. In this spot there was also a stone with red spots painted on it, representing the burial place of one of their number considered to be famous, in whose honor the performance was taking place. But I could not wait until the end of the performance; my head ached so much from the stuffy air that I had to leave.

18th Today in the evening I again attended a celebration in the kazhim. To start with five men came out one after the other. They all wore masks and some of them were draped in ferns. They blew on pipes suspended on threads from their nostrils, and each one cavorted about in a special way. One of them was daubed with red, another with black, two of them wore parkas, and the fifth a kamleika, and this last one carried charms in his hands. The naked men and the one in the kamleika wore something made of bird skin which hung down to their knees. Near the circle sat two Americans who wore no decorations and were dressed in their everyday clothes. What this performance was meant to represent I could not discover. The interpreter told us that these were devils deceiving people, but that, as concerns the rest, he himself did not fully understand, for the exact significance of these dances, especially when they deal with the activities of spirits, is known or revealed only to self-styled experts, called by the islanders *kasiats* or wise men. These are the people who plan the festivals which deal with the life of the inhabitants of Kad'iak and neighboring islands, and with devils and the like. If an islander cannot answer a question put to him, he answers, "The *kasiat* will know about this."

When the devils had cavorted about and gone the men began to drive out the women and children. This also happens after the festivals when the islanders from various villages gather for a celebration and at the end of it the talk turns to public matters, then the women are also sent out, but as this could not be the explanation for their behavior now but must of course be related to some kind of superstition, I was very desirous of learning its meaning. When the women and children had left a man appeared wearing a cape, a magnificent mask and carrying charms, representing the 'evil spirits'. He shouted and jumped from place to place in time to the singing which was produced by all the spectators while one beat on a tambourine. This was the end of the dance. After this there was to be another performance but I did not want to wait for it.

Later I learnt the following from the Russians about the dismissal of the women: when the performance was ending the women thought there were real devils, and were looking for somewhere to hide, since these spirits run everywhere and pinch all those they come across. In the past they had even stabbed people with little knives, wrapped round for this purpose with grass, except for the point itself, so that the wound made should not be very deep. Now the islanders no longer do this, but the women are no less afraid of the supposed demons, either because they are superstitious, or because they are afraid of being pinched.

30th The toion, or chief, of the wooded islet came himself to invite us to his festivities, and set off there after dinner. We squeezed our way into the kazhim with great difficulty. The roof of the kazhim or theater was rounded. Inside, however, the air was fresh and not stuffy. We were invited to sit on bearskins spread out on a bench. In the middle of the kazhim burnt a large torch and around the walls there were several smaller ones. The space for the performance and the roof above our heads were covered with dry grass. The dancers depicted hunters setting off on an expedition, in other words the same dances as we had seen in the kazhim at the harbor. Here also there were two men sitting near the torch with tambourines and two standing at the sides with small paddles and trinket-charms, naked with red stripes painted all over their bodies, but in masks and with sticks in their mouths. These masks were made from bent twigs so that almost all of the man's face was visible between the twigs, smeared with red and white paint. Above the torch on the cross beams, were bound crossed squares of branches from which hung arrows, baidarkas, decoys and other implements and, as before, all this was rocked by one man. But here, on the four corners of these crossbeams there was also a man sitting on the suspended boards, wearing a mask just like the first two and also with various stripes painted on his body. These also did some rocking. The performance was also the same. According to the toion the reason for its existence was the following: a certain islander had travelled for five years without killing a single animal, although he had previously been considered a great hunter. Then from grief he began to avoid people and he went and lived in the mountains. One night as he was sleeping on the top of a volcano he had a dream and when afterwards he returned to the village he arranged this dance just as he had seen it in the dream. Since that time he had been very successful in catching animals; that was why the islanders still celebrate the festival in the hope that it will also bring them successful hunting.

The spectators consisted of native inhabitants, dressed in their finery. The women were wearing their best dresses such as: cloth, parkas, or those made from marmot skin or cider-down, almost all had bones through their nostrils, or beads threaded onto sticks, while on their arms and legs, their necks, and in their ears were as many beads as they could fit in, or all they had. Everyone was very pleased with the performance. During the rest of the festival the women kept bringing in food and serving it to the people. They only had to look away for a moment and one of the young boys would grab the dish and run away; then the women would start chasing, and everyone roared with laughter.

When the performance was over, which the Russians call an igrushka, a kasiat came forward, and shouted something. Because our toion had not a complete mastery of Russian he could only tell us that it had something to do with three men who had just arrived. Then we left, but went back when we heard the sound of tambourines. Back in the kazhim we saw, jumping round the lampion, the four men who had earlier been sitting up by the boards. All this, it would appear, was only done so as to entertain the spectators with something while the next performance was being prepared, for the men in question did not dance for very long; they soon threw off their masks and sat down on the floor with the others.

Soon after this everyone sat down in the appointed place and the performance began. Two men began to beat tambourines in time to a song which was taken up by all those watching. Then there appeared the man with the painted body, wearing a mask, round which there was a semi-circular framework of carved twigs, and the final decorative touch was added by some eagle's feathers. He entered with his back to the spectators, and he knelt for a long while facing away from them, shook the trinkets quietly in unison and gradually turning round, then suddenly he leapt up, banged more loudly and, as though shaking all over, constantly shifted his position. After he had danced for half an hour he went out and in his place there appeared two men in masks similar to his, but in the middle was a woman with a half circle round her head. These also came in backwards and then knelt for a while. After this they stood up, turned to face the audience and made various movements of the body, skilfully keeping in time with the sounds of the charms. They were replaced by one man in a mask surrounded by a semi-circle and carrying trinkets. He, like the others, came in backwards but dancing with more skill. With this the performance came to an end.

I could not discover the significance of this performance and had not expected such harmony in the movements and dances of these savages. I have also forgotten to say that before the last performance began the kasiat came out and shouted something, then as the action continued he instructed them in what they should sing, and conducted the chorus.

My duties and exercises were always the same and consisted of reading, of walking along the seashore with my gun and visiting the natives in their huts. For this purpose I would take along with me some food and get into my baidarka and travel for five or six days and more away from the port.

I shall now describe some of these journeys.

15th Jan. As I walked along the shore to do a bit of shooting I came face to face with a bear but we parted without doing any harm to each other.

9th Feb. I was travelling by boat out to the wooded island and en route I shot an eagle with a white tail, one duck and several woodcocks.

27th Feb. I travelled in a three-seater baidarka and I took along three similar boats. To begin with the weather was quite warm and fine, but at five o'clock a strong contrary wind caught us in the middle of Kizhuetsk Bay so that in the evening we put into the village of Kizhuetsk, or a *zhil* as the Russians call it here, and we stayed with the *toion*.

28th Feb. There was a sharp frost and the wind was so strong that I found myself forced to spend several days with the savages. I would spend the evening and night with them and in the day travel into the interior.

1st March The weather continued cold, but calm. I set out on my journey. I travelled round many parts where it was possible to shoot duck and seals. In the evening we stopped in a small bay in which a blind for shooting deer had been built. It was made of grass and about one sazhen square, but no taller than one and a half arshins. Soon there was a strong wind with storms. We bedded down on some grass in the blind, brought in some warmed stones and thus spent a very peaceful and warm night.

2nd March There was a sharp frost, and great waves in the strait between Kad'iak and Afognak from the storm the day before. This prevented me from travelling on. I walked along the shore and shot some partridges and in the evening I caught some ducks with a net.

3rd March The frost continued and once again the wind was fierce. I crossed to some small islands where there were lots of partridges, but I did not manage to shoot any. In winter they are completely white which makes them extremely difficult to spot when they are sitting on the snow and not moving.

4th March There is still a frost but the weather is calm. At three o'clock midday I came into the harbor. On the way there I had shot more than a dozen ducks. The snow, which in the end became very thick, prevented me from shooting more.

6th March In the morning Khvostov and I set off to scale a high mountain near the harbor, but before we got to the top we had to rest several times. On the mountainside we saw two foxes; one of them, a black-brown, was so big that we almost mistook it for a bear. From the top of this mountain we could see the whole of Chin'iatsk Bay with its islands and its cliffs rising out of the sea, a part of the wooded island and Afognak, and beyond that the open sea. On the other side there were the peaks of many rocky mountains. A panoramic view always produces a pleasant impression, and I stood with great pleasure in the same spot for more than half an hour admiring this magnificent sight, and giving free reign to my excited imagination. This sort of enjoyment is more familiar to people who lead a lonely life and his hardly describable. A man becomes more content with his existence when he is standing on a high mountain breathing the excellent pure air and seeing a multitude of objects at his feet. He looks at the unencompassable width of the ocean and dreams of his enterprise, brings himself close to the whole world and to those distant lands that he has left behind. There, I thought, beyond these high and savage mountains, beyond the wide ocean, beyond the wide expanses of land are my relations and my friends, whom I will sometime meet again. Such thoughts afforded me great pleasure and brought my spirit into sweet agitation such as I had not experienced before and which it seemed to me an inhabitant of St. Petersburg can only feel in America, that remoteness where everything he meets is new and the imagination is prone to wander.

From here we climbed down the mountain chain to a stream, the banks of which we followed as far as the so-called Sapozhnikov dwelling [zhil'ia] which is seven versts from the harbor, and which is so called because the promyshlennik Sapozhnikov lives there, whose job is to raise cattle, fish and so forth. The mountains at this spot are fairly well back from the shoreline, and the valley in between consists of good, fertile soil, which is why, in addition to a great deal of hay-making, there were attempts made here at growing corn but, either as a result of the dampness or perhaps lack of knowledge, the results have so far remained very inconclusive. On the path from the mountains to the Sapozhnikov dwelling we walked into a rainstorm and we got even more wet by wading through several streams which flowed across the fields; therefore, so as to get back as quickly as possible to the harbor we set off by baidarka.

8th March At eight o'clock in the evening the northern lights began, running from northeast to north, while at four o'clock there were slight earth tremors; only two tremors were reasonably violent.

18th March The winds were blowing quite strongly from the southeast with snow, but notwithstanding this I set off from the harbor with a party of three baidarkas. I visited the Americans of the southern

Chin'iatsk settlement, and then travelled all round the bay in which this settlement is situated. Heavy rain forced me to return and spend the night in this same Koniaga settlement. This is what the inhabitants of Kad'iak are called.

19th March In the morning there was snow, rain and hail with glimpses of the sun in between; then the snow came on again without a break.

20th March When the snow stopped I set off on a shooting expedition in the hinterland behind the bay, putting in at the shore in various places, for there was a plentiful supply of partridges everywhere.

In the meantime the wind began to strengthen from the north, and I hurried back to the harbor. Soon the intensity of the storm grew and the seas became fierce. We were still some way from the harbor. Almost every wave broke right over us and we often got mouthfuls of sea water. But it was mostly our hands that suffered as they became numb with the wetness and intense cold. As we plunged the paddles in one side and then the other they were almost torn from our hands. Despite this the Americans in my baidarka rowed skilfully and showed no signs of fear, and as each huge wave came up they shouted: "koo, koo, koo!" in order, I think, to warn their colleagues of the coming danger. One wave tore off the covering from where I sat in the baidarka, and the boat was half filled with water, but luckily another baidarka quickly paddled over to us, and we were righted, although there was no chance to bail out the water. At last we drew near the cape in the vicinity of the harbor island, but we could not round it because of the great spray sent up by the waves breaking on the rocks. My comrades on the other baidarkas went further out into the bay, but I obstinately wanted to round the headland. My baidarka was almost dashed upon the rocks so that I too was forced out into the bay; there we portaged across a small isthmus and reached the harbor at one o'clock. We were drenched from head to foot and thoroughly frozen; it took a lot of rubbing to bring the feeling back into our arms.

28th March In the morning I set out from the harbor in excellent weather, which soon became overcast with a fresh wind, and within half an hour it was raining. I had to cross the strait separating Kad'iak and Afognak, a distance of some 18 versts. In Afognak we called in at Rubtsov odinochka where a Russian hut had been built. In these parts an odinochka is a place where there was no original native settlement, but where a hunter now lives with several kaiurs. In the summer this man supervises the fishing and in the autumn the trapping of foxes.

29th March A strong wind from the west prevented us from proceeding further. Today I dined very well, for I had shot many ducks and small woodcocks, and in the evening I caught a crab.

30th March The fierce wind forced me to remain here another day and a night. In spite of the bad weather I went out shooting near the seashore. To begin with I winged one duck which I chased for a long while, but eventually lost from view. As I travelled further on I killed several more birds, and on my way back I again saw the duck which I had wounded previously, and took up the chase again. It had already tired and began to sink when it suddenly appeared out of the water quite close to me. So close, that I tried to hit it with my paddle, but I leaned over too far, lost my balance and capsized the baidarka. For some time I hung in the water upside down until I freed my feet from the baidarka cover, kicked out, and came to the surface some way from the baidarka. The heavy clothing I had on dragged me down, added to which as I had swallowed a great deal of water I did not come round very quickly. Two of the Americans [who were with me] caught me by the collar, and pulled me to the upturned baidarka. We all clung on to this with our right arm and paddled with our left and in this way we reached the shore. After this we did in fact catch the duck which had been the cause of our mishap. My clothes, however, had begun to freeze on me, so I left my companions and ran to a Koniaga village about a verst away, where I dried my clothes and warmed myself.

31st March At six in the morning I set off in weather that was clear and calm but very cold. From the straits between the islands lying to the north of Kad'iak we could see the snow-capped mountains of Aliaska (or Aliaksa), many of which were sixty to seventy versts away and seemed to be higher than any of the highest mountains on Kad'iak. In fact, the whole shoreline of the Aliaska Peninsula is extremely high, and because of this the winters there are incomparably harsher than on Kad'iak, separated from Aliaska by a strait forty versts wide. Passing through the islets, we began to round the big cape of Kad'iak, which sticks far out into the sea. In the vicinity whales were playing, and several of them came to the surface so close to us that we could hear their breathing. Their breath had a revolting smell. After this we travelled to the island of Uganak and wanted to round Cape Kuliugum, but a fresh wind from the south and quite a heavy swell compelled us to put to Uganak Bay. In the evening there was a frost. My right arm got slightly frostbitten because the waves had been breaking across that side of the baidarka and I was very lightly dressed. It was already late when we reached the settlement on Uganak where we intended to stay the night in an empty house which the Americans had abandoned, because they said that noises could be heard under the floor at night and that an apparition appeared in the form of a woman with her hair hanging loose and her face covered except for her flashing eyes. But I was extremely tired from the hard paddling and I fell into a deep sleep and saw no ghosts at all.

1st April In the morning with cold weather from the east we set off and travelled round a long headland so as to get back into the strait separating the island of Uganak from Kad'iak. But as it was a long way across the strait to the settlement on that island we put in from the opposite side to a small bay and crossed the island on foot to the village, which was about three versts. We carried the baidarkas on our backs.

Here we were detained by a strong north wind, but I was not particularly dismayed by this for it was all the same to me whether I was in this native settlement or another one. In the evening some Aliaksans were staying here, and some of the villagers danced in the Koliuzh fashion. I treated everyone to tobacco and one old man stood up from his place and thanked me for all of them. In the afternoon I went walking with my gun or played with the natives at the game of *kaganak*, a description of which is given below.

It is well known that the Koniaga are not so much afraid of death as of being whipped. Soon after our arrival on Kad'iak one man was whipped with a cat-o'-nine-tails for rudeness and disobedience. This gave rise to a rumor amongst the Americans that we had brought new, more painful whips from Okhotsk. This caused one of the local inhabitants to approach a sailor who was in my company and to ask him: "Are these 'cats' painful?" The sailor invited him to find out. The islander went a little way off, but soon came back with a thin lash, plaited from whalegut. This he gave to the sailor, and asked to be whipped. The sailor considered this a comic request, but he made the American ready and then hit him with the lash three times with all his might on his bare back. The Koniaga leapt up and rushed off that instant, having naturally formed a very unfavorable impression of this kind of lash.

3rd April I travelled by baidarka to a small sheltered bay on the coast of Uganak Island. It seemed as though made by the hand of man. The mouth of the bay looks just like the open gates of a fort cut into the stone rampart, and no more than seven sazhens wide, although quite long. The current at this spot is very strong, and when there is no more than three feet of water at low tide it seems to have a discernible slope towards the sea, as though let out of a sluice.

The shoreline of this channel or mouth of the bay is steep all over and behind it is a bay shaped like a bucket, in the middle of which lies an islet. The surrounding area is wooded and bushes grow right down to the shoreline. It was with great difficulty that I made my way up this channel, though the water level at this time of year was quite high. As it went down into low water I had to hold on to the oars for it seemed as though I were floating over rapids where the disturbance from the speed of the water turned into a regular maelstrom.

4th April At three o'clock midday the wind dropped, and I set out towards the harbor. Until the current changed I had to wait in Bystryi [Fast] Strait, so named because of the very fast currents there against which it is impossible to paddle a baidarka. When the water began to fall we set off on our way. I slumbered in the baidarka, but I was awakened by an unusual noise. This was caused by a small whirlpool at the end of Bystryi Strait. We had to paddle across it with great caution, supporting the baidarka with our paddles so that it was not capsized by the waves. The night was very calm and clear. When the baidarkas became separated I would fire a shot from my gun as a signal so they could again come together. Our journey seemed very pleasant as we paddled diagonally across the strait between Kad'iak and Afognak, although its width following this course is about twenty-five to thirty versts. I shot a swan near the entrance to the harbor, where we arrived at about five in the morning. From Uganak Island to the harbor is considered to be some ninety versts. Thus we had paddled this distance in less than eleven hours, excluding the time we were standing to in Bystry Strait.

8th April An American who arrived today from the south side of Kad'iak told us that on isolated high rocks in Chin'iatsk Cape there were sealions, usually referred to as *sivuchy* or *siuchy*. These animals had not appeared in the area of the harbor for five years past. From curiosity I travelled to see them, taking with me a marksman, or *strelets* as they call them here. There was a fresh southwest wind blowing and there was quite a heavy swell left over from the weather of the day before; we therefore paddled along the coastline round partically the whole of Chin'iatsk Bay. En route the marksman, Brusenin, shot two seals, while I bagged nine ducks and several black sandpipers. We found no sealions, however, and we set off back straight across the bay for the wind had slackened quite a deal. As we approached the islet near the harbor, I took the cover off my seat in the baidarka and was paddling peacefully. But suddenly I heard that Brusenin was shouting something in Koniaga and my paddlers began to go at it for all they were worth. Looking astern I saw a great steep wave which, however, we managed to outrun. Another one soon came along, however, and as I had not managed to fasten the cover completely some water came into the baidarka. Such a disturbance often happens above underwater rocks which are called here *potainiks*. Above such rocks it is usually calm but sometimes a huge mound of water comes up which is extremely dangerous for baidarkas, such a phenomenon is described here as the potainik "playing". According to reports by both Russians and Americans some of these potainiks play once a day, others twice, others once a month and always at regular intervals. In a strong wind there is always a great sea above these rocks. Baidarkas occasionally founder when they are caught unawares by potainiks, as they begin to play. The Americans know where most of them are and try to avoid them, even in calm weather. Not all underwater rocks produce the action I have described; it must therefore be concluded that the so-called *potainiki* contain something particular such as funnels or the like.

10th April Today was marked by a strange incident. A ninety-six year old promyshlennik wishes to marry an extremely ugly forty-five year old native woman, who had for a long while been very unwilling to agree to this, but had eventually given him her word. When they were in the church, however, she said that she did not wish to wed him, thus the wedding ceremony broke up and the old man was very disappointed.

In the evening a party of Aliaksan baidarkas arrived. It had been going along the coast of America trading in sea otters. The promyshlennik with them had managed by deceit to bring along an Aliaksan who had murdered a Russian promyshlennik, and had said of him that he had died of boils and the other Americans who lived in the same village willingly agreed with this story. The murderer was a handsome young man who had previously been one of the hostages at the harbor and who had fallen in loved with the murdered promyshlennik's wife, a Kad'iak girl.

"Why did you kill the Russian?" they asked him.

"The girl told me to," he replied.

"What should we do with you?" they then asked him.

"Kill me in the same way," he answered boldly.

He and his accomplices where, however, simply whipped with ships' ropes, and they were then to be sent on the first vessel to Iakutsk as kaiurs.

On the say day news came from Chugatsk Bay that a ship's side, about four sazhens in length, had been washed up on the island of Tsukli, and from Ukamok they brought a trunk of blue-cloth and a straw hat of the kind normally worn in the Sandwich Islands which had been washed up by the sea. These last had been washed up in the autumn which therefore gave us to suppose that around this time some English or United States vessel had been wrecked.

In the winter they had brought in from the island of Sitkhinak a stub from a large wax candle which had been washed up and which could have come from no other ship but a Russian one, and probably from the company's vessel *Phoenix*. This vessel of the Russian-American Company was built in America and [in 1798] took the Archimandrite [Ioasaf] from Kad'iak to Okhotsk, where he was to be made a bishop. For the Archimandrite's comfort a special deckhouse had been made on the *Phoenix*, which was secured only with knees. Some itinerant Englishman [James Shields] was made captain of the vessel. It is not only in America that this very title gives people an idea that the bearer is a skilful navigator. The *Phoenix* set out in August [1799] from Okhotsk with the archbishop, together with all his retinue and eighty or more promyshlenniks, amongst whom there was an outbreak of yellow fever even before they left Okhotsk. The ship was fitted with three masts (although it was only 100 to 110 tons), simply so that it could be said that the company owned a three-masted ship, which are here generally ennobled by being called frigates. At the end of October the *Phoenix* was sighted off the island of Unimak. After that she became the subject of guesses and speculation about the cause and place of her wreck. It seems likely that the stormy weather and the unsoundness of the ship, sickness among the crew and negligence on the part of the captain were all contributory factors in the loss of the *Phoenix*. She was of great importance to the company, both from the point of view of the value of her cargo, and the number of men being transported to America, the non-arrival of which weakened the company's institutions and trade. The sea scattered the remains of the ship's cargo widely along the coast of America. Flagons of vodka were discovered, bottles of sour wine, wax candles, a samovar, a ship's wheel, upper beams and other articles--in an area extending from Unalashka right down to Sitkha and even further south.

19th April Towards evening a party from the south side of Kad'iak, numbering some 200 baidarkas, had gathered in the harbor; the Koniagas never come there from the northern side of the island, but they stock up with iukola at Karluk, and go straight to the island of Shuekh. There, or somewhat further on, they join forces with the other party and wait for the Russians who have been sent to supervise the hunting. After this they all travel together.

Today the ninety-six year old man, about whom I

spoke above, again persuaded his lady to marry him, and she finally agreed.

20th April At about midday the party began to set off from the harbor.

23rd April In the morning I set off for Afognak Island with several of the Russians. In the artel on the island there are eight to ten hunters and a large number of kaiurs. It is only here that iukola is prepared from halibut. I parted with my companions here and travelled on to Rubtsov odinochka, 16 versts away.

24th April A strong contrary wind forced me to spend a whole day in the Rubtsov odinochka. At this time the ducks were flying away to find somewhere to lay their eggs, and the geese and swans had begun to appear. In the sound I shot three geese and several ducks.

25th At sunrise I set off on the return journey.

3rd May The galiot *Aleksandr Nevskii* set off for Yakutat. Another vessel, called the *Ol'ga*, built on Kad'iak from spruce, set off for Unalashka. It is well known that spruce is highly unsuitable for the ribbing of ships: the *Ol'ga* may serve as a fresh illustration of this. When Baranov went on it for the first time the water had to be bailed out all the time so that afterwards seaweed came out with the pumps, and the ship eventually sank on a sand bar. But fresh planking was put on her even after this, and after this a third time, and they went on sending her to sea. This little vessel never goes far from the shore and always rides out a contrary wind at anchor somewhere. But despite its ramshackle condition Baranov has no better vessel.

12th May Today Khvostov and I took with us a marksman and set off to see the sealions which had again started to appear on the rocks at Cape Chin'iatsk. We travelled there at high water which is not a suitable time for shooting, because the breakers which reach the top of the rocks prevent the animals from lying on them peacefully. The weather was rainy. We arrived at Cape Chin'iatsk, where we spent the night, Khvostov in a straw lean-to [*shalash*] made by some islanders when they had been there, while I was in a kind of tent such as the local Americans usually make when they are on long journeys--from baidarkas and planking. The baidarkas are placed on their side on the windward side; then from the paddles placed upon them and parallel to the ground, one makes a small roof. Under this half-covered tent I was quite well sheltered from the rain and the wind. All night we could hear the sealions roaring.

13th May At 10 o'clock in the morning, when the water was at its lowest, we paddled out to the rocks. The marksman climbed up onto one empty rock while the sealions lay on another about fifteen sazhens away. These animals have very bad eyesight, but a very good sense of smell. It is, therefore, normal practice to approach them from downwind, otherwise they will catch your scent and jump into the sea. While the marksman was getting ready we had plenty of time to examine these animals. Their pelt is light grey in color, while the cows are lighter still. They have a short head with tiny ears that are just discernible. They roared all the time, lifting up their snouts and turning their heads from side to side as though sniffing something. Each animal had several wounds on it which it had got during the battles for possession of the cows. These sealions had no skin on their snout like the ones described by Anson on his journey to the island of Juan Fernandez. As these animals were lying there they did seem rather like lions, which is, naturally, how they came to get their name.

When the first sealion was shot it fell into the sea and sank. Whether it was alive or dead we could not tell, for when these animals are killed they do not stay on the surface. The sound of the shot caused another sealion to jump into the water, but the rest went on lying there. The second shot killed one sealion, another one lying near it remained on the rock, all the remainder leapt into the water. The third shot wounded the last one, but it jumped into the water. The east wind had whipped up a lot of spray, especially round the isolated rocks. It was impossible to get near the rock in question with one baidarka so we lashed two together, awaited a favorable moment, paddled up to the rock and put two Americans down on it. They cut the sealion's throat, inflated it, and bound it up with a rope so that the air would not escape. They pushed the animal into the sea where it floated. Then we took off the Americans and towed the sealion to the shore, cut it up into pieces, put the pieces in the baidarkas and set off for the harbor. The weather was all the time overcast with rain; on the way, however, we were overtaken by a fresh contrary wind with a large swell, which stopped us from getting back quickly.

17th May After lunch Khvostov and I went off by three-man baidarka to the wooded island. As we cast off from it we capsized, but we bailed out the water, and instead of ballast we placed another two men in the bottom of the baidarka and continued on our way.

24th May Today was Trinity Day and in the morning we went to church. We spent the evening with

Baranov. We sang, danced, were very merry and eventually dispersed at two in the morning.

30th May Today the *Sv. Ekaterina* left for Iakutsk [*sic.* Yakutat].

13th June In the morning we, that is Khvostov and I, set off for Elovoi [Spruce] Island. We had heard that a whale had been washed ashore there. This turned out to be of the striped type, and was no more than four sazhens long. I shall not waste time on the description of such a well-known animal. While we were there it was cut up into pieces, half went to the company, and the other to the hunter who had killed it. This could be determined by the stone dart still in the whale, and which bore the owner's mark. These marks are registered in the office on Kad'iak, but the hunters are able to recognize them anyhow.

We did not wish to spend the night on the open shore in such damp weather and so set off back for the whale when it was already dark. The mist was so thick that it was impossible to make out anything at a distance greater than nine sazhens. But the Americans with their amazing ability in such circumstances led us straight to a *shalash* some twelve versts from the washed-up whale. Here we spent the night and, next morning, we went on to the harbor.

17th June We were now quite ready to sail away from Kad'iak, but as Baranov had not yet prepared all the necessary papers for our departure for Russia we waited without much to occupy us. Today I went back to Afognak and Rubtsov odinochka. In the middle of the strait between Kad'iak and Afognak, water began to appear in my baidarka, but as there was little we could do about it, we simply tried to paddle all the faster. When we arrived and dragged the baidarka out of the water, we could see three holes in the bottom, right next to the keel, one of them as large as two and a quarter arshins, another a quarter of an arshin and the third two vershoks. There were also two little ones in the side. We all were amazed that we had not sunk, for we guessed that the baidarka had been holed right back in the harbor when we had grounded on a sand bar and pushed ourselves off with our paddles. One of the wooden boards which are normally placed inside the baidarka with a bearskin over it was the only thing covering these splits. If the sea had not been so calm the whole baidarka would have come apart.

18th June There we picked wild onion so as to salt it and store it for the voyage to Okhotsk. It is well-known that wild onions, wild garlic, spoonwort and several other plants are very efficacious against scurvy and also protect one from catching it. Thus, in order to collect enough wild onion (it does not grow on Kad'iak, at least not in the vicinity of the harbor), we spent all day at Rubtsov odinochka where they were laying in stocks of fish, for gutting, cleaning and preparation of which up to thirteen women and kaiurs had been brought. Iukola was being prepared in the same way as in Okhotsk, with the difference that in the beginning when the fish is going up the river and is very fat, the fat itself is cut off for it will not dry with the other parts and will simply go bitter.

At that time there were great numbers of red salmon going up the river. Out of sheer curiosity I ordered a dragnet to be cast and pulled in in the morning, and at one time more than two thousand fish were caught, most of which were, however, thrown back. We turned out the scoop and took out all the fish because it would be impossible to clean such a great number of them in twenty-four hours, as half or maybe one-third of them would spoil. Apart from this the people there were not strong enough to pull a dragnet with so many fish in to the shore, and it might burst of its own accord.

19th At five in the morning I set off home.

25th June Today, towards evening, when we had received the remaining papers from Baranov, we pulled up the anchor while it was calm and were towed out to the wooded island, and then again lay at anchor in a small sandy bay.

CHAPTER V

June 1803

THE VOYAGE. ARRIVAL IN OKHOTSK AND OUR RETURN TO ST. PETERSBURG.

26th Twice we dragged our anchor because of the wind, and both times we were forced to lay on it again when the wind dropped completely.

27th At five o'clock in the morning, with a light northerly breeze, we pulled up our anchor and were towed out beyond the island. The wind went to south-southeast, and we set course to the east, then an easterly wind came up and we went south-southeast. We rounded Cape Chin'iatsk and Ugak, and then went south. There was a swell from the southeast.

29th In overcast weather with rain and the same wind as before, we sailed south. Puffins and fulmars appeared round the ship.

30th The wind was from the northeast and our course was south-southwest. Towards evening we had to take in two reefs on the topsail. Puffins, fulmars and auks were flying round the ship.

1st July The wind was westerly and rather changeable. After midday the weather became fine.

2nd July The wind was southwest, and the weather was quite fine. At midday readings gave our position as latitude 53°45' and longitude 199°45'.

3rd July The wind was mainly southwest, with a few changes.

4th July The wind was easterly, and our course to the southwest. The weather was overcast. Puffins and fulmars could be seen, and porpoises swam round the ship.

5th July Until six o'clock in the evening we set course to the southwest in a fresh east-northeast wind with heavy rain; after this it became calm and a mist came up.

6th July When the mist had cleared we could see Unalashka, and with a southerly wind we set a course into the straits between that island and Unalga, so as to come out to the north of the Aleutian chain. But as there was a calm and then a slight breeze from the north-east we took a course south of Unalashka. Near the land we could see whales and sealions.

7th July For a day and a night there was a calm, or there were changeable light breezes, which prevented us from rounding Cape Unalashka. We saw a fur seal [sea-cat].

8th July With very light winds between south and east we sailed very quickly, near to two small islands to the south of Umnak. We saw sealions and birds which are normally in the vicinity of the islands. At midnight a whale surfaced so near at hand to the ship, and with such a noise, that many of the men thought that it was breakers hitting against an underwater rock.

9th July The incoming and outgoing tide would first bring us nearer the above-mentioned islands, and then take us further away from them. At about midday two baidarkas came out from Umnak and brought us some fresh fish from the hunter Krinkov who was there. These baidarkas are made differently from those on Kad'iak, especially the one-man types. They are as long as the Kad'iak two-seater ones, but are so narrow and thin that it is amazing how they manage to stay afloat in them in rough weather. The bow has no horns bent up and backwards but splits in the same way, with a stick fixed to either end, in order, I believe, to prevent seaweed from catching there and capsizing the baidarka. The stern is blunt and comes to quite a sharp angle. We took four arrows from these islanders and two little boards used for casting them, and we gave them a shirt, some tobacco, and several other trinkets, which they obviously had not expected at all, as they expressed great surprise. All day we saw many sealions and whales.

10th July The wind was variable between west and south-southwest. We saw fulmars and a whale chased by porpoises. The Island of Four Mountains was hidden from us when darkness fell.

11th July The wind was east-southeast and our course was westerly. The weather was overcast with rain. We sighted whales, puffins, one guillemot and some sea-cabbage floating in the water.

12th July There was a strong topsail reef wind from the west. At eleven o'clock in the morning, as we approached the island of Seguak, we turned through the following wind on to the starboard tack. The weather was still very cold. At midday the Reaumur thermometer showed plus $5\frac{1}{2}°$ and at six o'clock in the evening only 4°. It seemed more like the end of autumn than the middle of summer. Our hands froze on deck and went so numb when we were reefing the sails that we had to immerse them in cold water to bring them back to life.

13th July Towards evening the wind dropped and we turned onto a port tack, and again sighted Amlia and Seguak. Puffins and gulls were flying round the ship and two fulmars which landed on the sails to rest were caught by hand, but as we approached land they were released.

14th July There was a calm and then a breeze from the northwest. The weather was fine enough. We were in sight of the island of Atkha. We sighted whales, porpoises, puffins, fulmars and sea swallows.

15th and 16th July With a west wind we coasted along the south side of Atkha, in sight of land all the time. We were accompanied by the same animals and birds.

17th July The weather was clear and there were occasional glimpses of the sun. Towards evening we approached Atkha with a quiet southerly breeze.

18th July The wind was from the south. We lay on a starboard tack and then port, parallel to the islands of Atkha and Amlia. The currents in the sea here were drawing us noticeably closer to the shore. From midday it became fresh, and when we saw that there was no chance of going round either Atkha or Amlia, we decided at one o'clock, midday, to go north-northeast, into the narrow and unknown channel between Atkha and Amlia. At the very narrowest part of the passage we could see foam and we did not know what to conclude; was it a contrary current, or the surf breaking on a sandbar? The seaweed growing on the banks to the left of this foam made us fear that we were going straight onto a reef of rocks. Under topsail and jib our speed was about $5\frac{1}{2}$ miles an hour, and in addition the current doubled, if not more than doubled, our speed so that we were approaching the narrows very quickly. Soon we could see that the above-mentioned flecks of foam stretched across the whole of the straits. But when we were three cables' length from them (360 sazhens), we could not take any soundings, of course, because of our great speed. Eventually we took a sounding of seventeen sazhens, and then twelve, and then there was a calm and, when we noticed that the ship was drifting towards the Atkha shore, from which a bank stretched out, we dropped anchor straightway and let out seventy sazhens of cable. The ship made a very quick turn, but when the anchor pulled taut, it dragged, and we were carried right into the foam. We hardly had time, as it were, to blink, before we were already there, and then we saw that the foam came not from the sea beating on a sandbar but from the meeting of two opposing currents, or a suloi, as the hunters normally call it. At this very moment a fierce squall blew up from the south, because of which, so as not to be dashed against the shore of Atkha, we pulled up anchor, put on sail and set a course to the northeast. According to the log our speed was eight and a quarter miles, and if we add to this the six to eight miles an hour we gained from the current carrying us along, it may be imagined with what speed we were moving. In fact the coasts of Atkha and Amlia, neither of which was more than a verst away, just seemed to flash past our eyes. When we had passed this danger we strengthened the topsail and began to reef the main topsail. The wind became fresh with squally gusts, but towards midnight it dropped somewhat.

19th July With a fresh reef-topsail wind from the southwest, south and southeast, we held a course to the west. At four in the afternoon there was a little rain.

We were very relieved that we had managed to make our way north of the Aleutian chain, for the continuing strong southerly wind could have made a great deal of trouble for us. If in our bad ship in a moderate wind we had not even been able to pass either Atkha by going forward, or Amlia by going back, then what would have happened to us in this strong wind on the other side of the island chain? We would doubtless have been dashed against the shore. Then what chance would there have been on the open sea in a strong wind and with an unfavorable sea bed (for there are almost no favorable ones here) of riding it out at anchor? If we had lost our ship we would have had to cross from the Aleutian Islands to Kamchatka in leather baidarkas. Then the American Company would have lost a cargo worth in the region of two million rubles.

These circumstances provoke me to say something about the unfavorable qualities of merchant ships, which always have full holds and therefore cannot, by means of tacking, get away from the shore, and thus perish on it, while a decently constructed ship which, though capable of holding less cargo, may approach the shore with every confidence and can get off, even in an onshore wind. The citizens of the United States of America have realized this truth earlier than anyone else; they have begun to build better merchant ships, and to lose less of them than the Europeans.

20th July The weather was overcast with fog and damp. We lay west by south in a fresh reef-topsail wind from the south, which slackened off towards midday. At midday we took a reading of our position as latitude 53° 05' on the meridian of the Kaniaga Island.

21st July The weather was overcast with mist and damp. There was no wind at first but then a changeable breeze, which finally settled at midnight at west-southwest. At midday we calculated ourselves to be on the meridian of the western tip of the island of Tanaga.

22nd July We followed the same course. From midnight the wind came from the north and then from the northeast. There was quite a large swell, then the wind blew for a whole day and night from the north-northwest.

23rd July The weather was fine and warm; there was a calm until two o'clock midday, during which time we repaired the rigging and got out our baidarka. I paddled around the ship in this and shot eight fulmars, including one white one. The flesh of these birds smells of whale blubber, on which they would seem to feed, since we found pieces of it in the gullets of those we had shot. It could have been that a dead whale was floating in the vicinity. Our readings showed us that we were being carried by the current a long way to the northeast. We had also noticed this on our journey from Okhotsk to America. At two o'clock the wind was blowing from the south southwest.

24th July The wind was from the same quarter and light, and was followed by a calm. In the evening many fulmars appeared round the ship, several of which I managed to shoot. In addition we could see puffins and sea swallows (*Hyrondelles de mer*) which are here called *petushki*.

25th July Until midday there was a calm, during which time we lowered the baidarka, and I shot a fulmar and skua. This latter bird is somewhat like the guillemot, although it is completely different in its quick flight. It has a sharp beak and its belly and neck feathers are white; its back, wings and head are dark grey, while its legs are black and webbed. The skua has very sharp sight. It flies high and when it spots something it dives straight into the sea. It is given its name, sea-robber, by the hunters because it chases gulls and fulmars until they regurgitate the last food they have eaten.

After midday there was a gentle breeze from the south, and at seven o'clock in the evening there was a damp fog.

26th July With a wind from southwest to south we followed a course west-northwest. For a whole day and night the weather was overcast and damp so that at midday there was just a glimpse of the sun through the mist. Yesterday and today we sighted the usual birds and much sea-cabbage.

27th July In overcast weather with rain the wind was changeable and finally settled at northeast to east and eventually became fresh. We lay on a southwesterly course.

20th [28th?] July With continuing overcast weather and a moderate wind from the northeast and north-northeast we went southwest. We saw fulmars, puffins, sea swallows, whitish gulls which kept to the shore and a great number of plants floating in the sea. At one o'clock midday we sighted the island of Attu, and we set a course west by south, so as to pass the island to the west. Now we again noticed that the current was carrying us to the northeast. At four o'clock in the afternoon the weather cleared. The water, which was its usual bluish color, now seemed much greener, this this may have been the result of the sun. The declination of the compass through the amplitude we took was 9° east. On the mountains of the island of Attu we could see much snow which even showed white at some places in the foothills. At sunset the horizon was quite clear. Over the whole island hung great mountains of thick grey clouds, from underneath which could be seen the snow-covered wild mountain peaks. From the striking of the last rays of the sun the sky took on a very bright color which made it a beautiful spectacle.

29th July There was quite a fresh wind varying between north by west and northwest and we followed a course west-southwest and southwest. At midday we checked our latitude and discovered that on Captain Sarychev's chart the island of Attu was marked twenty minutes further north than it should have been. A small group of puffins followed the ship right up until dusk. In addition we saw several fulmars, sea swallows and one guillemot.

30th July The weather was reasonably good and with the wind variable between northeast by east and east we steered a course to west-southwest. The compass bearing was 7°30' east. In the evening a lot of porpoises came round the ship, overtaking us and diving out of the water in front of the bows, but they all went away as soon as one of them was wounded by a harpoon.

31st July With a wind changeable between east and southeast we followed a course west-southwest.

During the latter part of the day the weather was fine and at night for the first time on this journey we saw a clear sky full of stars. We occasionally sighted the usual birds.

1st Aug. The wind and our course remained the same, and there was a calm towards the end of the day. At midday we calculated our position as midway between Attu and the third Kurile strait.

2nd Aug. There was a gentle northeast wind and until six o'clock in the evening we travelled west-southwest. After this there was a very slight wind between north and west. Today we saw two whales, many sandpipers, several fulmars or sea swallows and one albatross.

3rd Aug. Until two o'clock in the afternoon there was no wind and after that a gentle wind from the northwest to north, which kept our course west-southwest. While there was no wind I shot eight fulmars and one albatross; the flesh of the latter did not smell of whale blubber and seemed to us very tasty. Here we spotted another species of fulmar: they are smaller than the other kind, have darker colored feathers, a sharper beak, and a more agile flight.

4th Aug. At six in the afternoon, as we were lying west by south with a wind northeast by east, we suddenly heard our ship shudder as though we had slightly scraped a sandbar. A few seconds later we felt a second blow and a sound rather like distant thunder. We assumed that this was an earth tremor, but we were not really sure whether the tremors could be felt so strongly in such deep water; there were also no discernible storm conditions, or any other change in the atmosphere.

5th August There was a weak variable wind between northeast by north and north-northwest, and we lay west by south. In the morning we saw some seaweed floating in the sea and growing on sandbars; this always serves, when it is fresh, as a sure sign of the proximity of land. At six in the evening we sighted the coast of Kamchatka, at first from the cross-trees and later from the deck. At night the sea seemed more than normally phosphorescent which it seems to me always happens when you are nearing the shore.

6th August There was a gentle breeze from the north-northwest and our course was west into the straits separating the island of Paramushir from the island of Annikutan, and usually referred to as the Third Kurile strait. At eleven o'clock in the morning there was a calm, and the shore was shrouded in cloud. During this stillness I shot fulmars which we preferred by far to our bad victuals.

7th August It was calm all day. In the evening there was a slight and changeable wind between northeast and east. We set a course to the northwest and west-northwest.

8th August Until six o'clock in the morning there was fog, but later this quickly cleared up and we entered the third Kurile strait with a light wind from east-southeast, which later freshened. There can be no more convenient passage between the Kurile Islands. It is everywhere clear, about five German miles wide and near the surrounding shore very easily navigable. On the southwest tip of Paramushir there is a high mountain; and not far away is the islet of Shirinka which looks like a stook or an extremely high ridge of hills. In the distance a view opens of the island of Alait, which appears before any of the others when it is on the western side, and sometimes only the peak of its mountain can be seen above the clouds. On Annikutan there are two mountains like sugar loaves, and to the west of it is the small island of Makaronshi. All the shoreline is generally very steep and in places always snow-covered. In the strait we saw many orcas and that night a small whale played around the ship for a long time.

9th Aug. In the strong topmast wind, sometimes blowing strongly, and sometimes dropping away, and varying between east by south and northeast by east, we lay northwest by north under a topsail reefed with one reef, a foresail, mainsail, jib and topsail gallant which we occasionally strengthened.

10th–14th August For five days there was no wind, or there were light changeable breezes. During this time we held a course northwest by north. Every day we saw the birds normally to be found in these waters, sometimes porpoises, and on one occasion a whale.

15th Aug. The wind was quite fresh and varying between southwest by west and west by south; we kept our course northwest by north and north-northwest. At about midnight we saw something bright on the horizon off the starboard bow which looked like the sun coming up. This ball of light then quickly neared the ship, and then just as quickly went back to its original position. While this happened the sea turned the color of pale flame. We were assured that such phenomena are quite common here and the hunters call them *spolokha*.

16th August The wind was variable between south and west, and then there was very little calm; what wind there was came from the same quarter: we followed a course northwest by north. In the morning, amongst the large number of the usual birds, we saw one eider, from which we concluded (as our calculations later confirmed) that we were not far from the island of Sv. Iona. The bird, which does not ever fly very far from the shore, soon flew back there. At times fish would leap out of the water, belonging naturally to the great numbers which go up the rivers that flow into the Sea of Okhotsk.

17th Aug. The slight breezes and lack of wind persisted, the breezes coming from southeast and northeast. At midday we calculated our position as fifty-five English miles from Okhotsk, on a bearing from it southeast by south and half a point east. We saw many puffins, fulmars and several albatrosses, or seven-sazhen seagulls.

At eight in the morning we saw between the north and northeast the coast adjoining the high Cape Shilkap. The night was such that it must be considered a rarity in these parts from the point of view of climate. There was a full moon, the sky was cloudless with a clear horizon, and we could see clearly the whole coast stretching from Okhotsk to Shilkap.

19th Aug. With a gentle wind from the southwest and west-southwest we travelled northwest, with the current, which normally flows here from the northeast along the coast. At about midnight the wind became northwest.

20th Aug. The wind was light, somewhat changeable, but always contrary, as we rounded Shilkap. In the last few days we had seen a great number of a certain kind of mollusk, here called *zhirki*. At midday there were many seals playing round the ship.

21st Aug. The wind, which had all morning blown from the north, later backed to northeast, and then there were very light breezes between south and east, which moved us towards the mouth of the River Okhota. At ten o'clock in the evening an American Company baidarka came out to us from Okhotsk. It brought us fresh meat and other foodstuffs. At about midnight the tide began to go out, so we dropped anchor.

22nd Aug. At eight o'clock in the morning we raised anchor and approached the mouth of the Okhota with the aid of a tug. Soon the wind fell to a light breeze varying between south and east. We put on sail and crossed the bar or shallows as the water was beginning to subside. Several sazhens from the southern headland our vessel yawed across some very tall waves which rolled her so much that she shipped water on both sides. We dropped anchor and wanted to use a kedge-anchor, hoping to get up the river against the current. But when we noticed that the water was very low we raised anchor again, went back across the shallows and stood at anchor some two and a half versts from Okhotsk.

I wished to know whether there was any mail for us in Okhotsk and so set out in my baidarka; but as it was a long way to the mouth of the river, I had to go ashore directly opposite the ship. At this point the surf breaking on the shore was high and dangerous. We had to wait for a really large wave which would carry us to the beach in one go. Once there I and the front oarsman leapt out and dragged the baidarka up the beach, so that only the stern oarsman was drenched from head to foot by the following wave.

The sea off the coast of Okhotsk is very shallow. Four versts offshore the depth is not greater than four sazhens. For this reason the noise of the surf can always be heard around the town. The surf is greater on the outgoing tide, especially when a wind from the open sea makes the surf high. Great white steep billows come rolling in with a tremendous crash. This noise alone makes Okhotsk's position an unpleasant one, for it causes boredom and depression. In calm conditions the inhabitants of this town always know what the weather is going to be like; for if the surf is strong and noisy on the spit of land running from the north bank of the Okhota or in other words: "when the Tungus cat is meowing" (as the townsfolk say), then the weather will be fine, but if the Uratsk cat is making a noise, i.e. the spit from the south bank, where the River Urak flows in, then the weather will be bad.

I spent about two hours with Mr. Polevoi and received from him letters addressed to myself and to Khvostov, and I then returned to my baidarka. The tide was already out and a fairly fresh wind was blowing from the sea causing a terrifying surf to break upon the beach. A crowd of people had gathered round my baidarka and all of them were talking about the impossibility of getting off and my oarsmen tended to agree with them. A certain peredovschchik who was there (a supervisor of the hunters) said that he had been sailing baidarkas for thirty-three years, and thus he could safely assure me that I would never get the boat off the beach. I wanted to prove to him that it could be done. I therefore persuaded the oarsmen to set off towards the ship, despite the protests of the assembled crowd. So we got into the baidarka on dry land, put on our kamleikas, our seat-covers and laced ourselves in. Then we waited until a very large wave came in, then we allowed ourselves to be lifted, and we began to paddle with all our might. The first wave to meet us broke only over the first paddler, the second covered his head and came up to my neck and tore off my seat cover. It was too late to turn back and it was not possible to repair the cover, thus nothing remained to us but to row for all we were worth so as to get away as quickly as possible. One more wave broke over us, but then we came out of the surf and saw so much water in the baidarka that it was hardly staying afloat. Those watching from the shore when we were in the middle of the surf could not see our baidarka and thought that we had perished, but when they finally saw us safe they began to wave their hats as a sign of their joy. I must confess that stubbornness forms no small part of my nature and it has several times cost me dearly. I cannot justify what I did. It deserves more to be called senseless obstinacy than praiseworthy boldness. That was what I thought of it, not when I was doing it, but afterwards. I must say that on this occasion only extreme good fortune saved me from the effects of my extraordinary foolhardiness.

23rd Aug. On the high midday tide we entered the mouth of the River Okhota and stopped at anchor at Kukhtui to wait for the current to slacken. We tried to cast kedge anchors in the Okhota but it could not be done quickly. In the meantime the current changed and became very strong in a direction downriver. The kedge anchor was not holding and was pulled to the ship when we began to pull on it. Then in order to withstand the river current we set topsail, mainsail and foresail. The wind was fresh from the south. Although the ship with these sails set had, of course, a speed of four and a half knots, it nevertheless began to fall back. The water level had dropped to such an extent in the meantime that we were in danger of running aground on the shallows and of losing the ship, so we dropped anchor at least to keep us in the river. But then, as before, we continued to drift, i.e. to be pulled back. So with the help of the sails we decided to make for the Tungus shore and go around there. When the water ebbed and the roughness died down we began to unload the ship. After two and a half to three hours we had unloaded the whole of the cargo. We let down the booms, took away all the flying rigging, topsails, topmasts, gallants, topgallant-yards, the barrels on the deck and poured all the fresh water out of the hold. When we had completed these tasks we raised anchor and the various kedges for the pulling of the ship. The wind became very fresh from the south and whipped up quite a swell, several cables snapped, but finally at ten o'clock in the evening we came off the sandbar and drew up to the Okhotsk shore where we made fast.

Our sea journey was over. There was nothing with which to *Sv. Elizaveta* could return to America so she would have to spend the winter in Okhotsk. For this reason Khvostov and I decided to travel to St. Petersburg, planning our route so as to be able to stay in several

Siberian towns and gain some acquaintance with this distant part of Russia.

5th Sept. Today there was quite a heavy fall of snow; we travelled with dog-teams.

23rd Sept. In the evening we left Okhotsk in the company of five of our friends and we spent the night near the River Okhota, without reaching the charcoal pits. The night was extremely cold.

24th Sept. At nine o'clock in the morning we saddled our horses, bade farewell to those who had come to see us off, and set off further on our way. We spent the night at Meta.

25th Sept. We stopped to spend the night sixteen versts beyond the Uratsk Crossing, at the Urak, in Topol'nik, where the fallen leaves from the poplar form the best food for horses at this time of year. When the snow lies so deep that the animals cannot reach the food underneath it the willow is cut down for them with other low bushes, and when there is not even any of that, they are encouraged to gnaw the bark from the trees. All day there were falls of snow.

26th Sept. We forded the little River Berezovka between the rapids and the muddy fords on the Urak, and beyond the latter river we stopped to spend the night. In the morning it showed and the air was freezing; then there was a mist, and in the end the day became quite warm. On the way I shot some partridges.

27th Sept. When we were still some twenty versts away from the *Plot bishch*(?) I rode ahead with a cossack. We picked berries and caught fish for ourselves and when we had gone another twelve versts we stopped to spend the night. The further we travelled the more snow we came upon and this made our progress very difficult. The merchant caravan proceeding in front of us from Okhotsk lost many of its horses.

28th Sept. We camped for the night only eighteen versts from the Iudoma cross. Lake Sis'kiul was completely frozen. In places the snow was very deep.

In the morning we were delayed for a long while because the horses had wandered away in the night. Today, however, we reached the owner of our pack-drivers, took good horses from him and left our exhausted ones behind. We forded the River Iudoma, down which floated a great deal of *shuga* or ice. The dog we had with us was unable to get across and so remained on the other side. We spent the night at the second burnt clearing, in snow that was more than half an arshin deep. The wood between the river swamp and the first burnt strip of forest is called the *Syl'ia-yiabyt'* (hang-your-pants-up) wood.

29th Sept. During this period the days were cold but for the most part clear; today thick snow was falling which blinded us as we crossed the clearings. We cross the Taskh-talon [the stone field] mountain ridge and cross the River Akachan two or three times. This river flows into the Iudoma. The Rivers Ognennaia and Lamkova, and the one where our horses had been drowned in the previous year, in fact the whole of the journey which we had made then, avoiding fording the flooded Akachan, was to the right side of us now. We avoided the Malyi Kogon-ippyt and stopped at the larger river of the same name to spend the night, in snow which was about an arshin deep.

1st October In the morning we were again held up by our horses, which had strayed, for this we were forced to leave the Iakut. Thick, wet snow continued to fall.

2nd Oct. We crossed a series of lakes called the Malyi, Srednii, and Bol'shoi Chzhergatalakh and entered the supply base Myrsa Saibata (the merchant supply store). The name derives from a Iakut *myrs* (merchant) who as he returned in the late autumn from Okhotsk, was overtaken by snow of such depth that he could find no way of getting through this ravine so he cut up his horses for meat and keeping the flesh in the storehouse spent the winter there. Beyond this wood is Kere-be-talon (chestnut mare's field). The origin of this is that an exhausted chestnut mare was left there by some Iakuts returning one year from Okhotsk. Against all expectations she was discovered alive the following year.

We too were forced to leave a horse here. On the journey there were many ravines. When we had crossed Bus'-Kiul', we stopped to spend the night.

3rd The night was very cold and in the day the frost often forced us to dismount and go on foot. Where the rivers were deep they were covered in thick ice. But where the current was quick there was still thick sludge-ice. We spent the night in Dylga-Asylyk (a feeding-place in Kochki) twenty versts from the River Allakh-Iun.

We forded the Allakh-Iun, although in many places it was already covered with ice which would have borne the horses. We arrived early at the post station but we stopped so as to rest and feed our horses, which were so tired that they could hardly place one foot in front of the other; for the snow in this area was fine and beneath it there was a fair amount of grass. The Iakuts asked us to remain here for another day and wanted to follow the River Berezovka by another route, since they did not think that, with the snow, it would be possible to follow the summer route across seven ranges and other high mountain ranges. We found this pasturage empty. The horses were led off to another place because the road stops and another begins to go through Aimiakon. We took over the Iakut kitchens. Although our camp consisted only of four moss-grown walls with a bark roof in which a hole had been made to let the smoke out, it still seemed very comfortable to us after having spent so many nights in the frost.

5th After midday two Tungus came to us saying that some twenty versts beyond the Allakh-Iun there were their nomad yurtas with their wives, children and deer, and that they had travelled to us on foot. A Tungus stroll! We gave them tobacco and they gave us in return two sacks of musk oil residue.

Musk comes from a species of wild goat, the kaparga, which are to be found mostly in the mountains. Their wool is black, or black with white patches--and is long like goat's hair. When its coat is long the kaparga looks like a large dog. It has small upright horns, no tail and thin legs; the meat is very tasty. Under the belly near the rear and under the skin is a gland with musk which is even exported to Russia. The Iakuts, the Tungus and the Russians who live here drink this musk, dried and mixed with oil; they rub themselves with the liquid as an aid against external rashes and they use it as a successful cure against the mange in horses. The Iakuts and Tungus call the kaparga by the same name--*Biugan*. This animal is always to be found in small herds.

Our Iakuts changed their minds about travelling along the River Berezovka for there was no cleared path there at all; this would have presented especial difficulties when we were crossing one extremely high mountain ridge, which was of course covered in deep snow. Thus we travelled the summer route where there was a path cleared by the merchant caravans travelling in front of us in convoy. During our crossing of the seven peaks there was a biting cold wind blowing, or a *khiuz*, as the inhabitants of East Siberia call it. This wind blew snow with such great force from the mountain tops that they seemed to smoke.

That night when we camped we were caught up by Polevoi and from then on we began to bivouac better at night; for now we could sleep not in the tents but under square pieces of canvas fixed at an angle to the ground; near these a large fire was kept alight all night and this was very pleasant in such a severe climate. I was extremely sorry that I had no thermometer with me with which to measure the exact degree of cold, which, of course, in the higher spots must have reached twenty-five or twenty-eight degrees Reaumur. When we arrived at our night's camp we usually dug away the snow from under the place where we wished to pitch our tent and start a fire, otherwise when the latter melted the snow all our bedding and clothing would be ruined. Then we would take care to pitch the tent lengthwise in the ravine as it ran between the mountains so that the smoke would not get in our faces.

From midday onwards the sky became overcast and snow began to fall; then towards evening it began to snow heavily. We travelled some thirty versts along the River Kunkui and then camped for the night. The name *Kunkui* means 'narrow place', and the river is so called because it flows in a very narrow mountain gorge. The pastures in the Kunkui are very good, as there is much grass of the mare's-tail species, which the Iakuts call *sibikhtia*, and this soon put some flesh back onto our horses. Sibikhtia is green even in winter. For this reason at the beginning of spring and towards autumn the route along the Kunkui is always preferred as far as its source even, but in summer they avoid this route for on the Kunkui it is possible to be pinned down in one place for more than a month if the rains set in. By the beginning of spring in this climate I mean that part of the year when the ice has not quite cleared from the rivers.

8th Towards midday the snow stopped and the sky cleared. At first we travelled along the Kunkui on the ice but now we sometimes had to ford it as well.

9th On and off it snowed. On the Belaia River we went through the ice with several horses, which we were only just able to save.

10th The mountains have noticeably become lower, which is a sure sign that we are approaching the Aldan. The weather was clear with a sharp frost.

11th The weather continued to be just as cold as before. Even before sunrise we reached the River Aldan which was dotted with large ice floes which were still just moving in the center--this meant that it would be impossible to cross the river with horses. Because of this we had to wait here for over two days and nights. At the feeding place many other travellers had arrived who had set out from Okhotsk and all of us had to be accommodated in just two cossack yurtas. At this time of year the Iakuts come specially to the Aldan crossing and they sell meat, butter and other food supplies at a great profit. In the local yurtas, as in the Iakut ones, there is ice in the windows instead of glass.

15th In the morning the water in the river overflowed its banks, which told us that the river must have frozen over a little farther downstream. In the evening we could hear the crack of the ice floes rubbing against each other. Around midnight this noise stopped and the river had stopped opposite the station as well.

16th There were occasional falls of snow and the weather was cold. The ice near the station would still not take the weight of a man, so the Iakuts went upstream a little way where the ice was thicker, broke holes in it in many places so that the water flowed up and froze and then, as they waited, the ice became even thicker.

In the evening a Iakut woman came to our yurta. When she saw anyone making some kind of unusual movement she would do the same, shout out and leap upon him. After this she would imitate anyone who did anything, then shout, and attack with her fists or with a stick. Finally she grew so wild that she sat on the floor and began to sway and chant as though she were casting spells. She was taken away, and went on shouting until she collapsed. Such women are often to be encountered among the Iakuts and they are known as *Ameriaki*. We were assured that they were ill, but I believe that to begin with they simulate this berserk behavior and then gradually become accustomed to it.

17th In the morning the Iakuts went across the Aldan on the ice with one pack-horse; around midday we began to cross in the same manner. The ice in some places was still quite thin, bent under us and made cracking noises, but we crossed safely. Only the rear horse went through but with great effort and no little danger to ourselves we were able to drag it out. From the Aldan we took post-horses and crossed the River Nokha, where we camped for the night at the station of the same name.

18th At five in the morning we set off on our way. At the start of our journey it was snowing but then it stopped as soon as the sun, around which a rainbow could be seen, rose a little above the horizon. At the Amginsk station we found some splendid crucian-carp. We camped for the night at Mel'zhege.

19th By nightfall we had reached Chuporga. The evening was bitterly cold.

20th In the forenoon there was a heavy fall of snow

and after this a biting wind blew straight into our faces. This cut down the distance covered to 64 versts, to be precise.

21st From the station at Chuchigiisk, where we had spent the night, we set off early and at five in the afternoon we arrived in the town of Iakutsk. We were to stay here until a good route had been settled along the Lena River as far as the landing at Kachugsk. Since the autumn the Lena had, as usual, become increasingly uneven so that until a road has been cleared it is very bumpy because of the jagged ice packs, here called *torozy*.

9th Nov. Towards evening we left the town and set off together with Mr. Polevoi, in three sledges in all. The great majority of the settlers living between Iakutsk and Alekminsk, and beyond even, at the present time have only kasha to eat. This is made from milk and pine bark with, on occasions, a little flour added, while yet others having nothing to eat but pine bark and water. The bark is stripped from the trees in the autumn, dried and mixed with flour. The results of such a diet are evident on the faces of each one of them for none of them has any color or any other sign of strength and health. In one place we came across a twelve-year-old girl who looked like an old woman. Passing merchants help these unfortunate people by sharing with them a little of their own food supplies. For this reason they always carry extra supplies with them. Our fellow-traveller, Mr. Polevoi, who was a generous and virtuous man, weighted down his sledge and ours with biscuits and all kinds of food supplies so that he could dispense them to the poor inhabitants, who were as a result closely attached to him. He often travelled from Irkutsk to Okhotsk and always treated these unfortunate people in the same way. It would be good if more Polevois were travelling along the whole of the route!

The kibitkas [covered sledges] in which we travelled along the Lena River are very small and light but so badly built that they rarely stay in one piece as they bump along over the ice. They cannot carry more than ten or twelve puds. Because we had no oats the horses could only be fed on hay and sometimes on brushwood, and so they quickly became useless. After a month of travel on the winter road they can hardly drag their legs along and travel is very difficult.

12th With every day the frost became more severe. As an experiment I travelled between two stations on the driver's seat and I can assure you that it was not easy. When the first blast of wind hits your face, it is as though you had been burnt. As you breathe you can hear the air crackling. A cloud of steam rises up in a column above the horses and this can be seen from behind, and the animals cannot move quickly because of getting out of breath from the density of the air. Every four or five versts it is necessary to halt the horses and clear away the icicles blocking their nostrils, otherwise their breathing is blocked and they come to a stop. The people living along the Lena wear chin-covers, nose-covers, forehead-covers, ear-muffs and cheek-covers, so that only their eyes and mouths remain uncovered. Around their necks above their top coats they wear neck scarves made from squirrel tails. Their coats are of hare or deerskin. Over this is normally worn the Iakut *sanaiakh*. On their legs above their deerskin boots they wear *suturi* and kneepads. The suturi have been described already above. Their mittens are made large and from some warm fur, backed with a coarser skin, such as deer-skin or fox paws and the like.

13th From Kharabalysk (44 versts) we travelled all the time at walking speed and the drivers walked beside the kibitka [conveyance]. Finally, some ten versts from Namana I walked as well and soon overtook my kibitka.

14th When we were a short distance from Alekminsk the runner under our kibitka broke and we abandoned it. Not much farther on another one tipped over and also broke. I almost got frostbite on my hands mending it. When we arrived in the town we sent men back after the one we had abandoned. The driver we had left guarding it had also nearly frozen to death for the cold was savage.

Here we had confirmed what I had previously heard rumored about horses purchased on the River Viliui--that if they are set free, even after two years they will still make their way home--even if it were a thousand-verst journey. The reason given for this is the good quality of the local grass. The River Viliui abounds in fish, especially in summer, when they swim up from the sea. Salt-water fish rarely go any further upstream than the Vitim and then only in small numbers. The iron found on the Viliui is considered one of the best for quality. The Iakuts very skilfully make various high quality articles out of it and the knives made locally are famous throughout the whole of northeastern Siberia, for the metal is very soft so that the knife-blades bend and spring back again when used for handicrafts.

20th At the Dubrovsk zaimka we found some Tungus returning from the sable hunting on the Vitim. We gave them vodka and in return they wanted to give us sable fur, but as we would not accept this gift from them they thought that it was not enough for us and they threw in more sable and several squirrels, and when they saw that we still did not want to take it, they were amazed and could hardly believe that we had entertained them with vodka without having the slightest intention of acquiring any of their sables. The Tungus have been taught to think in this way by the Russian merchants who, before they get down to trading, normally give out vodka and presents--this places an onus on the Tungus to return the gift.

25th From Kirensk onwards the horses were good everywhere. Towards evening we arrived in Irkutsk, having been sixteen days and nights on the road from Okhotsk, or excluding the times we had camped overnight in one place more than once, thirteen.

20th Dec. At night we left Irkutsk. The Angara was so thickly covered with floating ice that it was impossible to cross. Then we were told that forty versts upstream the river was already frozen over so we went along the right bank to this point. We spent the night at Urik, that is, some eighteen versts from Irkutsk.

21st In the morning we set off, and by a roundabout route we came out at Mal't onto the high road.

23rd At five in the morning we arrived in Nizhne-Udinsk.

We arrived at Krasnoiarsk. Our journey thence from Nizhne-Udinsk had been most unpleasant, first because a snowstorm which went on for several days in a row covered up the road, and second because we were travelling at Christmastime when many of the drivers are drunk, do not feed the horses, harness them wrongly, and this all causes various accidents and delays.

28th In the evening we arrived in Tomsk and drove around the streets for some time before we could find anywhere to stay the night.

30th We left Tomsk, and at midnight we arrived at a station called Krutye logi [steep dens]. We saw the New Year in in the Barabinsk steppes.

1804 3rd Jan. At dawn we arrived in Kop'evo where the Barabinsk steppes come to an end. From here we turned in the direction of Tobol'sk, forking right from the Ishim road. That evening we passed through the town of Tara. Frost and blizzards continued and the road was very bad; actually it would be more preicse to say there was no road and we were travelling over open country.

In Tobol'sk gubernia there was hardly any rye but corn everywhere; the rye this season had not taken at all and it was selling at a whole *griven* a pud more than corn.

From Tara to Tobol'sk we went by a different, shorter route, forking off at Aevsk station towards Tatarsk settlement. This route takes 440 versts, the one we had been travelling, 560.

About 300 versts this side of Tobol'sk, in an area about 200 versts around, last summer a great multitude of rodents had appeared which the local inhabitants called moles, but which, if the descriptions are to be believed, must have been a kind of rat because they were the same size, had the same kind of tail and some were covered in spots. The color of their fur was for the most part black, but grey ones had also been seen. These rodents ate nearly all the wheat, even that which had been cut and stored in elevated store-houses. They had remained right up until the first snows. In the winter many ermines had appeared and the people hoped that they would exterminate the above-mentioned rodents.

Because the road here is too narrow our four or five horses were harnessed up one behind the other. Such a harness is in no way compatible with fast travel.

7th In the evening we arrived in Tobol'sk. On the following day we lunched with Governor-General Ivan Osipovich Selifanov and on the day after that with the Governor, Ivan Fedorovich Shteingeil. Towards evening on that day we again set out.

Tobol'sk is built on a steep bluff and when seen from below and at a distance looks very attractive: but it must be even more attractive in summer for the town stands at the confluence of the rivers Irtysh and Tobol', which both meander through the surrounding areas.

14th We passed through Perm stopping in the town but using the time only to change horses.

17th We entered Kazan, where we stayed until the 24th. From then until the 26th it rained, washing away the road, which seemed all the more boring because of the intermittent bouts of fever I was having.

We stayed one day in Moscow to repair the wagon. Our journey became happier with each hour, for in almost every town we came across acquaintances, and we were all the time nearing the end of our journey. I cannot satisfactorily describe the joy which I felt as we entered St. Petersburg at nine in the morning of 5th February. Was it not long ago (for what signified the past twenty months) when we left here that our hearts had been emburdened by the anguish of parting from our relations and near ones? Was it not long ago that we saw in our imagination the immeasurable distance, the innumerable dangers, an alien world and alien sky? Was it not long ago that we had the desperate thought that perhaps we might never return, and this gnawed at the very depths of our soul? Now all these earlier fears were past. We have satisfied our curiosity, performed certain services and with a pleasant memory of our past difficulties, now we hasten on to see our relatives, our well-wishers, friends and acquaintances. Anyone who has been on a long journey will know this joy, but he will appreciate it even more if he never expected to live to enjoy it.

End of Part One

TWO JOURNEYS TO AMERICA
BY THE
NAVAL OFFICERS KHVOSTOV AND DAVYDOV
WRITTEN BY THE LATTER

PART TWO

Printed at the Naval Topography
at St. Petersburg
in 1810

PREFATORY NOTE

In the account of the first journey on page 254, Mr. Davydov says that the two travellers found an error in Vice-Admiral Sarychev's map concerning the calculation of the position of the island of Attu--to be precise, that on the map the island is placed 20 minutes further north than it should be.

The Department has not let this remark go without notice. Subsequent research has shown that the calculation made by Lieutenants Khvostov and Davydov itself contains an error of 14 minutes. Consequently the difference between the two measurements is reduced to a mere 6 minutes. In the circumstances the Department, since it cannot be sure that Khvostov and Davydov's calculations did not contain further error, has decided to confirm the charting of the island according to Vice-Admiral Sarychev.

The following articles include a description of the island of Kad'iak and its inhabitants.

I

THE POSITION OF KAD'IAK AND ADJACENT ISLANDS. THE NUMBER OF INHABITANTS, KNOWN AS KONIAGAS.

The island of Kad'iak, or as it is normally called *Kadik*, lies between latitude 56°48' and 38° north and in length occupies an area, so far not precisely calculated, between longitude 206°30' and 208°30' east from Greenwich. Previously the Russians called the place Kykhtakh, which is what they understood the islanders to say. In their language it means large island. The inhabitants of Kad'iak, Afognak, Tugidak, Sitkhinak and the other small islands adjacent to Kad'iak speak the same language with some small variations in pronunciation which distinguish those coming from the east, and west of the group. Tugidak and Sitkhinak lie to the south of Kad'iak and are separated from it by a narrow strait. To the north is Afognak, which is about a quarter the size of Kad'iak. The inhabitants of all the above-mentioned islands and the other islands near Kad'iak were calculated in 1803 as being not much less than seven thousand --this includes adults and children of both sexes. On Shuekh, which lies north from Afognak, there are no permanent inhabitants, but the islanders sometimes visit there to hunt seals and sealions. In the autumn a fair number of fox are trapped there. The island to the east of this one is called Evrashech'ia [Ground Squirrel, later misnamed Marmot Island] Island, after the name of the small animal which is caught there and for which the islanders occasionally visit the place. On the islands north of Shuekh the Russians shoot sealions. Vancouver said these islands were barren, for they consisted almost entirely of bare rock. The Russians call them *Peregrebnye* [crossing] Islands because they lie almost halfway between Shuekh and Kinai Bay and serve as a resting place for the islanders hunting beavers [otters]. They paddle across the wide strait and stop there to rest. Sixty English miles south of Tugidak lies the small island of Ukamok on which several islanders and Russians live all year round, catching squirrels and birds.

II

THE APPEARANCE OF THE ISLANDERS. THEIR ARTIFACTS AND ADORNMENTS.

The inhabitants of Kad'iak and of all the islands described above call themselves Koniagas, but it would seem that this term is often applied to the Aliaksans as well. They are of medium height, very few of them being tall. They are generally well-built, probably as a result of their very healthy upbringing as children. Their skin is dark-copper in color, a result, it would seem, rather of their being constantly in the open air, as well as of the fact that in summer they sail their baidarkas. naked and also, when it is warm, sit naked in their houses. It would thus seem to me that this skin coloring is not inborn. This is borne out by the fact that many of the women have a very pale skin, which results from the fact that they are in the open air less. They eyes are dark, and their hair also. The men wear their hair either in a plait or hanging loose. Others, imitating the Russians and the English have begun to cut it at the front, but this fashion is not widely followed. The women have very long hair which they wear in bunches at the back of the head and cut it at eye-level in front. Many cut it short all over except for a small patch done up in bunches. The children are shorn completely except for a patch on the top of the head.

The standard of health in both sexes seems good and even in old age the people do not seem feeble, for they can be found performing the same duties as the young, so as to provide their daily bread. Among the islanders there seem to be few old men, perhaps because they lead a difficult life and are in constant danger so that few of them live to enjoy old age.

There is nothing particular in the faces of the Koniagas which might distinguish them from other peoples. They have round, flat and long faces, but in both sexes there are few of attractive appearance, and if anything, the men are better-looking. The children born to Russians and islanders are generally good-looking. Many of the women would also be attractive, if they did not decorate themselves in what seems to us an ugly way. For in addition to the beads, about which mention was made earlier, they pierce their nostrils through at the bottom and wear there bones, beads or corals. It may easily be imagined how such a 'bone mustache' might disfigure the most attractive woman. But their taste is not satisfied even with this idea for they then make several holes in their lower lip from which they hang a loop into which are placed beads and small white bones. These holes vary in number between two and six. Their lips are pierced by close relatives and there is a great deal of respect, therefore, for the girl islander who has the most. In addition to this method of decorating themselves they also specialize in sewing themselves beards. For this they rub a threat in soot and add a black mixture, and by means of a needle they draw this thread under their skin, making in this fashion a black design on their chin which remains there all their lives for there is no way at all of removing it. Others have two designs running from their ears to their chin. When a girl gets married designs are drawn on her body as a sign of love, or on her arms. Many people have a line drawn across their whole body running from one shoulder under their bosom to the other. In these circumstances the designs are according to the taste of the person concerned. Their ears are pierced all round, and they hang beads, coral and many other ornaments there, the most precious of which are pearls. The Koliuzhes relate that these come from the mainland opposite the Charlotte Islands and perhaps from a place even further removed. By a process of barter the pearls pass from hand to hand until they reach Kad'iak, and they were even seen on the Aleutian Islands before the Russians reached America. It was thought at the time that they came from Chugach Bay, but it is now known that they were not to be found in any of the places reached by the Russians. The Koliuzhes maintain that at one spot on the mainland, opposite the Charlotte Islands, there is a particular lake where special worms are bred by the natives by immersing in the water the body of someone who has died, or of a slave killed specially for the purpose. After several days the body is removed with the worms clinging to it. The shells of these worms are called *tsuklei*. They are normally about a vershok long, sometimes more, but rarely as much as two vershki. The shell is round, as thick as a small goose's feather, somewhat curved, and one end is always narrower than the other. This ornament, as I have said, is considered the most expensive so that for a pair of good *tsuklei* on Kad'iak it is possible to receive a whole squirrel-skin parka. The women wear them in their noses or ears, where they also hang pieces of mother-of-pearl which are occasionally washed up by the sea. Many wear earrings. On their hands the women wear as many rings and stones as they possess or as they can accommodate there. On their neck and wrists and ankles they wear jewelry made from beads and multicolored stones, but they prefer yellow amber to all others. Their taste for the color of the beads varies, but they show a predilection for black, and red bugle beads are preferred to beads.*

Nowadays the customs of sewing beards and piercing

*Beads have lost most of their value on Kad'iak because the inhabitants have accumulated a lot of them and have nowhere to dispose of them. This commodity goes mainly to the Kinaitsy, to the Chugaches and to the Copper River people, who trade with other peoples of the interior.

the lower lip and nostrils is beginning to die out altogether, and some islanders have even forsaken their bunches and are beginning to wear plaits when they see how the Russian women dress.

The men on Kad'iak also decorate themselves. Some of them pierce their lower lip like the women and others slit it completely, so that they look as though they have two mouths. When they drink or eat, the food drops out of their lower lip which makes this form of self-adornment even more repulsive. A large proportion of the men pierce their ears right round so that they may wear beads in them. The islanders have small beards, which begin to grow later than those of Europeans. It is not so long ago that people who had never travelled farther than the door of their study stopped maintaining that the American peoples did not have beards. In Laperouse's writings we read that in Chile even the Spaniards cannot agree amongst themselves about this.

The islanders generally have an unpleasant body odor, so that it is always possible to tell by the smell when one of them has come into the room. There are many enough reasons for this: their clothes are always badly made and smell of fat, the savages eat a great deal of whale blubber and are often even stained with it and, in addition, because of their slovenliness they rarely wash themselves.

All the peoples of northwestern America paint their faces on various occasions and each one does it according to the workings of his own imagination. When a Koniaga is about to embark upon some important undertaking, either hunting or rowing a long distance at sea, he paints his face with red graphite (found on Cape Iakolitsk and in other places); he does exactly the same thing when he is about to receive his guests.

III

THE ISLANDERS' DRESS AND ITS MANUFACTURE.

Before the Russians came both sexes dressed in the same way, and their outer garments consisted of kamleikas and parkas. The latter were made either from the skins of birds, squirrels, otters or other animals. Parka, kamleika and many other words have no meaning in the language of the islanders and have been introduced by the Russians who heard them in Kamchatka and Eastern Siberia. The parkas are like those in Kamchatka, in other words, like long shirts with very narrow collars only wide enough to allow the head to pass through. A kamleika is cut the same but it also has a head flap which can be put up when it rains.

Gavriil Ivanovich Davydov

Okhotsk in 1786

Unalashka Settlement, about 1804

Pavlovsk Harbor, Kad'iak, about 1804

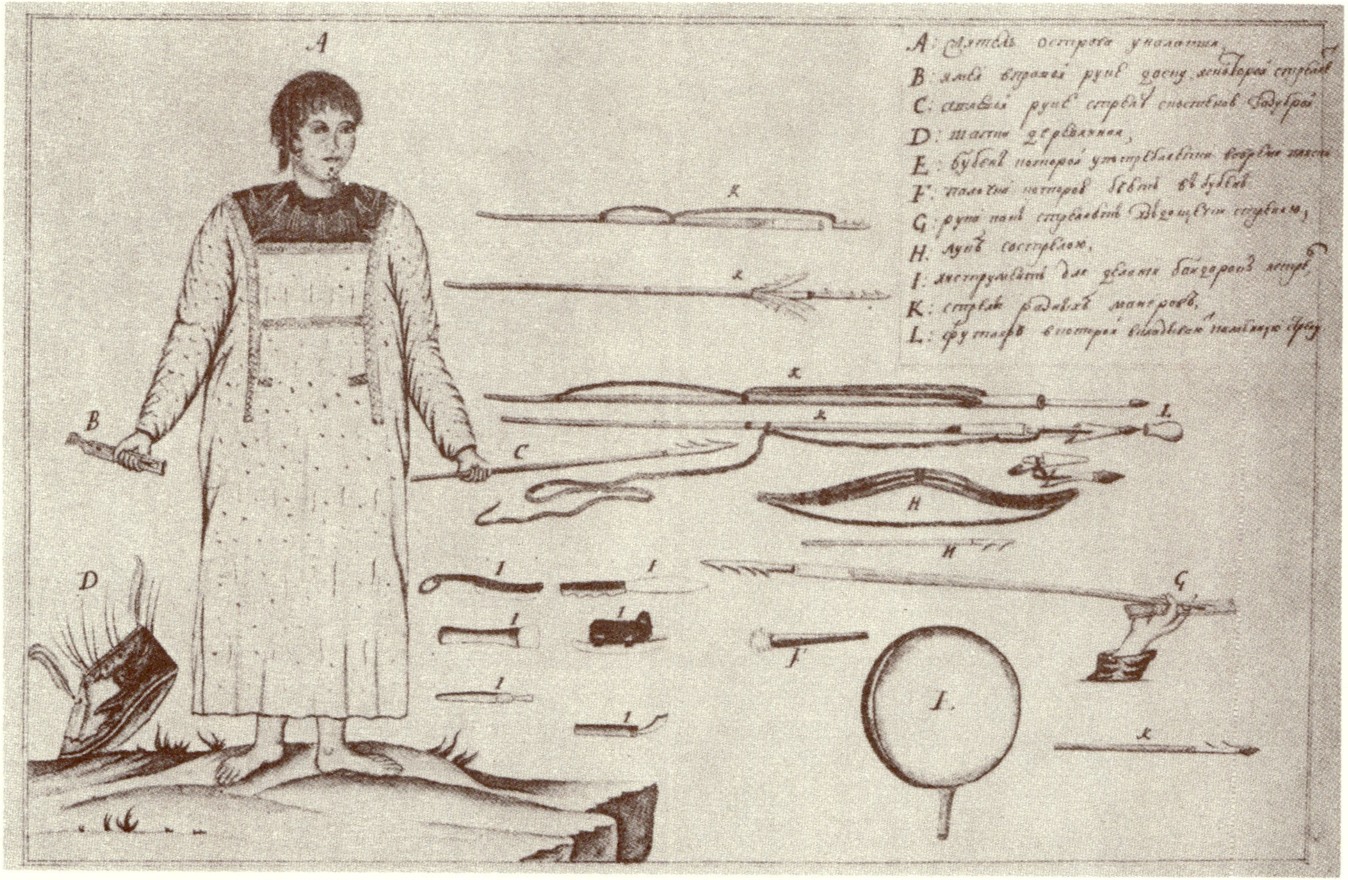

Aleut man (by Levashov, about 1768)

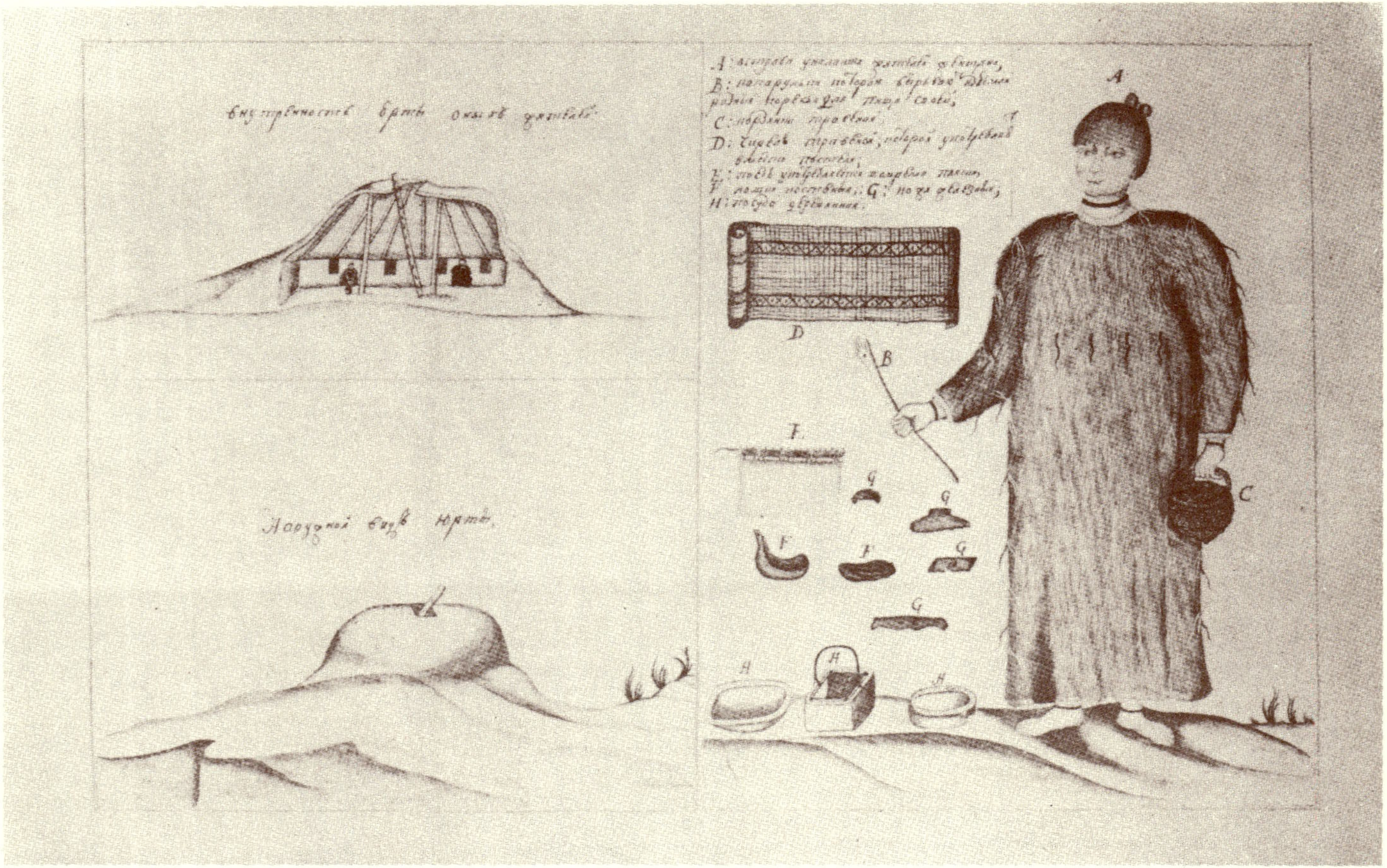

Aleut woman (by Levashov, about 1768)

Toion Nankok of Kad'iak (by Tikhanov, 1818)

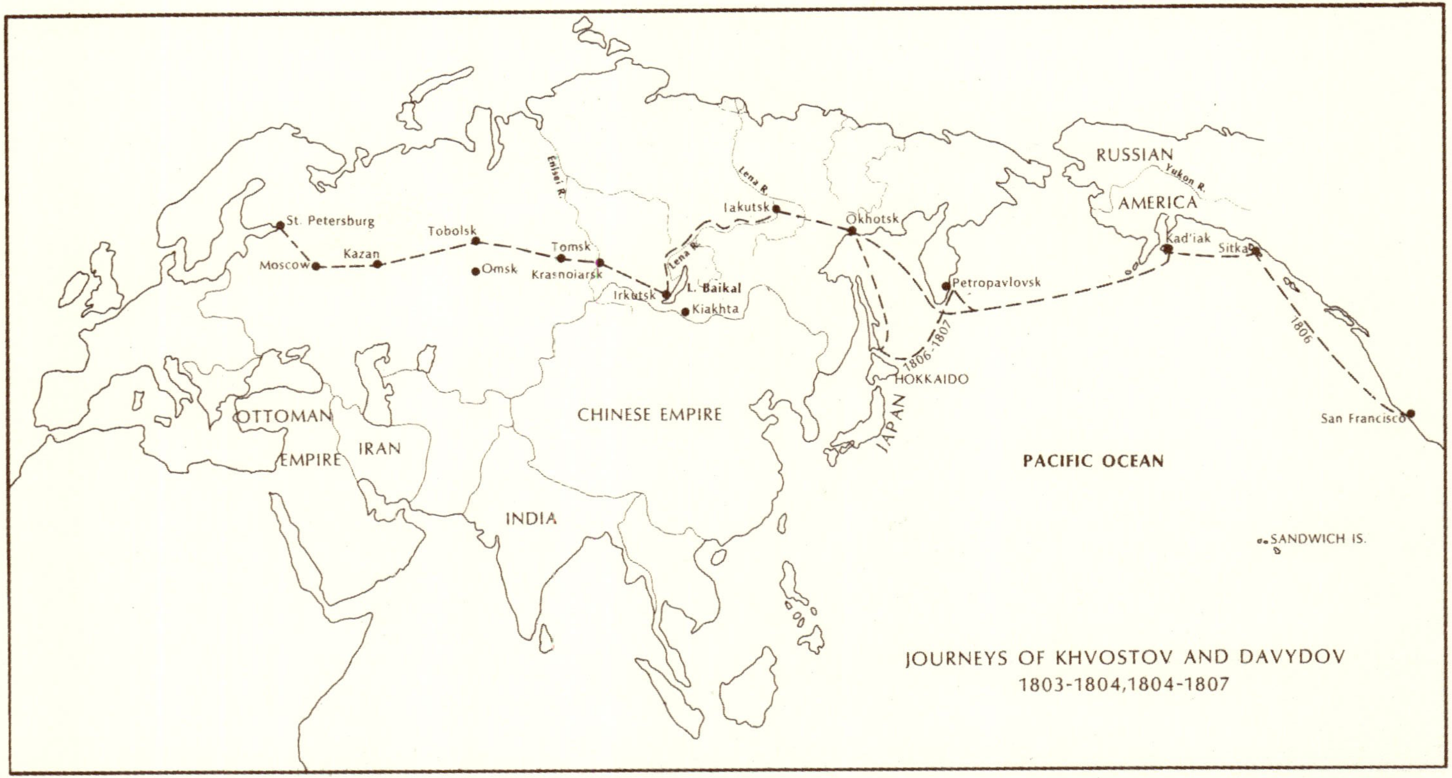

Map, routes taken by Khvostov and Davydov, 1802-1807

Birdskin parkas are made from murres [*ara*], puffins [*toporka*], cormorants [*uril*] and horned puffin [*ipatka*] skins, which are removed with the feathers. The women suck the fat out of them and then smear them with fermented fish eggs. After some time they scrape it off and squeeze out the skin until it is dry. The islanders have another method of preparing birdskins; they soak them for two or three days and nights and then wash them over and squeeze them dry. When they have prepared the skins they sew them together with threads (these they acquire from the Aliaska Peninsula) made from spun deer or whale gut. Great patience is needed in making these threads, for first the dried gut is torn into the thinnest of threads before being twined and dried.

Of the birdskin in parkas only those of the cormorant [*uril*] are considered good quality and they are really very handsome. They are made of the birds' neck feathers which are small and soft, so that it is hard at first to recognize it as birdskins. They are difficult to collect, however, for it is necessary to kill some 40 cormorants to make one large parka. These coats are worn by the women, they are decorated with every good ornament, for example: red and green worsted torn into strips, deer or goat-hair, ermine or otter cut into thin strips, puffin beaks, eagles' feathers, and other articles which have great value in the eyes of the savages. All this is sewn by one end to the parka and forms rows of various objects hanging from it. In the spring the guillemots have on their necks long, thin, white feathers or whiskers and these, because of their piebald color, are preferred to those collected at any other time of the year. On simple birdskin parkas the top around the neck is colored red and decorated with several sewn-on cormorant necks. If these are in short supply two are sewn on at the front and two at the back and if there are none to be had the parka remains unadorned. Of the coats sewn from birdskins those of puffins are preferred to murres. In damp weather they are donned with the feathers to the outside so that the rain runs off the feathers and does not wet the coat; those made from cormorant necks are always worn with the feathers to the outside.

Squirrel skins are sewn into parkas without even the heads and tails being removed, only the latter cannot be seen. These coats are made like two together, one with the fur on the outside, the other with the fur on the inside. Only the skins on the outer surface are sewn with the heads; those inside remain unsewn, so that the parka looks like it is made of many rows which are not joined together. Before beginning to stitch a squirrel parka each animal is cut in two--on backs and bellies--as they say here. The former are used for the outer surface, the latter for the inner one. In squirrel parkas the sleeves are very short and hoes are cut underneath them where the hands may be put or kept under the coat, but they are never kept in the sleeves. These parkas normally belong to the womenfolk, but men sometims wear them too.

The clothing of the islanders described above is far from sufficient; in addition they have marmot and deerskin parkas; the former are bartered from the Kinaitsy, the Chugaches and other peoples living farther to the east; and the latter from the Aliaksintsy, who sell ready processed deerskins and kamleikas sewn from them. Deerskin parkas, like cormorant, are decorated with various trinkets. Bearskin and beaverskin [sea otter?] parkas have now completely disappeared as the islanders are obliged to deliver instantly the pelts of these animals to the company.

Kamleikas are made from the intestines of whales, seals, bears and the throats of these animals, of which, however, the Russians use the sealion throat mainly as kneepieces for boots. Kamleikas are also made from whale intestines and the skin flayed from the tongue and liver of this animal, but only when the whale washed up by the sea is still fresh. From the skin of the tongue of a large whale eight kamleikas may be produced. Although these, it would seem, should be better, since because of the size of the whale there are fewer seams, so that when kamleikas are made with skin from the tongue they consist of only two or three strips, they are only worn when there is absolutely nothing else, for they are heavy and tear easily. In all these coats the gut is sewn in lengths across the coat which is therefore known as a gut coat, while those made from throats are known as 'throat coats'. The latter are heavy, thicker and coarser but they keep out the damp longer and are more reliable to wear; consequently the Russians wear them on shore and at sea, but they are completely unsuitable for wearing when travelling by baidara. Of the gut kamleikas the best are from bears, for they are cleaner, finer and stronger; the worst in quality are seal excluding, of course, whale.

For the preparation of the gut one method is always used. They are turned inside out and the fat and offal are scraped off with a sharp shell; then they are washed and rinsed in urine, squeezed in water, allowed to dry and squeezed by hand.

A kamleika is a very necessary possession for an islander for, in addition to affording him protection from the rain, no Koniaga can travel by baidarka without one. When this coat is finished then its sleeves are tied together and it is filled with water, and if there are no leaks then the kamleika is pronounced good. If, in fine weather, a storm forces a Koniaga to don a kamleika, then he sprinkles it beforehand and afterwards with water so that the heat of the sun will not crack it. The kamleika, as has already been said, is decorated with plucked-out threads of red and green worsted and with goats' or deer hair. Others stitch a strip of ribbon-like colored skin round the hem and the cuffs.

Their hats are woven very skilfully and stoutly for fir-roots, with wide brims and a low crown slightly pointed at the top, and they are decorated with various designs. At the top of the hat they draw a crab, seal or some other animal. If they want the colors of the hat or anything else to stay there for a long time, they mix the paint with a solution of blood let specially by punching on the nose. Some young gallants wear hats with a high crown like a flower pot. The Kinaitsy wear ones which are even more strange for above the ordinary hat is a woven cylinder to which is fastened the effigy of a mink.

Other Koniagas wear wooden bonnets, which are sharply pointed and painted. In the top of these are fixed sealion whiskers onto which bears have been threaded. Others again cover just their eyes with a shade into which are set various stones. Many have wooden painted hats shaped like seal heads and these are very often worn when hunting this animal. In short, the islanders make various kinds of hats from thin wood and bark which they paint in different colors and decorate according to taste.

The islanders wore no other kinds of clothes before the Russians came to them, but now they barter animal skins for silk or cotton material and the women prefer this made up in the old style, that is to say as parkas. Now they are getting used to shirts, of which until now they have had no conception. Many, just as in Siberia and Kamchatka, make the upper part of it better than the hem. When native girls marry Russians they sometimes wear jackets and skirts, and even long dresses, which do not seem to suit them at all, but what is even more comic is to see a native woman wearing high-heeled shoes. Like women everywhere, they love dressing up. They may sometimes be seen in all their finery, walking through the mud, holding their shoes in their hand. But however much a local girl may dress up, beads, bugle-beads and multi-colored stones do not cease to please her. An idea of luxury is furtively stealing into the savage mind, for the Americans love dressing in European clothes, if they can acquire them.

Almost all the islanders go barefoot winter and summer, and not many of them have shoes made from seal or walrus skin, but even these are rather sack-like objects with crude whaleskin heels and soles sewn to them. The rich, especially the women, have warm shoes made from squirrel or marmot skins.

IV

THEIR DWELLING.

The Koniagas build their houses in the following fashion: logs are sunk into the ground, sometimes hewn planks are used. These slope slightly to the inside. The roofs are made either flat or rounded. Then all this structure is covered with grass and earth. This is their communal kitchen, entrance to which is gained through a small doorway, screened by a curtain of sealskin. In the middle of this hut a fire is kept burning and a hole is left in the roof above it to allow the smoke to escape. Instead of a floor dry grass is strewn upon the ground and several domestic utensils are placed around the sides. In others there are cupboards, but this *shalash* [hut] is always dirty and presents an unpleasant spectacle to a European, for the food waste, fish bones and shells are very rarely removed. At the side of the kitchen there is a small round opening, covered with a board, only wide enough for a made to crawl through with great difficulty, which gives access to a warm shelter called by the Russians the *zhupan*, occupied normally by two or three families, and more rarely, by one. Two or three such zhupans surround each kitchen, depending upon the number of families living together. The floor of this shelter is always below ground level and its walls are sloping. The roof projects above ground, and in it, or in the side of the structure, is a window. Otter gut or the thin translucent membranes from other animals serve as glass and instead of frames there are four pieces of wood, but a reasonable amount of light comes in. The zhupans are kept clean; they have a board floor if wood is readily accessible, otherwise dried grass or clean bast matting are used.

In each settlement there is a large shalash called a *kazhim*, in which festivities are conducted. Its roof is rounded and there is a large window covered with sewn-together gut, and there are tables and benches around the walls inside.

If several families are living together each has its own separate place for sleeping, marked out simply by a blanket spread on the ground. It is so narrow that it is impossible to sleep in it without crouching oneself up into a ball. Cradles are made for babes-in-arms and these are placed on the floor. But older children sleep together with the adults and even the dogs join them there. Bear or sealskins serve as beds. If these are not available then they spread out grass matting and sometimes simply dry grass. There are bathing zhupans and baths which they had before the arrival of the Russians. Steam is produced in them by means of water poured on heated stones, and instead of a switch a certain kind of seaweed is used. This is so coarse that it would quickly flay the skin off anyone with a tender skin [surface]. The Koniagas take such baths in steam and wash by going down to the nearby sea or stream, both in summer and winter.

What is more revolting than all else is the filth around their huts, for the islanders do not go far away to do anything--and this gives one a very bad impression of their tidiness.

The Koniagas choose a site for their dwelling usually near a stream--so that they will have a ready supply of fish to lay in for the winter stocks. Also necessary is nearness to the shoreline which, when revealed by the outgoing tide, becomes a sandbank with shellfish on it, for this is the islanders' foodstore. On the wooded island, and in several other places, there are no streams near the settlements, but the islanders will not move away because, they say, that is where their fathers lived.

V

THE KONIAGA CHARACTER.

Having made a close and careful study of the islanders, under various conditions, I have become convinced of the wit and inventiveness with which, despite poverty of means, they have perfected their artifacts, and with these qualities in mind it is impossible to call them complete savages. True, the scope of their activities is very limited, but what they have fashioned is skilfully and thoughtfully executed, regardless of the crudity of their tools, with which a European artisan could do little. In earlier times the stone ax, bone needle (which had in itself to be manufactured), the shell, and the rare piece of metal were the only mechanical equipment they possessed. Even now they do not have many more instruments yet they have been and are still able to work bone and other materials very well. They have adopted some practices from the Russians and excel at these too, often as well as their teachers.

Habit, or perhaps an absence of salt in their diet, may be the reason for their excellent and reliable sense of sight. When engaged in carpentry an American knows without a thread just what is level and what is not. They travel in their baidarkas in the thickest of fogs, when the visibility is down to five sazhens, but they can always point out the shore to you, and they will come in exactly where they intend to. If you are on a ship in dangerous waters at night, or when there is a fog, then you can be reassured if you have an American in the bows [forward part of the ship], for he will always be able to see the rocks from an ample distance; and it is remarkable how they manage to make them out in stormy weather, when the sea is so white and rough around the underwater rocks.

Their memory, unburdened by learning and knowledge, is very reliable. During the festivals they will relate deeds performed by the fellow countrymen in far-off times, as they have been handed down orally. They only have to hear a thing once, or set eyes on some place, and they will never forget it. Going through a bay which a Koniaga has already crossed, he will know every rock and you can rely on him as much as on any pilot.

Since they use all their senses to their maximum all the time they have developed them to a point of perfection unknown to Europeans. They travel about the sea with such self-assurance that they might as well be on dry land. On several occasions I have had the opportunity of making quite long open sea crossings with them, in fog, snow and storm, and always we have arrived at just the settlement for which we had set course. Many of them can forecast accurately fine or stormy weather. Any one of them who intends to trade farther off across the sea will rise early before the sun is up and sit on top of his shalash or on a hillock, and depending on how the sun rises over the horizon he will decide whether to go or not. They have become accustomed to doing this. It has, to be more exact, become a way of life forced upon them, so that a fine morning rarely goes by without the savages greeting the rising sun with all their attention, as though to perfect their experience, to know what weather was being foretold. Others might think that this was the result of a certain kind of religious feeling, but I am firmly convinced that this is not the case.

Such qualities in the Koniagas are completely praiseworthy, but unfortunately in comparison to them there are others which, when they are revealed, will hardly give anyone cause to laud the condition of savage man. Ungratefulness, impacable vengeance toward their enemies, the savagery with which the latter are treated, lack of devotion to their relatives and indifference to the sufferings of those nearest to them are also part of their nature. The islanders are very deceitful and sly; you will never see a Koniaga in a rage; he is capable of masking even the strongest hatred, and all his revenge is calmly plotted. If they arrive at a settlement in the company of a Russian who understands their language they go first into the shalash and say that the Russian is a good man who understands their language. In this way, they warn the others not to say anything they should not in his presence. They show him every courtesy and even carry him from the baidara as they land. But they will not provide any useful information, their very courtesy is nothing but an act of weakness and fear, without which of course it might become evil savagery. Several years ago when a party of Koniagas was returning from Sitka, four baidarkas had gone on ahead. They became tired from the long paddling and they stopped to rest on a small island near the new harbor. Three or four days later all these people were discovered murdered, by whom was not known, but it was thought that other islanders, who had a grudge against them, had come across them by chance asleep, and had not missed an opportunity of taking their revenge.

Taking all these above-mentioned qualities into account, the Koniagas, like all savage peoples, are prodigal to the ultimate degree, and are so idle that they are only galvanized into activity by the extremities of need. Living the winter in the islanders' settlements I have seen how for a whole day almost no one will do anything. They all lie in their warm shelters dozing and even conversing a little. One of them might take up a tambourine and begin to beat it, as though driven to do it against his will, and he sings through his yawns. From time to time, also as though unwillingly, the others may join in. Sometimes in the evenings they will all sing like this to the sound of the tambourine.

Sometimes on a hot day, after a long time paddling, the islanders will come ashore near a stream and lie down on its banks to rest. Each one will say: "*Tana-iukhtu*"--I want water--but none of them will stand up and get it. If any Russian happens to be there and orders one of them to bring water and then offers him a drink the islander does not thing of thanking him. The same may be observed when they are lying in their zhupans: although the headman of the settlement may say that he wishes to drink even then no one moves an inch, unless his son or some other boy is there. If you arrive in a settlement in winter you will surely be told that there are many starving people there. If you ask one of them why they do not go out and catch some fish, you will hear that there are none to be caught. If you insist and say that there are, then the native will go on to tell you that he cannot go because his wife would miss him. But if you force him to go he will catch fish--and even thank you for it.

Now, however, the islanders have become more industrious. If it seems strange that such a short number of years have produced some changes in these savages, then I must say that it is not the number of years that is important, but the articles to which they have been introduced. Frequently an article which seems to us of little consequence produces a vast change in the habits of these savage peoples. The ax when brought to them produced great progress in their conceptions, so that now they complete in a week a task over which they would formerly have labored for a year. They have grown accustomed to tobacco and they will work harder in order to obtain it. And there are now a great many trinkets which the Koniaga considers as luxury items and his wish to acquire them forces him to use his wits to think up all possible means of achieving this end. Luxury is gradually creeping in: in former times a savage would not have longed for a birdskin parka if he did not have one, yet now he wishes to dress in squirrelskin or cotton. The wives of the leaders, or toions, as the Russians call them, buy red velvet or red cotton for their parkas, but it should not be thought that by wearing such fine clothes they take more care of them; they sit down on the ground just as carelessly and spatter them all over with grease and fat.

The Koniagas are naturally carefree in their domestic life, but when they go out hunting animals, or on some other undertaking, they change completely; then they can perform any task and they bear hunger and all kinds of deprivation with patience.

Sometimes a storm will force them to stay in their baidaras for several days and nights on the open sea, yet their talk about this afterwards as though it were some quite normal occurrence, and they treat it with their customary indifference.

From early childhood the islanders train their bodies to withstand pain and, when they wish to boast, will often punish their children till they bleed. Sometimes at the end of a festival a young boy is ordered into the kazhim. He carries a jagged piece of broken shell. He goes up to one of those watching and asks: "Am I brave?"

The person asked normally replies, "Yes, brave, and your father and grandfather were as brave."

Then with the sharp edge of the shell the lad cuts his arm from shoulder to wrist and then he begins to dance, boasting of his brave act, worthy of his ancestors. As a result, on many of them you can see scars on their arms, chests and backs and some (especially among the Koliuzhes) have so many that there hardly seem three square inches of unmarked skin anywhere.

Almost all Americans walk barefoot all the time, even when there is more than twenty degrees of frost. I have already described how after their steam bath, even in the harshest cold, Koniagas will go into the sea, stay in the water for a quarter of an hour, clamber out onto the shore, and sit there for some time, completely naked. It would seem as though they do not feel the cold at all. Sometimes when a Koniaga has been in the sea for some time during a frost he will, when he comes back into the kazhim, summon all the occupants outside to beat him--if he bears this voluntary punishment he has the right to choose any woman he likes.

Sometimes the Koniagas will seem full of curiosity--they will look at everything with rapt attention and they will ask each person coming up from the harbor what is new.

The islanders are very fond of games of chance, and I have seen them gamble away everything they possess in a day. The difference between these prodigal acts and European ones is that whatever their losses the savages maintain their nonchalance.

I have said that their indifference to misfortune, even of their fellows, is one of their normal cruel qualities. It is so great that when they are travelling in many baidarkas and one of them capsizes then the others will pass by unless the person in the water is from their own village.

Those who live on the northwest side of Kad'iak are bolder and more daring than their fellows. This results from the fact that, before the arrival of the Russians, the islanders were constantly at war amongst themselves, but more often with neighboring peoples such as the Aliaksintsy and the Kinai. So these people, because of their geographical position nearest to the enemy, had more often recourse to caution and bravery. To this day they shoot bows and arrows very well, and not many know how to do this on the other parts of the island.

The indifference of these savages to life is worthy of great amazement. Suicide often occurs here for the most trivial of reasons and few care about preventing it. If someone says that they wish to kill themselves, or drown themselves, no one makes any move to restrain them or to dissuade them from their intentions, and even if they are seen drowning, no one will go to their rescue.

In general all the local tribes love freedom and independence. The term *kalgi* [slave] rouses the most craven coward to despise death. When the Russians first came to Kinai Bay the commander of the ship sent a landing party to capture some savages so that their acquaintance might be made. The party found seven or eight families of Kinai and brought them to the ship but the savages, believing they were being taken into bondage, murdered all their women and children on the way and then killed themselves. Such examples are not infrequent here.

One of the interpreters asked one of the savages about the members of his household.

"I have had a son," said the savage. "I wanted to kill it but my wife took pity, and stopped me."

"Why did you want to do such an evil thing?" asked the interpreter with horror.

"Better it should die than become a kaiur [slave]," answered the Koniaga.

One young American invited his friends and treated them to everything he had in the house--and it must be understood that in such circumstances he guests ate heartily. His father asked him what would happen when all the food was gone. "Surely," he said, "we shall all go hungry afterwards."

"If you begrudge me it," said the son, "I shall drown myself and thus remove the source of expense for you."

And the next day he did indeed take a baidarka, row out into the bay and overturn it, and was drowned.

Another American, aged fifteen to sixteen, who was apprenticed to the coppersmith, one day stole some trifle from his master and was caught in the act. Afterwards his colleagues would not stop reproaching him. The lad became thoughtful and remote and sadder with every hour. One day a shot was heard on the outskirts of the village. People ran to where the sound came from and found the unfortunate criminal shot dead with a pistol lying beside him.

The Koniagas lack the sin common to nearly all savages--theft. I have rarely heard of it happening amongst them. It is quite possible to leave an American in charge of a great number of things which to him are treasures and he will of course take nothing, apart from a necessary quantity of tobacco. This causes no harm; it has come to be such a necessity for them.

Such rejection of the fear of death could threaten with complete destruction the small numbers of Russians scattered over this large tract of country, if there were amongst these people general agreement and mutual trust about taking the necessary measures. Even without this trust, however, they have several times attacked our settlements, killed the people there, and destroyed the buildings.

The islanders are lazy and phlegmatic, and even appear stupid, but they know how to look after their own interests without offering any thanks. If you give them more, they will always ask for more. In winter when there is no fresh food they bring duck and fresh fish to the harbor and sell them for various trinkets which they need, especially for tobacco. When they saw that our people bought very willingly from them they at once put up their prices. When an American brings several ducks then he shows just one for sale and then the next and, when he has sold that, he takes out another in the hope that he will make more that way than selling them all together. Sometimes they ask for ducks or other trifles more than the company pays them for otters, and when they see that no hunter will buy them they subsequently give them away for several leaves of tobacco. Never will a

Koniaga take all his cod to one customer, or all his ducks, but he takes them to various people in the belief that in this way he will get more for them.

On Kad'iak none of the Russians has been curious enough to collect the islanders' artifacts; as for example: thread made from woven gut, sewn pouches, and so forth. We ordered such things to be brought to us; at first trading was very orderly, but eventually when the Americans saw that we were collecting lots of them they began to put up their prices. One man had brought along a carved helmet like the ones they wear at the festivals, and asked a great deal for it. When he realized that there would not be a sale he went to the fort and sold it there for a small amount of beads. One of the hunters gave him what he asked for it, and the Koniaga was very pleased with this, but when he learned that the article had been brought to us he came and said that he had been given very little for it and demanded more from us. We gave him back the helmet and forbade him to come and trade any more.

When the Koniagas had no ducks or fish to sell, then they would bring berries and whale blubber, although they knew that we did not eat them, and that there were many in the area of the port. Sometimes they would propose for sale ashes for rubbing tobacco, or something else which was in no way useful to us. Some came with gifts with the intention of getting more in return than they would have got by selling. If you start paying an American with tobacco from a box, or with money, when he sees large amounts of it he begins to ask for more even though this would involve paying him ten times more than the article is worth; so that in these circumstances it would be impossible to satisfy this savage. If you given him a very valuable present he will come to you the following day with some trifle and demand more for it than he would from another.

The priests have had more opportunity than me to observer the habits of the islanders, but although they defend them, they do admit that it is difficult to recognize any feelings of gratitude in the islanders. To justify this somewhat they argue that the savages are very childlike in their greed and that our things are completely new to them. I will readily agree with this conclusion.

When the islanders were assembled to swear loyalty to the Tsar they asked, "Has he sent us any presents?"

The Koniagas will sacrifice even the life of a friend for the acquisition of some trifle which pleases them. When the Aliaskintsy are cursing them they often reproach them saying, "When we kill we kill openly but you kill your friends when they are weaker than you and often only for the sake of a parka." And in fact in earlier times if one islander saw another one fishing he would stain himself with his murder just to acquire his parka, or some other possession which took his fancy.

Before the arrival of the Russians the islanders warred amongst themselves for various reasons; sometimes they were driven to it by hunger, sometimes by the desire for booty, consisting of clothes, baidarkas and other items. Sometimes they would fight to capture the enemy's women or to take prisoners as slaves. But more often than not the cause of their taking up arms was the deep-seated hatred between tribe and tribe. The prisoners are condemned forever to be slaves.

The Koniagas consider corporal punishment a great dishonor; they are more afraid of it than of death itself. One day they got together and refused to go on a hunting trip. Then the Russians arrested a chief who was widely respected by the savages and they threatened to take severe measures against him if the savages did not change their decision. At this the chief said to the manager, "We are not afraid of death! You can contest this by thrusting a spear into my heart or under my arm (the savages maintain that it is just as easy to kill a man this way as in the heart or head), then you will see how calmly I die." He asked them only not to order him to be flogged with ships' ropes, which would dishonor him.

Several Koniagas on a hunting trip spent several days idle when the Russian in charge of them was away, or it could have been that they were prevented from hunting by the weather. Fearing that the hunter would inform the baidarshchik (the senior Russian in the artel), and that the latter would beat them, they killed the Russian and said that he had died in an accident. Their crime was discovered, however, and one of the murderers was taken to the harbor and whipped, then placed in irons and told that he would be whipped again the following day. That night the American quietly escaped from his guards and jumped off the cliffs; as the tide was in he was not killed, but he had the tenacity to dive under the water until he drowned.

One day when a hunter had killed a seal he struck one of the islanders there present for not pulling in the carcass quickly enough. The savage was angered by this act and at the first opportunity revenged the insult by killing the Russian. When this crime became known the Koniaga was brought to the harbor and asked: "Did you kill the Russian?"

"I killed him."

"Why?"

"He struck me."

"What punishment do you deserve?"

"Death."

They flogged him and kept him in chains, but the savage found by chance a sharp shell and cut his own throat.

One young Koniaga who had also killed a Russian was placed in irons together with his mother who, as it later turned out, had had nothing to do with the crime. His mother was also his wife. Because of the lack of vigilance of the guard this young American escaped from the fort and threw himself off the cliffs and into the sea, but as it was low water he did not drown straight away, so his mother or wife, fearing that he would be dragged out and beaten, then jumped in and throwing her arms round him she pushed him under the water until he expired, and then clambered out onto the shore. Could anything more awful be imagined?

But it is impossible to describe all the instances of the islanders' indifference to life and their hatred of the Russians. They always kill the hunters whenever there is a chance of covering it up and they might be even more brazen if it were not that they fear being beaten which to them is worse than death. When one Russian only is in charge of a group of them they look after him well, knowing that they will not be believed even if he dies a natural death. But when there are two or more Russians with a hunting party they make no effort to save anyone who suffers an accident, counting on the survivors to say that the Koniagas were not the cause of his death.

VI

THE UPBRINGING OF CHILDREN.

But we shall cease to be surprised at their bestial morals when we see the way they bring up their children. In earlier times they often had before they eyes examples of unheard-of savagery. When the fathers brought in prisoners they often made the children stab them or shoot at them with bows and arrows, thus prolonging the suffering of these unfortunates, for weak childrens' hands were not strong enough to deliver a fatal blow. Sometimes (it is difficult to believe such evil deeds took place) they cut open the prisoners' stomachs while they were still alive and made the children pull out their intestines! How could the children not become savages if they had grown used to such bestiality from a very young age?

The local women rarely give birth to more than four or five children, and for the most part less, and many do not bear any at all. When an islander feels that she is about to give birth she makes one of her companions pummel her belly, or stretch her stomach, so as to quicken the delivery and decrease the birth-pains. It may be imagined how dangerous this practice can be, both for the mother and for the child, and for this reason obviously some are born dead. For all this the women giving birth recovers very quickly and soon goes about her normal duties again. The children are fed at the breast until they are three years old and sometimes for longer if no more are born. The babies have cradles made for them which do not rock but are simply placed on the floor. They never swaddle children.

It is very strange that not a single islander has ever learnt or knows how to swim, although this would seem a necessity for a people who spend a major part of their life in baidarkas and who are so often in danger of drowning. As far as they are able they try to teach their children to withstand illness firmly and the rigors of the climate. From the first very day they purposely keep the child in either a dry or a damp place. If the baby cries they put it in water, even though it may be winter and then keep the child there until it stops crying. When it begins to walk they no longer watch over it and it is free to run barefoot over the rocks and grass, in warm weather or in the bitter cold. After this it is able to stand damp and bad weather perfectly well. In winter, even when the frost is severe, the children are driven into the sea and they stay there for some time. The Koliuzhes do the same but with the addition that as the children come shivering out of the water they are whipped. A father is proud when his son throws a rock at him or at his mother and draws blood. From their very early years the children begin building baidarkas and launching them; they also fashion bows and arrows, learn to shoot at birds or simply at a target. A father places his son when he is six or seven in a baidarka with him and teaches him how to paddle it. Shortly afterwards he makes him a small paddle and places the baidarka in the sea where large waves are breaking on the shore with noise and spray. To start with the father ties a rope to the baidarka so as to draw his son into the shore if it overturns, but later he does not even do that.

I have said that when they are still small they boast of how they have slashed their own bodies, and this penchant for suffering seems to grow with their strength; for not only children but also adults never pass a bird without throwing a stone at it. If a fish is lying in low water stranded by the tide then no one will pass by without stopping for the pleasure of hitting it on the head. When they catch a crow or jay the poke out its eyes or break its legs and then let it go. When there is an abundance of fish, for fun they jab them with sticks or poke out their eyes and then put them back in the water. If they wing a duck then instead of finishing it off with a knife an American will bite off his head.

The girls are taught to sew, to make patterns, sew bags, plait thread, bindings or *mauty* for arrows, to make hats, basket work bonnets, *shkaty* or buckets, in short all that belongs to the handiwork of their sex. The cut and tastefulness of some of the work of the women is to be admired. It is true that all this is done rather sluggishly; often a woman will spend several months over a headress to be worn at one of their festivals and after all that will part with it for a few leaves of tobacco.

The parents not only pay little heed to their daughters' chastity but for the most part in return for trinkets they will themselves encourage the girl to transgress, even though she may not be of age to do so.

VII

MORE ON THE HABITS AND CUSTOMS OF THE KONIAGAS.

When one is describing a newly discovered people which is near to its primeval state one must take into account not only the pleasure one may give the reader but the benefit that may accrue from the accuracy of one's observations. In connection with this I propose to lay out here everything that I was able to see for myself or learn about.

Among all savage peoples the women are more slaves than companions of the men; here, in contrast, they wield a lot of power and the girls are not chosen by the men but they choose their husbands. There are accounts of similar practices amongst the inhabitants of the Mariana Islands, but there according to these accounts, the men are ugly, but here apparently the male sex is considered superior to the female. Even given this apparent ascendancy of the women, however, they are not allowed to attend the councils when matters of public interest are being discussed, and they do not even sit down to eat with the men.

The Koliuzhes, on the other hand, treat their women almost as domestic animals; they are given all the arduous work, but they are allowed to participate in discussions of important matters. How can one reconcile such opposites? Love between males and females begins here very early; when the girls are ten or eleven they already show affection for boys of the same age. The effect of this is that it is virtually unheard of for girls in this area to remain virgins until they marry. It may be that fish, which is almost the only thing the islanders eat, helps to develop these tendencies and speeds up the action of nature. In addition to this the fathers and mothers not only do not restrain their daughter from this sort of behavior, but they even encourage them by example and teaching. Is it surprising, therefore, that the first and foremost female virtue, chastity, is here completely unknown? The local women on the contrary put all their vanity into pleasing a large number of men. It would seem as though they considered it a sin to refuse anyone who importuned them even if it was an old man; they are in no way ashamed of revealing to each other all their lovers, and they even boast about it. Because of this the women are often bitterly jealous of each other; the men, however, are rarely jealous of their wives. There was, however, a savage example of this here: the wife of one of the chiefs fell in love with a Russian, for which her husband cut off her nose, saying: "Now no one will love you!" A little while later when this woman found a chance, she cut off her husband's privy member, saying: "Now, if anyone loves you, you won't be any use to them." True, such instances here are very rare and although a woman without a nose may occasionally be seen it can be almost guaranteed that this is the result of venereal disease and not that her husband has cut it off because of her infidelity.

There are many more examples which prove the opposite. As proof of the Koniagas' indifference in these circumstances, I shall quote one. Several women have two husbands each: the first is their actual husband and he chooses the second with the agreement of the wife. The second husband becomes at the same time a kind of servant, that is he carries water, firewood and performs other various tasks. He can sleep with the wife only in the absence of the real husband; when the latter returns he is deprived of this right. Such husbands are nicknamed by the Russians *polovinshchiki* ['sharers', 'halftimers'].

Depravity and violent lust are even more widespread amongst this half-savage people: there are men with plucked beards who only do womens' tasks, they live with the women and like them they sometimes have two husbands. Such men are called *akhnuchiki*. They are not despised, but on the contrary the villagers obey them and they are often wizards. A Koniaga who has an akhnuchik instead of a wife is even considered lucky. A father or mother will consider their son an akhnuchik from the time he is a baby if he seems like a girl to them. Sometimes the parents forecast that they are going to have a daughter, and if they are mistaken they make their son into an akhnuchik. In addition Koniagas sometimes marry their mothers although such cases are extremely rare and are frowned upon even by the islanders themselves. As the proverb says *Shto gorod, to norov, shto derevnia, to obychai* [as the town so the manners, as the country so the customs]. Almost all the women here have a very strange way of behaving, for when someone declares love for them they begin to play-act and pretend to resist, and to weep and laugh out loud. If a man who is unfamiliar with this custom takes this for a sign of rejection and leaves the woman alone, she later speaks of him as a dishonorable man with whom no other woman will want to be associated.

In earlier times, the men would offer their wives and daughters to those Russians they wished to entertain, and they still offer them, especially their daughters, for small gifts. There seems to be nothing a Koniaga would not sacrifice for his own gain. Every beauty becomes saleable for a small amount of tobacco, beads, red worsted or similar trifles. For such a collection of items a husband will agree to sell his daughter and his wife.

It is difficult to say for sure whether the islanders love their family or not; the latter would seem nearer the truth. There have been cases of vengeance being sought for them, but this can be found amongst other peoples. One case was very extraordinary; a bear killed and ate a little girl and her two brothers proposed to take vengeance on the bears for this; they would kill them all until in the stomach of one they found the earrings which had been in the girl's ears, or some other sign. Both of them were famous hunters, and they killed many bears on Kad'iak, and then crossed to the Aliaskan Peninsula where in one bear it is said they found the things the girl had been wearing. It is difficult to know how the bear, which ate the girl on Kad'iak, came to be in Aliaska, because the straits separating these two places are forty versts wide; but it could be that some unfortunate girl there, wearing the same things, was overcome by the same fate. I do not deny the veracity of this tale, but it is almost the only one which illustrates the love of the islanders for their relatives. Many examples which show the opposite could be proved. Often orphans who are left with their uncle's family on the death of their parents, or with another close relative, live without any kind of supervision at all; they are not clothed or fed, and are given bones like the dogs. When they grow older they are sold as slaves. The Koniagas love their wives more than their children. When the latter are given as hostages they forget all about them in the belief that now they will be looked after by someone else, but if their wife is taken (as has happened in the past) they will pay a large ransom for her.

The son of the chief of the Ugalakhmiuts was held by the Russians as a hostage; when his father came to the new harbor his child was brought before him. I was a witness to this meeting of theirs after a three-year separation. The Ugalakhmiut did not even look at his son, and maintained his normal calm equilibrium. I have also been present at a reunion between husband and wife and these were overjoyed and embraced each other.

The conditions of the poor are everywhere hard and amongst these savages they are even worse than amongst more enlightened peoples. Perhaps one might ask who is considered rich amongst the savages and who is poor: the answer--he who has a baidarka is rich. Such a person is even now regarded with respect by the Russians; for a Koniaga who has a baidarka always has a source of food. He can hunt animals for which he will get, not very much, but at least something from the company, while his comrade who travels with him and does the same amount of work, must consider himself lucky if he is well-fed and clothed somehow or other.

VIII

MORE ON THE HABITS AND CUSTOMS OF THE KONIAGAS. THEIR SUPERSTITIONS. SOME EXAMPLES OF THE IDEAS OF THE SAVAGES OF NORTHWEST AMERICA.

In earlier times the islanders still thought of ridding themselves of the Russians at some juncture. In this belief they placed a great deal of hope in one of their leaders who was greatly feared by all the neighboring peoples. The Koniagas proposed to him the daring venture of destroying the Russians. When Shelikhov came to hear of this he summoned the chief to him and reproached him with his evil intentions. The savage gave him the following answer: "You know that I am not afraid to die and that I can move the islanders to destroy you--but if, after this, more Russians come in larger numbers, what will happen to our wives and children? In addition, you have prevented us from fighting amongst ourselves and thus, for as long as I am alive, the Koniagas shall live in peace with the Russians." He kept his word, which was only broken when he was unable to prevent it.

The Koniagas had an extremely odd conception of the Russians. When they first saw them arriving on Kad'iak they thought they were devils coming out of the water. It was not surprising that our huge vessels (by comparison with their boats) moving across the water without the aid of oars, which the people had never seen before, the firearms, and all that was completely new for them frightened them and gave rise to their ridiculous assumption. To begin with the islanders had no idea at all that the Russians were going to settle amongst them for good, but when, subsequently, the number of visiting ships increased, they began to suspect that this might be the case. Even at the present time they have a very unclear understanding of Russia. I referred earlier to the fact that when not a single ship came from Okhotsk for five years in a row and then several old men were brought over from Unalashka, the Koniagas concluded that these Russians must be the last ones, and they were so firmly convinced of this that they began to talk about wiping out our hunters; but the arrival of the *Sv. Aleksandr* and the *Sv. Elisaveta* dispelled their illusion. But with all this they do not believe that there are very many Russians, as they are unable to count above twenty. They often ask if all the Russians could be placed in the large sandy bay on the west coast of Kad'iak, and are usually told that even the whole island would not be large enough.

When something is too difficult for the savages to explain then to express their ideas they use simple but strong expressions. Once it so happened that there were very few Russians in Chugatsk Bay. The local inhabitants appeared to be friendly for they gave hostages and thereby made it impossible to undertake anything since they dare not endanger the children of their chiefs or others whose lives they held dear. The baidarshchik (the head of the Russian artel) in Chugatsk Bay sent one of the hunters to the Copper River, so called because about four hundred versts from its mouth it is joined by another river on whose banks natural copper is to be found. The discovery of this metal, or of the place in which it was found, was the object of the expedition. As guards the hunter was given several of the savages who lived around the mouth of the Copper River and from whom hostages had also been taken. When they were some distance from the mouth of the river these Americans proposed to kill the hunter and return to Chugatsk Bay to say that he had been killed when they were attacked by savages from another tribe. And if, at the same time, the remaining Russians were to be so incautious as to meet them unarmed then they would strike them all down with daggers then had hidden under their capes. The chief of the savages resisted this plan for a long time, saying that the Russians would naturally return and seek vengeance for the death of their fellows.

"We shall kill them also," they replied. "The Russians will come again and we shall kill them again and then they will come again--for isn't the river already flowing with them?"

At last the chief was persuaded to fall in with their plan, and then they fired an arrows from a bow at the sleeping hunter. The latter leapt up and grabbed his gun but he could not get it to fire because it was damp. While this was happening he was wounded in several places; then, falling to the ground, he pretended to be dead. The savages placed him in the baidarka and returned to the artel. The baidarshchik who came out to meet them asked: "Where is the Russian?"

"He was killed when some people attacked us."

"And were many of your people killed?"

Their spokesman had not anticipated this question and was embarrassed, so he hesitantly answered that not one had been hurt. This made the baidarshchik suspicious and he ordered all the Russians to come forward with their guns loaded. When the "dead" man was brought forward he stood up and revealed the evil intentions of his guards. Proof of the evil plan was given by the weapons they had concealed about them.

The Chugaches appear to be more cunning, more daring and more cautious than the other tribes. When they learnt that Baranov was travelling to Chugatsk Bay they disappeared from their settlements so that none of them was visible anywhere. All that could be seen everywhere were poles with sticks bound to them at right angles. The Russians believed that these sticks indicated the direction which the fleeing villagers had gone--and that they were left as a sign for their comrades who might have been caught out of the village or unawares and would not know what had happened. This guess proved to be correct. However, when the direction indicated by the sticks was followed there was no sign of anyone there. And the Chugaches have kept the mystery of this a secret, even to the present day.

All the savages are prone to superstition from which, it is true, even enlightened people are not immune. The Koniaga women will not pick up or touch wood which is red or painted red because they fear that this will cause heavy menstrual flow. There are many such examples.

The Koniagas set much store by magicians and they will not embark on any weighty undertaking without their advice. In winter, at the end of the festival, the magicians tell fortunes and forecast whether the hunting will be good or bad. Because they are cleverer and more enterprising than the other islanders they often set them against the Russians, towards whom they are always hostile.

At one time on the Andreianov Islands the Russians in their baidarkas approached one settlement and asked for hostages at gunpoint. The Aleuts ran to their medicine-men, two of whom advised them to defend themselves, while one old medicine woman advised them to do as the Russians wished. All the time they writhed about with twigs in their hands and uttered unintelligible sounds. Suddenly one of the medicine men was killed by a gunshot. The islanders ran up to him and could not make out why he had fallen. They were even more surprised to see the blood flowing when there was no sign of any arrow. They stuffed the dead man's wounds with grass and stood him on his feet, but to no avail. In the meantime one of the other medicine men and the old woman went on magicking. The former was still advising them not to yield and made several sneering grimaces in the direction of the Russians, saying: "What will they do to us? We are bold, the dog-god brought us into the world--like it, we run quickly," and so forth. The old woman clapped her hands in triumph because she had foretold the truth exactly. It was then that the Aleuts agreed to give hostages.

As I have said earlier, the Americans on various occasions paint their faces--in particular when they have to undertake a long journey by canoe; but at these times in addition to this superstitious ritual they have another which they learnt from experience to be very useful. It consists of their eating little or nothing at all before they set out, for it is quite true that a hungry man rows more strongly and easily and can endure this task for much longer.

On Ukamok chestnuts are sometimes washed up by the sea. Anyone finding one believes it to be a sign of good luck and goes off hunting boldly and hopefully, wearing the chestnut round his neck.

During mestruation the women leave the village and live alone. Special little huts like dog kennels are even built for this purpose. During the whole course of the period the woman does not leave the hut and food is brought out to her. When everything has finished she washes herself and is only then allowed back into the village.

When you speak to an islander in Russian and he does not understand he points to his ear and says: "*Asitok*"--that is 'bad'. In similar circumstances the Iakuts say '*kulga sokh*'--'I have no ear'. It must not be forgotten that the majority of unenlightened peoples confuse hearing with understanding. The reason for this is of course a poverty of language with which to express abstract thought.

The Chugaches have a special custom unlike that of any of the other local tribes; they exchange names with the people they select as friends. A similar custom is to be found amongst the South Sea Islanders--yet there is no other similarity between them and these distant peoples. One Chugach asked Baranov's permission to exchange names with his "son"; this was how they referred to Baranov's big dog, Sargach, because they could see how devoted he was to his master. And so the old man began to call himself Sargach and brought his friend fish and other things to eat, and tried to please him in every way. One day the Chugach came to visit his friend while Baranov was not at home; the dog flew at him, knocked him down and stood growling at his throat, in spite of all the man's protestations of tender friendship. Some hunters who were nearby came to the old man's rescue, but even then the latter's feelings for Sargach did not alter, and he was very upset when the dog died.

The Koniagas' former way of life, when they were

constantly in danger from warring amongst themselves, and the present tutelage over them by the Russians have taught these savages to simulate and rarely to tell the truth. Never ask an islander where there are most animals, or what is said of the Russians or such like questions, for he will always deceive you or say that he does not know.

The Koniagas, like all savages, frequently use any unusual occurrences or phenomena they come across as omens for the future. They will foretell, for example, whether a party setting off to hunt otters will drown or be killed. But the Russians give little credence to them in such cases and always send out the hunters regardless of whether the prophecy might come true or not.

All the islanders confirmed to me that a strange phenomenon had recently taken place on the island. In the month of January, 1801, there was an extremely violent storm on Kad'iak, which is a rare occurrence there. At one village at that time there was a festival when suddenly the savages were brought the news that near their cabin there was a rock which was jumping up and down. They all leapt out of the kazhim to look and saw that from time to time an oval-shaped rock on the hillside was lifting itself up and moving uphill. The Koniagas were very frightened. The boldest amongst them struck the rock with a spear, but even after that the rock went on moving throughout the whole duration of the storm, so that it changed its position by something like ten sazhens. When Baranov heard of this he ordered the stone to be brought to him and he found it to be of about three puds in weight. When it was placed in a fire a certain amount of sulfur was extracted. A small quantity of iron filings were attached to it. I shall leave it to students of natural phenomena to decide whether the action of the thunder could have had such an effect.

The Americans know how to work things to their advantage. Out of many examples perhaps this one could be told: the islanders almost never accept tobacco from the company for otters, especially when there is a great amount of it--since they are assured that they can get it in winter in return for ducks or cod.

When the Koniagas catch cod for themselves they kill it at the nose so as not to spoil the head, which they consider the most tasty piece. But if they are catching fish for the Russians they cut off the head straight away.

IX

LIFE-STYLE AND DIET OF THE ISLANDERS. SOME NEW CUSTOMS.

It is said that in earlier times the Koniagas, because of their constant wars with neighboring settlements, always lived in the summer on lonely and inaccessible rocks from which people were lowered by ropes even to go and fetch water. This seems highly likely as such fortifications are still to be seen in isolated parts. Such caution seems to have been all the more necessary because in summer nearly all the men would go off hunting animals, or fishing, or fighting, so that not many of them were left at home. But I do not intend to go on relating what used to happen although one has a fair idea of it from other people's accounts, but I shall begin to talk about the present.

The islanders always get up before sunrise. Each of them, before he gets up, has obligatorily to sit on his bed for a few moments and then he comes out and washes himself. But as a love of cleanliness is not common to all not everyone does this. The fashionable women wash not only in water but in urine, to which they ascribe the quality of making the skin whiter and clearer. After this each one sets about his tasks--some go off hunting, some repair their baidarkas or tasks of this kind. The women also perform some kind of work. Such general activity is, however, much more noticeable in summer. At this time the women are laying in stocks of berries and roots while the men, when they are not hunting in the employ of the company, help to dry fish which are sometimes hung on the end of poles. Then they start to eat those at the other end which have hardly started to dry, although they have only to reach down with their hand into the stream to catch even fresher ones. Each family builds up its own stocks of fish and foodstuffs, but these hardly last them until January, that is to the end of the festivals. At this time the sandbar with shellfish becomes the main source of food for them. In addition to this they glean what they can where they can, in a random fashion, whenever the weather permits them to put to sea.

In the winter the islanders do almost nothing and for most of the time they stay in bed--the only exception being during the festivals. Then, with tireless energy, they go about visiting each other and exchanging gifts. The gifts have to be of equal value, so that no one remains in debt. Sometimes they exchange presents even though they have not seen each other for a long time. The headmen of the villages sometimes only return visits after a lapse of two or three years, and then they are made with great ceremony. The hospitality consists of a large feast--the eating goes on day and night so that some are physically exhausted.

But the islanders indulge much more and with great pleasure in the catching of sea animals. In the main they try to catch seals, the skins of which are more needed by them than any other pelts. Those who live on the northern shore of Kad'iak go out to catch porpoise (*marsouins*) while others sail out to fish for cod or to catch birds.

There is almost nothing which the islanders do not eat. There is hardly a shellfish or crab or shiny sea worm, and virtually no growing plant, which they would not use in their food. When an American is fishing and he feels hungry then he catches a live cod or plaice and eats the head or tail while the fish is alive. Rotting or, as the local expression goes, bitter fish, just as in Kamchatka and Okhotsk, is more popular in Kad'iak than fresh fish; the Kinais deliberately let it lie in a heap for several days until it begins to rot and smell nice to them. In Kamchatka and all of northeast Asia and even amongst many Russians such fish is considered a delicacy. This food, however, creates such disgusting flatulence that it is impossible to stay under the same roof as a man who has eaten his fill of this splendid repast. Rotting, or bitter, fish heads are treated with special reverence. Amongst the islanders an even greater delicacy is rotted or fermented caviar which gives off a revolting and unbearable smell. When they kill a deer the Americans immediately eat any filth that is in its stomach, and this is also considered a great treat. The Russian hunters have grown accustomed to almost all the above-mentioned splendid items of diet--because, naturally, there is nothing else for them to eat. The Koniagas are so uncouth or rather have such dreadful tastes that they have even been seen in the summertime to collect bears' droppings and cook them with berries as part of their diet. They even eat bugs which they pluck out of their own heads. I did hear that one islander, during a festival, ate human excrement to show his prowess--but he was ill for a long while afterwards. I have also been assured that when Shelikhov was in Kad'iak, and a Russian was killed at Afognak, one woman ate from the body; though if this were proved true it could better be described as vengeance, for amongst all the peoples of northwestern America known to the Russians there are no cannibals. There is only a rumor that the tribes living in the upper reaches of the Copper River practice this bestial habit.

After all that has just been said does it not seem amazing that the islanders will not eat pork on the grounds that pigs eat dirt!

The main staple of the islanders' diet is a fish which they prepare as winter stocks and which is called *iukola* or *kachemas*. Their stocks, however, rarely last for more than half the winter. For the remaining time they eat whatever food the sea provides them with and shellfish which they eat raw or warmed a little over a fire. The islanders are at all times, even times of plenty, great lovers of shellfish.

Amongst the Koniagas' delicacies whalemeat is one of the first. The islanders are very fond of whale blubber and any kind of fat, without which they could barely exist and would never be happy--though they had great quantities of fish and meat. Whale fat smells revolting and that is the very reason why it seems you will never get used to it, but you will be even more revolted when you discover how it is cooked. For this there is a gathering of old men, old women and children--that is, of all those who are not fit for any other work. They cut the blubber into strips, chew it and spit it out into some kind of receptacle. Then they cook it with berries and add several ground roots to this mixture--they place it in so-called *tolkushi* and use it as food.

The islanders also prepare themselves food from *makarsha* (snakeweed), mixing it with cranberry and whale blubber. The Russians on the other hand use the whortleberry and fern roots to make kvass.

All the berries stored by the islanders for the winter are cooked with fat, even for the hunters--only a small part of them is set aside for those Russians who do not like this preparation. In addition to this the Koniagas put in supplies of alder bark boiled in fat--this is also one of the less tasty dishes.

The Koniagas (like the Iakuts) show off by eating a lot, so that they are often ill from doing so.

If in earlier times the Americans suffered from a shortage of foodstuffs because of their idleness, then today this happens as a result of other factors, namely: the women lay in stores of fish, berries, sarana lily, etc. for the company during the whole period when the fish are running in the river; the men on the other hand are away all summer hunting sea otters and birds, returning only in the autumn, shortly before the fish go out to sea. Thus, since they are working for someone else at the best time of the year, they have practically no chance of drying fish and laying in stocks for themselves. True, in cases where islanders are literally starving the company helps them with supplies of iukola; but it should happen, in accordance with the laws of truth and good sense, that the labor of others was so sparingly used that our interests and profit were based on their well-being.

The Koniagas are very fond of our garden vegetables and the radish is even treated as a medicament. I believe that if they led a peaceful life and if the Russians attempted it, they could be taught how to cultivate gardens. But the company never directs any attention to this matter because sending the islanders off to hunt otters is vastly more profitable.

The Koniagas, and especially their women-folk, when they are not eating or sleeping, are always chewing spruce gum.

The islanders have an extreme passion for tobacco; they could hardly exist without it and those who live in remote districts and have no chance to acquire any are always cursing the Russians for having made them hanker after tobacco so much. Both men and women keep the tobacco in their mouth--few of them sniff it, and none of them smokes it--for they believe that this makes breathing more difficult and then they will not be able to move about so easily. The inhabitants of Kad'iak, and indeed all the savages of northwest America, are also in the increasing grip of a passion for strong drinks. However, the Koniagas did get drunk before the Russians came, on the fermented juice of raspberries and bilberries. The Russians distil a very good vodka from this--but a barrel of berries gives only a bucket of vodka.

The Koniagas at times suffer greatly from lack of food. They are very fond of sweet grasses--though they often die from eating them. During my stay in Kad'iak whole families of Americans have died as a result of this. It must be assumed that amongst these grasses there is one particular species which is highly toxic, for all the Koniagas eat a great amount of them without coming to any harm--but they always try when eating not to let the grass touch their lips as they always split from the sharpness of the juice.

Several Koniagas have died from eating the flesh of whales washed up by the sea because they had died from infectious diseases. But most fatalities occur as a result of eating shellfish--not all species of which they can identify. In this respect is sometimes happens that the same shellfish can be harmful at one time of the year and at other times harmless. In 1797 a hunting party returning from Sitka stopped to spend the night by the mouth of a stream where there were large quantities of shellfish. The Americans at once began to eat them. Within half an hour one Chugach had died, and he was soon followed by five Koniagas. Then all those who had eaten the shellfish grew very frightened--but no one knew what to do to help. Some ate sulfur, others rotting iukola, others tobacco or powder to induce vomiting, and all these were saved. During the next few hours over eighty men died. What was strange was that of those who had eaten shellfish from one side of the river, where they were not covered by seaweed (fucus), nearly all died--and even those who survived still feel a numbness in their limbs, both summer and winter, during the greatest festivals. On the other hand, those who ate from the other side of the river where the shellfish were under the seaweed were completely unaffected. It must also be noted with amazement that all those who suffered from the shellfish began to feel relief with the ebb tide and felt completely well when it came back in.

I am assured that pepper boiled in water is an effective antidote in such cases.

X

ILLNESSES AND METHODS OF TREATMENT.

It appears that the most prevalent illness amongst the islanders is boils, which are dangerous everywhere that fish forms the main part of the diet together with fat and other raw foods. Sometimes the boils do not burst but spread and sometimes cover the whole of the back. In such cases the skin is lanced with a sharp shell and the pus is sucked out. But if the core is very deep then they take a hard, sharpened stone set in wood so that the point of the stone is sticking out; this they place on the core or center of the boil up to the very handle and they twist it about. The pain produced by this action can well be imagined. When the pus is reached in this manner it is sucked out and the remainder comes out later of its own accord.

If the back has been painful for a long while then the sufferer is made to sit on a table or some kind of plank and two such stones are attached to the base of his back, either side of the backbone. Then he is told to lie back and to remain lying down until the blood stops flowing.

At the onset of any illness whatever the first precaution an islander takes is to eat as little as possible --even in cases of venereal disease this is almost the only cure. Recently one woman has gained a reputation in Kad'iak for her skilful treatment of this disease. She washes each patient's wound twice a day and the whole of the rest of the body--either in sea water or urine. She gives them roots to eat and they drink juice boiled from the same roots. These roots, according to Baranov, are somewhat similar to sarsaparilla. This woman has given to no one the secret of her doctoring which is reasonably successful. She has cured people who had the disease for several years and were in the advanced stages.

This scourge of humanity is not so virulent amongst the Koniagas, from which it might be possible to conclude that they have been subject to this infection for a long while and that it has weakened as time has gone by. The Russians in America soon began to perish from it, though the methods of treatment seem to be effective. The patient is usually made to sit in a very warm room. He is surrounded by cinnabar smoke and told to breathe it in--he is rubbed down with mercuric chloride and quicksilver and given an infusion of mercuric chloride to drink. Is it not surprising that the most persistent condition cannot stand such a mercurial storm? In addition the hunters, because of the lack of bread here, eat badly and often drink bitter liquids. Besides, venereal disease is not nearly so widespread in Kad'iak as many Russians say--for they take every illness, be it a cold or such like, to be venereal disease and they go through the cure described above.

The islanders quite often suffer from pains in the chest--which is naturally caused by the continuous and energetic rowing of the baidarkas, which they sometimes have to do during stormy weather. When a party leaves Kad'iak to go otter hunting some distance away, then on the longer stretches of rowing it happens that the kaiur (the Russian hunter normally seated in the middle of a three-man baidarka never rows) begins to bleed from the nose and ears. Many such rowers, once they have made two such journeys, fall into a fever and are completely without strength. A three-man baidarka, which is much heavier than a two-seater, demands correspondingly greater effort from the two rowers so as not to fall behind the main party.

In the case of some illnesses the Koniagas let blood from various parts of the body; such as the arms, legs, forehead, etc. But their method of letting the blood is very effective. They cut the skin near the vein from which they wish to take the blood, then they place below the vein a needle or sharpened bone and let the blood with a sharp shell. The office of barber is for the most part occupied by the women. For shortness of breath the Koniagas let blood from below the chin.

They perform some surgery. If they are wounded, for example, they will cut out the ball or arrow-head. They will also set broken arms, legs and so forth. I saw one islander, chopping wood, cut himself across the stomach; it was immediately sewn up and he quickly recovered.

One islander had suffered for some time from stones but could find no one who would cut the stones out of him. In the end one old man offered to do it and although, after the operation was performed on him, the Koniaga lay for a week in such a condition that he was barely distinguishable from a corpse, in the end he gradually began to get well and eventually he recovered completely.

Many Russians have assured me that they have seen with their own eyes how the islanders remove cataracts from their eyes. But once this method has been described I leave everyone free to believe it or not, because as I have not been a witness to it I cannot confirm its veracity. The Koniagas are said to take a large louse, to which they attach a hair. This is then lowered into the person's eye and the hair is jerked so that the louse will grasp the cataract.

Fever is completely unknown to the Koniagas, and even the Russians very rarely go down with it.

I have seen several savages suffering from sores, mostly on the legs and feet. One had had them for seven years; all of the right leg was covered in sores and in between them the flesh was raw. All those infected with this disease give off an unbearable and noxious odor.

On the island of Sutkhum the Koniagas dig up a root they call *shishkuk*. This plant has a very short stem with four or five longish leaves. Shishkuk smells quite good; they smoke the leaves, and expectant mothers drink the liquid boiled from it.

XI

BURIAL RITES.

When a person dies the house is abandoned, it is broken up and a new one is built. If someone is very proud of his house then a mortally ill person (naturally, one who has no relatives) is placed alive in a hole dug specially for the purpose. During my stay in Kad'iak in one village in the winter time one poor old woman who had no relatives became so ill that her death was imminent. The owners of the house in which she was living, in order to save themselves the trouble of having to build a new house at such a stormy time of the year, dug a hole for the old woman, placed her in it and covered it with wood. Three days later the unfortunate woman's cries could still be heard, but the hearts of these American savages contain no pity. The Koniagas place their dead in the earth simply--the rich dressed in all their finery. The grave is covered with earth and stones are rolled over the top, and the area is marked off with low boards--but there is no roof. The dead man's broken baidarka is placed over the grave. Incidentally, I have never heard of any food being placed in the grave, or arrows, or anything else. This indicates the difference between their view of the after-life and that of other peoples. The Koniagas, however, are so secretive about the rites of the religion that it is impossible to find out any details about them.

It is not so much the burial rites of these savages which are worthy of note as their indifference when death is approaching. They will discuss this very cold-bloodedly as though about someone else's affairs. They await calmly and without special desires that boundary that everyone has to cross. Close relatives show sympathy and as a sign of grief at a death they cut their hair--both the men and the women. But you may be sure that distant relatives will only do this for show. The memory of the dead who have distinguished themselves in war or in hunting animals is held very dear. During the festivals speeches are made in their honor. The islanders have not been known to offer sacrifices on the death of their relatives; the Koliuzhes, on the other hand, do this all the time. If a tribal chief or a rich man dies then several slaves are chosen to serve him in the other world. These slaves are summoned to an assembly of the tribe and made to dance, having been told beforehand that they will be killed. Arrows are fired at them and the children are made to stab them with spears, as they grow weaker and can dance no longer they are struck down with spears.

When the islanders celebrate the memory of their relatives all those present are given presents at the end of the ceremony. During this ritual one person will give a speech praising the dead man and for this he will be given expensive presents.

XII

THE SPREAD OF CHRISTIANITY. THE ISLANDERS' RELIGION.

When the Archimandrite and his brother monks arrived in Kad'iak they set about converting the islanders to the Christian faith, but they encountered many obstacles to the fulfillment of this. In the first instance this was because of superstition and the fear which every people has of changing its beliefs and, secondly, because the priests did not know the Koniaga language. Because of this the priests had to spread their teaching through savage interpreters who knew a little Russian. These latter could not understand the concepts which were completely new and too elevated for them, nor did they know how to explain them to their comrades. Because of this the priests found that the following measures helped to cut down their heavy work in fulfilling their obligations, namely: they would drive the adults into the sea several at a time, read a prayer over them and place crosses round their necks which confirmed the savages as Christians. To baptise the infants the priest would travel round the islands for some time, carrying out his other functions at the same time, however badly understood by the Koniagas. It can be imagined that such a method of introducing them to Christianity left very little impression on the minds of the savages, who would probably not have accepted baptism if they had not also during the ritual received a cross, a shirt and an undergarment. The priests forced the new Christians to get married and because they did not understand their language, they sometimes joined together very close relatives. This did not accord with the Koniagas' ideas and the savages in the settlement ceased to be Christians; they started to abandon their wives, as before, when it came into their head to do so, nor have they any respect at all for the printed ikons they are given. I myself have seen them being used to roll tobacco. It is true that in the presence of Russians they try to make it seem as though they know some customs, such as crossing themselves before they undertake a job of work; but because they do not fully understand the meaning of this they cross themselves before embarking upon acts that any Christian would consider sins.

Only those Koniagas who are brought up by the priests from childhood have learnt to read and write and receive the necessary understanding of Christian morality from daily example. A school has been re-established to take one hundred boys and could of course help to spread the Faith were the means available for the upkeep of this establishment. But in 1805 many children there died of hunger and scurvy and this will almost certainly happen again.

If only those who had been converted distinguished themselves in some way from the other islanders, then the others might accept the faith more willingly, since there is nothing which encourages the savages more than prospects of profit in the here and now without any reference to the fleshness bliss of the future. But as both Christians and heathens are, without distinction, sent far away to hunt and are used by the company for other work in equal numbers they no distinction is visible to the islanders who thus see no need to adopt the Orthodox faith. In addition there is no respect for the priests, some of whom are very worthy men, although not all of them, and the general depravity of the Russians are not factors which would encourage the savages to forsake their superstitutions.

I was never able to discover if the Koniagas had any idea of God; all that is known is that they are extremely afraid of evil spirits, although they do not offer any sacrifices to them. During festivals they imitate how the evil spirits tempt people or harm them. At the end of such performances the women are frightened even to look at those who played the part of the devils.

The islanders believe that man has a soul but they have no conception of what happens to it after death of the body.

XIII

MARRIAGE CUSTOMS.

These are extremely brief and unaccompanied by any kind of superstitions. The bridegroom gives presents to the father and mother of the bride and to the girl herself. Then he asks her if she will live with him, for in these cases only the girl's consent is required. Subsequently the son-in-law becomes virtually a servant of the father-in-law, and always brings him the best hunting catch--the best things he barters and the best part of what he receives. After some time has elapsed the newlyweds go off to their own house--but if the girl does not want to she remains living with her father. Separations take place by mutual consent and without any quarrels--but such separations are rare. In such cases the children live with the mother until they grow up, and then wherever they wish. Immediately a husband and wife are 'divorced' they are free to 'marry' again at once. As I said earlier, marital fidelity is not always considered a virtue by the islanders, and in many cases a husband will sell his wife for a small present.

Koniagas consider themselves luckier having daughters than sons, for the latter leave home when they marry, whereas a father-in-law is obliged to keep his son-in-law.

XIV

SPORTS.

In their games of chance the Koniagas will gamble away all they have, though it must be said to their credit that they are extremely honest about this and never argue, though the game might provide many excuses for this; and it also happens that if someone wins a lot of a certain commodity from a man he will give away his own in return.

The principal game is known as *kaganak* and consists of spreading two deer skins on the ground, slightly bent at the center and about 3½ to 4 arshins apart. In the middle of each is placed a bone dish about the size of a small coin marked round the rim with four black dots. Either two or four can play, forming two teams, each side staking something as a wager. The players, or both teams, have an equal number of small sticks which are used as counters. The number of these varies between 21 and 26 depending on how cold or hot the players are. Each player has five flat wooden rings, one side of which has been sharply curved towards the middle. From the edge of one skin they throw these wooden rings one after the other, trying to land them on the bone dish or to knock someone else's ring out of the way. When all ten wooden rings have been thrown they go up to the skin to see how they have fallen, for they all score. If someone's has completely covered the dish then they say he has 'gone out' and he gets three points, but if someone's ring covers only the black spot on the edge of the bone dish then he gets two marks and those lying nearest take the remainder. Then they collect the wooden sticks and begin to throw from this skin back towards the other one. If two are playing they throw again; if four, then the second pair take their turn. If one side wins all the sticks four times then the game is over. This game is the most extravagant amongst the Koniagas for it sometimes happens that all ten or more sticks may be won at once so that the game does not go on for very long.

Good hunters are careful not to play in the evenings, thinking that they may bring themselves bad luck in the hunting.

For one of the other games some ten to fifteen people assemble in teams, facing each other. Two thick, dry straws are set up at a distance of 25 sazhens. Then one side begins to fire arrows at them, first a man from one side, then one from the other, until they hit the straw. If all the arrows have been fired (each man has one) and no one has scored a hit--then they look to see who has got nearest. Then the arrows are gathered up and they begin to fire again. This game can go on for a long time, and often the people will disperse without a hit having been scored. Two straws are used and two skins in *kaganak* so as to be able to play on without first retrieving the sticks or arrows.

The Koniagas will play at throwing a seal's shoulder bone and laying bets on which way it will fall.

Sometimes a group of men at sea will decide to fire bows and arrows in the following way: one fires his as far as he can and the others try to beat him, and whoever succeeds take the bone and *maut* which is a thread woven from gut. Thus each one fires his arrow at the target in turn.

XV

FESTIVALS, DANCES AND SONGS.

The Koniagas' superstition was the prime reason for setting up the festival which usually begins in December. They begin with some kind of mysterious ceremony during which the women and children cannot be present.

They gather bundles of straw and smoke it with fir-cones and then they set fire to it and the hunters ask the spirits to give them a good catch of animals. When this ritual has been performed the men come out of the kazhim. Then all the inhabitants of the village, young and old, light torches and run shouting through the fields and the houses. After this the festivities begin in earnest; all may attend and the festivities will go on for almost as long as the Koniagas have food to entertain their guests.

In order to have the right to be at such celebrations a young girl or boy must be brought by their father, who cuts strips from his garments and gives them to them. The father's place is sometimes taken by the mother or a near relative. The kazhim in which these festivities normally take place belongs to the whole village. At the end of the festival it is demolished, the torches are broken into pieces, the helmets are cut up and everthing that went to adorn the participants is smashed and thrown into the forest. Sometimes the Koniagas, after a festival has taken place in their kazhim, will cut up their best garments and give a piece each to their guests, so as to thank them for honoring the host with a visit.

Some of the Koniaga rituals have already been described in the first part of this travelogue so that I do not think it necessary to speak of them again. I will mention merely that they are very varied, both in the reasons that give rise to them and in the way the ceremonies are carried out.

The Koniagas dance only during the festivals. The movements of their dance are so uniform that it cannot slake the curiosity of those who wish to have the pleasure of seeing them. The women's movements are hardly more satisfying. The Koniagas are very fond, however, of the dances of other tribes which are incomparably more lively and varied than their own.

The sound of the islanders' voices in singing is quite pleasant and has a range of emotion, though it is mostly mournful. The women's voices are especially good at the latter mood.

The Koniagas have poetry which consists solely of love poems, sometimes praising and sometimes satirical--these savages find the latter kind most to their taste. The *Kasiats* are for the most part the composers of this poetry and this gives them quite a reputation amongst their fellows. More often, however, the Koniagas, like the Iakuts, will take some short statement and sing it repeatedly solo, such as for example "I love you and you love me." From boredom a savage may sing this very short song for an hour or more.

XVI

HISTORY, GEOGRAPHY, ARITHMETIC AND ASTRONOMY.

Naturally, with a people so close to their original state, knowledge of the sciences will also be at a primitive level. About their own origins the Koniagas have the oddest of ideas: some say that a baidarka with the first people in it fell from the sky; others that on Kad'iak there was a bitch and on Aliaska a large spotted dog which swam out to the islands where the inhabitants are the descendants of these two; yet others believe that on Kad'iak there was a girl and that a dog swam over from Unalashka, and that they gave birth to the Koniagas, and to dogs. There are other similar absurd versions, all of which contain the common factor that these Americans believe themselves to be the original inhabitants of Kad'iak.

The Koniaga conception of geography is very limited. Before the coming of the Russians, they already knew of them from hearsay from the Aleutian Islands. They had also heard of the Aliaskans, the Kinaitsy and the Chugaches, of the Koloshes in the other direction, and of other peoples on the mainland of America.

Further than this their geographical knowledge does not stretch--or at least their understanding of further matters is very vague. If you ask them if the world ends somewhere they say no. When you as why, they say that people had sailed away young men in the baidarkas and came back old and still not having found the edge of the world. They say this in accordance with some kind of legend about an alleged continuous undertaking on which the Koniagas embarked and from which all their historical events derived. These tales were embroidered and added to as they passed from generation to generation. The history of savage peoples, just like the history of civilized nations, contains more about war and heroic deeds in this field. These events seem everywhere to be brilliant and to instil fear or amazement.

The Koniagas count on their fingers and toes, so that they count no further than twenty. When they wish to signify a larger quantity they add one, two or three to twenty or they count on the fingers and toes of a second or third person. An occasional person can be found who can reckon up to forty; and the women can count no further than ten. If an enormous quantity has to be conveyed then the Koniaga says "very many" and grasps his hair to show that he means as many as the hairs on his head.

The islanders can distinguish some constellations in the sky, as for example: the Great Bear, the Pleiades, Orion and others. They call the Bear '*Kab'iakhtakh*' and the Pleiades '*Pugat*'. They tell the time by relation to midday and midnight and consider their meager knowledge of astronomy to be perfectly adequate.

Their year begins in August and is divided into twelve months--which are generally called '*iagalup*'. Each month has its name and meaning, as listed below:

August: Kab'iakhgun; i.e. the Pleiades begin to rise.
September: Tugakhguch or Tagagun; Orion rises.
October: Kanchaun; hoarfrost falls on the grass.
November: Kangushauchi; snow appears on the mountains.
December: Kaklagvik; the rivers and lakes freeze.
January: Agvynikh; the sixth month from autumn.
February: Kypnyakhchik; cutting the iukola into strips.
March: Kvigit-annit; the ice breaks up.
April: Manikhehikhvak; the crows lay eggs.
May: Manikhchichak; the birds which have wintered round the lake, ducks, etc., lay eggs.
June: Kaig Yaat; the seals give birth.
July: Managkhat; the porpoises give birth.

From this it will be seen that the months are named after various phenomena in nature, and this in its turn produces months of uneven length. For example: Kypnyakhchik is the longest month for it covers the whole period during which the islanders are short of food supplies and eat only shellfish or pieces of the remaining iukola--which, however, few have left.

The Koniagas pay little attention to counting the years and none of them can tell you his age.

XVII

HANDICRAFTS.

We have seen from the foregoing that the inhabitants of Kad'iak make all kinds of clothes for themselves, some of which are quite tastefully made up. They also twist their own thread, bast mats, hats, sails and so forth.

In earlier years the Koniagas used as work tools a stone ax, sharpened shells, or sharpened pieces of iron. This metal was known to the savages long before the arrival of the Russians; they occasionally found metal objects washed up by the sea, and prized them greatly. The ax-heads were made wedge-shaped from a hard black and green stone, and were attached to a short, curved handle and looked like our large axes. The Americans have grown so used to working with them that they fashion metal ones nowadays in the same way.

The effort involved in making a stone ax can well be

imagined, as can also how tedious it must have been to work with one. This is why metal axes, knives, needles and several other articles must have produced a great change in the Koniagas' work habits.

The islanders make and decorate wooden platters, dishes and so on. Rocks for the paint can be found at various spots on the island or acquired by barter from the mainland of America. They are baked, crushed and mixed with an infusion of fish roe, or blood, and sometimes with water, which is, however, not so reliable. They use wooden spoons, which are decorated; or they are fashioned from the horns of wild sheep, which they acquire from Chugatsk Bay or Kinai Bay.

They make lanterns out of clay, in which they heat whale blubber. In the past they also knew how to fire pots but now the art has been lost; maybe because the Koniagas found our pots more convenient. It is good to enlighten them by importing more convenient raw materials for their handicrafts but it seems pointless, for what would happen to the Koniagas if the Russians go altogether? They would no longer be able to get our tools or raw materials and it would be difficult for them to go back to their old ways.

The Koniagas work very well with bone which they fashion with a small, bent knife. They always try to make the bone they use for arrowheads clean and smooth. They are constantly measuring it and checking it by eye. To cut the bone up they simply use a small piece of metal which has been wetted or smeared with fat. For drilling the bone they use a small chisel constructed so that it turns by means of a piece of string twisted round it.

They make fire by using a sharpened stick which, like the wood chips used with it, is from the chaga [redwood] tree which is thrown up on the island by the sea and which grows on the mainland of America. In the middle of this stick, the end of which is smeared with fat, a string has been twisted round several times. They take the ends of the string in their hands, and turn it as quickly as they can in both directions, until smoke comes from the end of the stick which is poked into the woodchips. Then they pick up a smouldering chip and put it to some dry grass; this they wave in their hand until a flame appears.

XVIII

FORMS OF WARFARE. TREATMENT OF PRISONERS.

All the tribes of Northwestern America are warlike; but they never conduct war openly, but attempt to attack their enemy when he is unprepared. To carry out such attacks the savages need all the great patience with which they are gifted, and they are capable of waiting several days and nights in long grass or behind rocks until a favorable opportunity occurs. When the attack occurs they kill all the males and take only the women and children as prisoners. The inhabitants of Kad'iak have sometimes taken male prisoners as slaves and sometimes, like other tribes, they torture their prisoners on the way back to their village.

Of all the tribes known to us in northwestern America the Koniagas are the least suited to warfare. If they have sometimes killed our hunters then it has always been singly. Also plots to exterminate all the Russians have always been uncovered in good time. Lack of unanimity amongst the islanders has been the main factor in this, rather than caution on the part of the Russians. Other tribes always present greater danger. In 1760, or shortly thereafter, four Russian ships had put in to various of the Aleutian Islands; the ships belonged to various trading companies. The Aleuts agreed together to kill the Russians, and this had to be done suddenly and in several places at once, so that when the others found out about the fate of their compatriots they would not have time to defend themselves. So they divided amongst themselves an even number of splinters and each day they threw one into the fire. When the last one had been thrown in then they attacked the Russians from all sides and killed all but six of them who shot their way out, and retreated to the caves of Unalashka. They remained there until the arrival of *peredovshchik* [foreman] Solov'ev, who, in reprisal, killed more than 3,000 Aleuts, burying some of them beneath the ruins of their yurtas in whole villages, for on Unalashka there was always a large number of people living in each house.

Shortly before the arrival of Shelikhov on Kad'iak, four baidaras of Fox Island Aleuts arrived in Uiatsk Bay (on Kad'iak) with the intention of killing and plundering the Koniagas, and attacking them at dawn. But the Koniagas had seen their enemy and crept up to them at night. They killed all the men, and took five women prisoner.

The Russians in America have often suffered for their lack of caution. The Lebedev company collapsed because of this, for all its settlements were destroyed one after another and the settlers killed. In Kenai Bay the savages gathered near the fort and asked to be allowed in to trade with the animal skins they had brought with them. Once inside the fort they sat on the ground as was the custom. When they saw that the Russians were not armed, at a signal from their chief they suddenly leapt on them and stabbed them all with daggers they had hidden under their cloaks.

The inhabitants of the Copper River killed all the Russians, except the baidarshchik, their commander. They nailed him to a cross and cut off his genital organ and put it in his mouth saying: "You took away our women--now see if you can anything with them." Then they put out his eyes and brought before him the pelts of various animals and said, "We went into the mountains to get these for you, in winter, and you did not feel the cold and hunger we had to go through. Here are your fox and sable furs." Eventually they said to him, "You were a good man; since you were fair with those under you we have tortured you little; otherwise we would have done more." After this they killed him and threw his body in the water.

In 1801 the Koliuzhes destroyed the company's settlement on the island of Sitka, where the Russians were small in number, badly equipped, constantly careless and had committed many unjust acts on the savages in the surrounding area. Several hunters settled in the same place form an artel, and the company administration selects one of them as baidarshchik. These people usually either embitter the savages through their own actions, or are not powerful enough to prevent the others from doing so. The behavior of the Russians in Sitka cannot have made a very good impression on the Koliuzhes, for the hunters started to take away their young girls and offend them in other ways. The Koliuzhes in neighboring districts reproached the ones in Sitka for letting such a small number of Russians get control over them so that in the end they had become slaves. They advised them to kill the hunters and they promised support in this. One chief would not agree for a long while, asking "What would happen afterwards? There are more of them than the blades of grass."

A little while later, however, the Russians, on some trivial suspicion, arrested the uncle of this chief who was so devoted to them, and it was then that the savages decided to kill them without delay. In the artel there were living several sailors left by United States' ships and receiving food and clothing, etc. These aided the savages by setting fire to the fort and shooting at the Russians during the Koliuzh attack.

The promyshlenniks defended themselves in the fort but were forced out when the fire took hold--some were cut down, and others taken alive while the rest fled to the forest and after much suffering escaped. Those taken prisoner were treated in a most barbarous way--they were first scalped--the Koliuzhes keep scalps as trophies, then the children were made to stab them or they were burned in various parts of the body, or their bodies were hacked about with fish-bone saws, in short these unfortunates had to bear every possible kind of suffering. The corpses were transfixed on spikes as a sign of shame, or thrown onto the seashore for the dogs and crows to eat.

Soon after this three ships belonging to the United States of America arrived in Sitka Bay (the English call it Norfolk Sound). Some of the unfortunate promyshlenniks made their way to these vessels. As usual the savages came out to the ships to trade and their chief, at the request of the Russians, was seized and held as a hostage for the prisoners. The Koliuzhes agreed to this but almost all the people they returned were Kad'iak women. The Americans from the United States began to demand all the remaining prisoners, threatening to hang the trembling chief if they were not returned. The Koliuzhes decided to recapture him by force, and a great number of boats converged on the ships--but these were capsized and their occupants killed by musket fire so that the savages found themselves forced to return all the prisoners and to include some otters in order to ransom their chief.

These savage tribes are very cunning. Vessels calling to trade with them must be armed and constantly at the ready. Five or six ships on the northwest coast of America have been captured by the Koliuzhes. The Americans of the United States have a healthy hatred of them and each vessel considers it a duty, once its cargo for Canton has been obtained, to burn a few native settlements.

XIX

METHODS OF GOVERNMENT.

Their villages, situated on the coastline of the island, each has its chief, called by the Russians a *toen* [pronounced 'toion']. Some of the chiefs rule over many settlements and are all descended from one tribe, and named after the bays or capes near which they live. The power of the chief of a village is quite limited. The islanders frequently give more respect and obedience to some rich person or good hunter. Nowadays the company's administrators have taken the place of the native toen and they nominate others for the post at will--but they do not command the same respect as those that have been ousted. The administrators, knowing the respect the islanders have for their native chiefs, do not make their wives or children work. In earlier times the status of the chiefs was hereditary--but the choice of a successor rarely fell upon the sons but more likely upon one of the nephews. The Koliuzhes have exactly the same custom.

On Kad'iak many of the islanders possess *kalgas*, or slaves, received either by barter or taken as prisoners. When Shelikhov visited Kad'iak, many slaves, in the hope of a better life, fled to the Russians. Then these people were used to kill suspicious islanders. They were also sent out to work alongside the Russians. Hunters sent off to catch foxes in traps were allowed to take them along with them. Almost every hunter did this for this does not cost many tobacco leaves. Afterwards when the Russians found themselves in sufficient numbers on Kad'iak they took all the slaves from the islanders to work for the company and the name *kalga* was changed to *kaiur*, which is a Kamchatka word meaning hired laborer. Then when the number of kaiurs declined because of work and various accidents the islanders began to be enlisted for committing minor offences. Naturally after that the number of criminals on Kad'iak was bound to increase. Only the chief's children were excluded from this category. Although the kaiurs were clothed and fed they were always glad to return to their villages so as to escape from the unending work. Living constantly together with Russians and not being suspected by them of evil intentions, they often used the opportunity to wipe out whole artels of our promyshlenniks. But this has not prevented the company from always having large numbers of them in its employment.

In former times each Koniaga considered himself a member of the village in which he lived, and as having an equal share in matters of general concern with all the others, when they were decided at public assemblies, by bravery or some other means. In his personal affairs each follows his own will. Nowadays the manager of the company rules over the islanders through the baidarshchiks, while little distinguishes the chiefs from other savages, except his name toen or, what is worse, he can be a means for the oppression of the other islanders.

XX

HOW THE RUSSIAN-AMERICAN COMPANY ADMINISTERS THE KONIAGAS, ALIAKSINTSY, KINAIS, CHUGACH AND OTHER PEOPLES.

The company administration for all these peoples is the same. The manager for the company in America spends most of his time in Kad'iak. At various places along the coast of the island there are small posts in which groups of hunters live--this is called an artel, and is supervised by a baidarshchik. The baidarshchiks receive their orders from the manager and pass them on to the savages. In addition to the artels, in some places there will be one promyshlennik living with several Americans--either for fishing or for fox-trapping, or for some other reason; and such an organization is called an *odinochka* [one-man post].

There are four artels on Kad'iak, in Igak [Ugak] Bay, in Three Saints Bay, or in the old harbor near Cape

Alitok, while the largest is on the Kurluk [Karluk] River. On Ukamok Island, lying to the south of Kad'iak, there is a Russian and some kaiurs who catch evrashkas from which parkas are made and which are used to pay the Koniagas for otters. On this island and Evrashech'ia Island the islanders are forbidden to catch evrashkas for themselves; they are also not allowed to shoot evrashkas and seals in these places where they are shot for the company. If they do their catch is confiscated by the company. The kaiurs on Ukamok are given tobacco to sniff only twice a week. On Afognak there are two artels: the Igvetsk, or Afognak, and the Malinovskii. There are also two on the island [peninsula] of Aliaska: at the native village of Kakmaisk [Katmai] and on the island of Satkhum [Sutkum]. In the latter place large stocks of lakhtaks (sealion and seal skins used for covering baidaras and baidarkas) and they also shoot deer and bears and trap foxes. There is no native settlement here and the place is inhabited only by some hunters and some Kad'iak kaiurs. The baidarshchik in Kakmaisk receives by barter animal pelts from the North and from the hinterland of Aliaska. Earlier there had been another artel on this peninsula, near Lake Iliamna. However, it was twice destroyed by the savages and the company did not have the resources to establish it again, although it was a rich source of pelts. In Kinai Bay there are two artels, Aleksandrovsk at the mouth of the Bay, and Nikolaievsk much further to the north. From both of them, and especially from the latter, there is a good supply of furs--the best ones being bears and black otters. In Voskresensk [Resurrection] Bay, where the Chugaches live, there is also an artel; further on there is also one in Chugatsk Bay, or Prince William Sound, on Nuchek Island. From time to time the inhabitants of the Copper River come here in huge boats to see the hostages that have been taken away from them, and to sell the furs and raw copper which they have brought with them.

In the Bering Bay or Yakutat, where the Koliuzh settlements begin, there was quite an important post for trading which was destroyed by the savages before it was completed in 1805. The main company fort is now on Baranov Island, or Sitka, and this will be described further on. In addition to these the company has small settlements in Unalashka, Atkha and on some of the other Aleutian Islands, and on Bering and Kitovye Islands. But so few original inhabitants remain in the Aleutian Archipelago that the Russians are able to live there in complete safety. But because of the drop in the number of men there and the killing off of the animals the the company itself and other commercial merchant companies, the company draws very little benefit from the posts there.

Having given some idea of the disposition of the company's settlements I shall now say something about the native peoples administered by them. They are in general forbidden to wear clothes made from expensive furs, which they are obliged to give to the company. They are allowed to make clotes from hares, marmots, squirrels and birdskins. Kaiurs are recruited from all the tribes for life-service with the company. The Kad'iak kaiurs are sent to all the company's settlements in America. Because of this the Koniagas have more to put up with than the others, for they are compelled to feed not only the Russians on Kad'iak, but also in other places where there is a lack of fish or, for some reason or other, no food to be had. In addition kaiurs are recruited from all over for the harvesting of fish and berries. Towards winter they are allowed back to the villages so that they do not have to be clothed and fed. The kaiurs catch fish in fish-ponds, trap foxes for fur, work in the salteries and the brick works, cut wood, carry supplies to the harbor, are used as rowers when Russians travel in three-seater baidarkas and, in a word, are used for all kinds of work. If a kaiur goes lame or loses an arm, or in some other way becomes unfit to carry on working, then he is found work scaring away the crows from the iukola hung out to dry, or some other such task.

Almost every married hunter has several kaiurs in his service. The company uses them for work until old age or the money raised by relatives, or a replacement, buys them out.

The Russian-American Company does not buy animals from the Koniagas or other peoples subject ot it, but sends them off hunting on long journeys far away. It rarely pays them in European goods (i.e. tobacco, axes, knives, needles, nankeens, varicolored stones, silks or other trinkets). In the main they are rewarded with evrashka or birdskin parkas, kamleikas, seal skins, nets, various objects woven from gut and even sometimes with fat. All these are used by the wives and children of the Americans who hunt animals, so that the payment for a pelt is very small.

Although the company has numerous kaiurs in its service, the remaining Americans are enslaved by it and have no less obligations laid upon them. Among the most onerous is the sending of men to hunt sea otters, known in the Siberian trade as sea-beavers. These animals used to breed originally off Kamchatka and the Kurile Islands, then they were hounded by the Russian hunters along the whole Aleutian chain and gradually driven to Kad'iak; but as they finally began to disappear from the shores of this island as well, the company began to send Koniagas, Aliaksintsy and Chugaches along the coast of America and even as far as the island of Sitka, which is more than 1,500 versts from Kad'iak. The savages are forced to row this distance in their leather baidarkas, landing on shore at night to rest. On the journey many are drowned or die as a result of other mishaps, to such an extent that now on Kad'iak of 30,000 inhabitants (an estimate by

Shelikhov* when he arrived on the island) very few are left. During my stay on Kad'iak (in 1803 and a short period prior to that) these hunting expeditions were organized in the following way:

The main party, consisting of around 500 baidarkas, left Kad'iak in April, followed the American coast as far, perhaps, as Bobrovaia [Sea Otter] Bay, and returned at the end of August. Although each Koniaga, when he sets off on such a lengthy journey, makes himself a new baidarka, it will hardly hold together for the return journey, especially if the summer has been wet, because this causes the skin to rot. This party is controlled by a Russian, called the *partovshchik*. Seven or eight promyshlenniks are attached to him. The partovshchik names the place where the baidarkas stop and where and when they begin hunting. He collects the sea otter pelts, pays for them with the goods he has with him, or gives promissory notes which can be exchanged on Kad'iak. The partovshchik barters furs from those peoples from whom the company does not dare take them. The fittest men are chosen to make up the party, for in addition to the difficulties of the journey, there is great danger from the Koliuzhes. For this reason all the baidarkas travel together and to the Koniagas are joined Aliaksintsy, Chugaches and a few Kinai people. The latter are not so accustomed to baidarkas and only those living near the mouth of Kinai Bay normally travel in them (the English call this area Cook River). In Yakutat the lakhtaks are taken from the baidarkas and smeared with fat and the Americans are issued guns, which they had not been given earlier for fear that they might use them to kill the promyshlenniks in the party and then return to Kad'iak. On the return journey they also travel together as far as Yakutat and there the guns and other objects are taken away again. After this they all hurry home as fast as they can in order to catch the fish still going upstream in the rivers and to lay in stocks of them as winter food. Others remain on the islands near Voskresensk Bay to hunt birds for parkas.

A second party, called the Tugidak party, is made up of less than 200 baidarkas under the command of a partovshchik and his assistant. As Yakutat is very near to Kad'iak itself, old baidarkas are used for this expedition and the hunters are old men and boys. The party assembles on Tugidak in the first days of April and on calm days makes trips to the sea for otters. Then the baidarkas in better condition are hived off and dispatched in the charge of the assistant to Ukamok Island. There they also hunt otters and catch fish so as to lay in winter stocks for those who are staying behind on the

*There have never been so many inhabitants on Kad'iak. Shelikhov exaggerated, presumably to draw attention to his 'important discovery'. During Mr. Sarychev's stay on the island in 1790 there were reported to be only about 3,000 inhabitants there.

island for the winter to hunt evrashkas, since there is not one stream on this island. The Tugidak baidarkas set off in August. Those in Ukamok, when they have caught sufficient fish, to go Simidi or Sutkhum and even as far as the island of Unga, where they are sent to catch birds.

A third party, consisting of 50 or so baidarkas, under the supervision of a Russian marksman, hunts sea otters off the islands of Shuekh, Evrashech'ia and the Peregrebnyis and in the mouth of Kinai Bay. But as there are very few animals there these Americans are used more for transporting sealion meat to Kad'iak and to Aleksandrovsk.

A fourth party consisting of 50 baidarkas travels between Kakmai and Sutkhum. For this Koniagas from the north coast of the island are used, and Aliaksintsy and Kinais, for the most part feeble old men and young boys. Because of this they are allowed back to their villages half-way through June.

The remaining 80 aged and weak Koniagas are sent in company baidarkas to catch birds from whose skins parkas are made. They hunt in the bays and islands near Aleksandrovsk where they are joined by old men of the Chugach and Kinai tribes. Others hunt birds in the islands near Sutkhum. Each native has to catch enough birds to make seven parkas and each parka consists of 30 to 40 skins. If for reasons of age or ill-health a man does not catch enough then his number is made up by adding someone else's surplus catch. The company pays nothing for the basic supply of these parkas. Bird hunting is very dangerous, especially for the old men who can hardly walk on level ground, let alone climb up the steepest and most overhanging cliffs for birds. Sometimes they have to use ropes and poles. Sometimes even young people fall and are killed in this hunting. In September the old men are allowed back to Kad'iak; there they are employed in carrying food stocks to the harbor; those who are somewhat fitter trap foxes.

Each one who provides seven parkas is given one and told to pay for it with five black fox furs or eight so-called *sivodushki* [red and dark brown] and red ones.

Every spring some 30 to 40 old men are sent to the harbor. They put out to sea and fish for cod and halibut until the salmon enter the river, which happens at the harbor at the middle of May or the beginning of June, while in other spots it starts somewhat earlier.

The whale hunters kill whales in various places; half, although by far less, is given to the hunters and the rest is taken by the company as well as all the gut and three parts of the whales. All over Kad'iak the company has been stocking up fat--in the past as many as 200 barrels. A native who kills more than three whales is given multiple quantities of tobacco and beads; for less they only fill a tobacco pouch once. If a hunter finds a whale washed up by the sea then the company claims the whole carcass, but if the whale is found by an American then half of it is given to his village.

When the menfolk spend all summer hunting otters or catching birds, the womenfolk and the older children, excluding those of the toen, do not stay idle from work for the company. The widows and wives whose husbands do not have baidarkas, but who have gone hunting with their comrades, are used for preparing fish: the former until well into autumn and the latter until the return of their husbands. Those remaining in the village process birdskins and sew them into parkas for the company. When the sarana lily ripens, then each woman is given the task of digging several ishkats (a measure approximately equal to a chetverik) of the roots. The gathering of sarana lilies is very hard work, and the time when it is most easily done is very short so that pregnant women or ones with a child feeding at the breast cannot dig the required amount and are forced to buy the remainder from others. When the berries ripen then the women are also sent to pick a certain quantity of them, depending upon the crops, between four and eight ishkats. This continues until well into the autumn, and there is no payment at all for this work. They pick cranberries and raspberries or crowberries, and because these do not grow everywhere they sometimes have to go as much as fifteen versts or more on foot to find them.

For this reason the Koniagas do not manage to lay in sufficient food supplies for the winter and they often go hungry. But even then they are not allowed to escape working. The women process birdskins, sew parkas and kamleikas, make yarn out of nettles, and threads and wicker baskets from gut, and the like--the men make nets or do something else.

The Aliaksintsy go hunting in large parties on the same basis as the Koniagas but their wives are required to harvest much smaller quantities of sarana and berries. Of the savages living in the hinterland of Alaska only the Ugashintsy go out to sea to hunt sea otters off Sutkhum Island; the remainder catch otters, river otters, hares, foxes and other animals. Their children are taken into bondage and when they are of age they are used as sailors on the ships and sometimes they stay on as kaiurs.

The Kinai people are not good sailors and no more than twelve baidarkas of them go on lengthy hunting trips. The remainder have birch bark boats and large leather baidaras in which they take food supplies to the Russian artels. Their wives gather berries and sarana, which they did not do for themselves before the Russians came. For the Russians the Kinai people hunt reindeer, martens, lynxes, black bears, wolverines, river otters, beavers, muskrats and minks. They also catch hares, marmots and evrashkas, and from the skins of these animals they make clothes, which are used by the company for paying the Koniagas and bartering pelts from the Koliuzhes. In the summer these tribes are sent into the hinterland of America with beads and other trinkets, so that they may barter them there for animal furs and prepared deer and elk skins with peoples still unknown to the Russians. The remaining tasks of the Kinai are the same as those given to the Koniagas.

The Chugaches are sent with the main party; those remaining are occupied with bird hunting while the womenfolk gather sarana and berries. Each spring all the baidarkas with the young girls are sent to the island of Kuchok, eighty-five versts from the coast, to dig sarana there, where it is considered to grow the best. On this island there are also many seals. Also in the vicinity of Chugatsk Bay, in the spring, a large number of birds breed there and a great multitude of eggs is collected for the Russians, and they are preserved in fat. In winter each Chugach is obliged to provide the company with three sheep or three marmots.

The people living between the Copper River and Chugatsk Bay are called the Ugaliagomiuts which means "the village to the east" in their language. From them hostages are taken, but they are not given any duties. Bondsmen are also taken from the Koliuzhes of Bering [Yakutat] Bay, but those living farther away are so strong and well armed that they have remained completely independent.

Those living on the north coast of Aliaksa, on the River Ugashik travel, as I have said above, to hunt sea otters, but several years ago they disappeared, even abandoning their hostages. The people living to the north of them at the mouth of a large river are known as the Aliagnagomiuts. The people living further north of Bristol Bay are called Aglagomiuts and those even further off Kuikhpagomiuts, and in the interior beyond Lake Iliamna there are the Ktsialtans. The Russians know very little about all of these tribes.

XXI

NOTES ON THE KINAI PEOPLE, THE COPPER RIVER, AND NORTHWEST AMERICA.

The inhabitants of Kinai Bay (which the English call the Cook River) speak a different language from the Aliaksintsy, the Koniagas and the Chugaches. They have intermingled with all these peoples, yet their customs and life-style are not so different.

The Kinai people have no conception of God and are frightened of evil spirits. Like the Koliuzhes they believe that the sky and the earth, the people and all that is to be seen were created by the Raven, and that it is he who visits people with sickness. At the same time they not only do not respect ravens but chase them and hit them, yet the children are forbidden to hunt the raven's young, because it is said that something evil will happen, rain will come or a great storm.

The Kinai, like the Tungus, place their dead on a platform raised off the ground by four posts; there they are cremated. The rich are usually dressed in some of their clothes, since the belief is that the spirit may need them in the other world. The remainder of the clothes which are not burnt are divided up amongst the relatives. At the burning they dance and sing songs composed in honor of the dead man. These savages believe that the souls of those who drown or die live their death under the earth, while those who are killed live in heaven. This superstition can easily be read as a device for encouraging people to be brave against the enemy. Also the Kinai do not believe in reward for good or punishment for evil in the after life.

When a Kinai woman gives birth the father cuts his clothes and keeps those living with him in one hut [*shalash*] for these tribes, despite the harshness of the climate in which they live, do not have warm shelters like the Koniagas and Aliaksintsy, but sit all winter in front of a large fire which is kept going in the middle of their large huts. Each year they rebuild their huts and often even choose a different site for the dwelling.

The Kinai also do not count farther than twenty, that is no higher than the number of fingers on their hands and toes on their feet.

When the Kinai wishes to take a wife then he makes presents to her, and to her mother and father. Then he goes into the hut and sleeps with her. If the wife does not wish to leave her father's house then the husband comes to live with his father-in-law and to work with him. Divorce is achieved by mutual consent and the children live with their mother until they are of age.

Neither the Kinai, nor the Koniagas know a word for goodbye; when they leave they simply say 'I am going'.

The Kinai have no tambourines; when they are dancing they beat on pieces of wood.

The Kinai despise bird-skin parkas and dress more like the Koliuzhes, in cloaks made from the skins of marmots and other animals made into mantles [*nakidki*]. The Russians call these articles of clothing *nakidki*; they are like rectangular blankets worn over the shoulders and secured at the neck like a cape. Their bows are the same as those of the Aliaksintsy, while the arrows have points of various material, such as: deer-horn, copper, iron or hard black stone. Metals are normally obtained from the inhabitants of the Copper River; arrow shafts are made from larch which does not grow in this bay but is washed up by the sea or brought by the Kinai, who go into the interior of America to hunt marmots and other animals.

In June the Kinai set off to catch marmots, and to begin with they go up the Sushitna River, flowing from the hinterland of America, on the right side of Kinai Bay. They travel on foot along the river bank, for the current in the river is extremely strong, and on the way they catch many beavers. From its source the Sushitna flows to the west for two days' journey, then it begins to bend to the north and the Kinai travel for ten days in that direction. When they cross the mountain chain which runs parallel to Kinai Bay, they can see beyond it flat spaces of tundra which consist mostly of moss-covered rock. After a twelve-day journey they catch sight of the Sushitna bending to the right amongst the mountains. Where it flows out of the mountains they catch marmots.

After 14 or 15 days' journeying they usually reach the mountains. Here the Kinai meet up with the inhabitants of the Copper River who have made the journey for the same reason. They trade with them and barter copper, iron wedges (which they use instead of axes), prepared elk skins and some other goods. It is well known that copper can be found in a raw state in the interior of America, but the iron wedges naturally have been passed from hand to hand and originated either in the United States or from Hudson's Bay.

Assuming that the Kinai cover twenty-five versts every day, the distance from Kinai Bay to this mountain range must be 375 versts. The inhabitants of the Copper River have a journey of roughly the same length; thus it can be computed that the Copper River lies some 700 or 800 versts from the head of Kinai Bay.

On the return journey the Kinai make their way home when the first frosts come. If the Sushitna is still not frozen over they make small rafts and at the end of three days' journey arrive at the mouth of the river on them. If there is ice they wait until the snow falls and travel on boards which act as skis. The boards are much shorter than skis and consist not of single pieces of wood but of a strap binding round a wooden rim, the front part of which is twisted upwards.

In Kinai Bay there are black and red graphite, a stone which gives a green color, in some places there is carbon and in others mica. In the region of the volcanos beyond Kamyshatsk Bay, they collect burning sulfur.

The Kinai people are usually prone to eye diseases and they quite frequently go blind. The reason for this is not hard to find. In the spring the snow covers the ground for a long while and the sun's rays, reflected from it, harm the eyes and even cause blindness. In Kamchatka exactly the same thing happens if a person travelling in the spring does not wear an eyeshade of woven hair or a net of hair over his whole face.

The main part of the Kinai diet is made up of fish which they catch by making weirs in the river. This method of fishing is described below. But when there is a wet summer the water-level of the rivers rises and the weirs are washed away; then the Kinai lose their food supply and go hungry.

The exploration of the Copper River, or of the spot where raw copper can be found was a constant preoccupation of Baranov's. The hunter who was sent from Chugatsk Bay for this purpose and was brought back wounded, had volunteered a second time to try to find the source of the raw metal. He made his way more than 300 versts up the so-called Copper River which enters the ocean east of Chugatsk Bay, then he followed another river, which joins the Copper River from the right, but he found nothing. He heard various rumors about the place where the copper was, and since he encountered a host of obstacles he returned to Nuchek. This second Mungo Park was not dissuaded either by the difficulties or the dangers he had already suffered, and he set off a third time, only to die at the hands of the savages.

The objective of all the merchant companies with trade in America was to discover tribes and obtain animal pelts from them. Once the Lebedev Company, which had many settlements in America, sent off north of Lake Iliamna several promyshlenniks accompanied by a sizeable number of savages who had had bondsmen taken from them. In the Kad'iak office of the present American Company I found a report on the journey by the hunter Ivanov, who had been in charge of the expedition. Here is what he says:

> Towards Christmas we left Lake Iliamna on skis and followed the River Nugulna which flows into the lake. Then we crossed Lake Klichikh out of which this river flows. From there we travelled north for seven days, past four villages in which we saw between forty and sixty men, as far as the River Bamadna, flowing out of the high mountains. After leaving this river we spent a whole day crossing the mountain ridge, and in four days we arrived at the River Khakhlitna after passing a densely populated village. From the Khakhlitna we travelled eight days to the north through flat, open country as far as the River Khagylin, which flows into the sea. On its banks there is a village in which we saw seventy or more men. It is eight days' journey north from this

> village to the River Galtsana and past the small settlement of Krolikova toiona (it is not known why the chief was called this name--Rabbit Chief). From Krolikova to the Tutna, an extremely broad river, is six days' journey, past the village of Mandychatsk in which there were up to ninety warriors (adult and capable of fighting). We went down the Tutna for two days as far as the village of Ukhagmak, where there were more than two hundred inhabitants. From there, following the same river, it is a day's journey to the village of Tuliuka where there were about one hundred and fifty people. Then we went through a portage (a narrow place where in the summer the boats are carried from one river to the other) to the mouth of the Balsanda, where there is the large village Izyntylkhuk with more than seven hundred inhabitants in it. From Izyntylkhuk we travelled for a day along the coast to Ikgeetsko which stands on the river of the same name and which has some seventy people in it. Thus it can be seen that both the Tutna and the Balsanda flow into the sea with a day and a night's journey between them.

But then Ivanov says the following:

> that the mouth of the Tutna is further north than the Balsanda, that the width of the Tutna [at its mouth, I believe] is between 4 and 6 versts, and that there are many islands along the river.

He was told that on the length of the Tutna there were forty-four villages containing up to seven thousand inhabitants. All the other rivers, with the exception of the Balsanda, mentioned above, flow into the Tutna.

Everywhere Ivanov saw many freshwater fish such as burbot, pike, nelma and others with the exception however of sturgeons. When the rivers are icebound the fish are caught with fish pots. Stocks of iukola are not laid in until the spring, since in the winter they catch many caribou and live on the meat. There are many other animals, such as: beavers, river otters, foxes of all species, martens, wolverines, grey squirrels, muskrats and hares. In the forest there are many birds--partridges, grouse, quail and other species. In summer there are great numbers of geese, swans and ducks.

In winter these peoples travel by large dog-sledges. They always live in one place; their houses are of logs, round and often sunk in the earth. In the houses he saw large knives with copper embossing, narrow axes and large ones, but for the most part blunt. He also saw large clay pots, cups carved out of wood and bark, large stone knives and arrowheads made from walrus bone.

Ivanov also saw several iron choppers which were like Iakut hatchets. He did not see many beads and the inhabitants always bought eagerly, especially the white kind; there were also white beads and various metal articles.

There are the following trees in these parts: a straight, thick fir tree, a small larch, poplar, cherry and a very thick birch. Along the Balsanda there are said to be mica, blockstone and whetstone.

Ivanov returned to Iliamna just before Easter. On the journey he crossed many lakes both large and small.

XXII

THE KONIAGA BAIDARAS, BAIDARKAS AND HUNTING IMPLEMENTS.

Large baidaras are rarely used by the islanders and then only for transporting iukola, or some other cargo, from place to place. They are rowed by means of short, single-bladed paddles, and the rowers sit facing the bow of the baidara, two to a seat. The forepost of these canoes is more inclined than in Russian ones, which can be seen more clearly from the attached drawings [not published--Ed.]. The framework of the baidara consists of thin wales pressed into the keel and joined to each other with thin ribbing. When they are building these boats the Russians and Americans use no iron; everything is lashed together with split and scraped whalebone. When the wooden skeleton of the baidara is complete then a sewn-to-measure leather skin is pulled over it and this takes the place of planking. As I have already said sea-lion skins, dressed and smoked beforehand, are considered the most suitable for this. Sometimes the Koniagas make sails for these dugouts out of bast-matting or of the very thinnest leather.

The normal vessels for the islanders are the three-man, two-man and one-man baidarka. These are used by the Koniagas, Aleuts, the Kinai living near the entrance to Kinai Bay, and the Chugaches. But the baidarkas vary in all the different places, and the one-man Aleut baidarka is so narrow and light that hardly anyone else would dare to put to sea in them, although the Aleuts fear no storms when in them. On the other hand the Kad'iak one-man baidarkas are shorter, broader and easier to get used to. The two- and three-man baidarkas of the Aliaksintsy go better than the others for they are made shorter and narrower.

First of all a web or hull of the baidarka is built which is very thin and light. Its measurements have to be exact and it must be symmetrical. A small round aperture is left at the top for the man to sit in. Then a sewn skin with a corresponding aperture is stretched over the frame. Inside the baidarka the floor is laid with old skins (which are therefore called the seat), so that the rower does not sit directly on the framework. The rower sits upright in the hole with his legs stretched forward; the Koniagas, however, for the most part, row in a kneeling position by simply placing piles of grass under their knees. The Chugaches build in small benches and instead of a litter they fit wooden knee plates (wooden slats which cause calluses on their knees and ankles).

In calm weather the holes are left open, but when the weather is bad the Americans wear a kamleika, attaching its hem to a cornice round the edge of the hole in the baidarka; then they pull on a leather bag (called a covering), one side of which is wrapped round the body. When the American is strapped in in this way no rough water can get into the boat. The Koniagas use single-bladed paddles, and the Aleuts two-bladed ones, which the former people use very rarely.

An American in his baidarka can withstand the most violent storm. With no protection but his own agility he sets to sea and will travel hundreds of versts from the shore when the weather promises to be calm. But if a storm breaks when they are far from shore, and they have no chance of reaching shelter, then they gather the baidarkas together in two and threes and ride out the storm. They try to come alongside each other so that the sides of the baidarkas do not touch, for it would be easy to chafe through the leather. No more than three gather together in case there is a large wave and many of them are dashed together. If just one baidarka is caught in a storm, then two large inflated bladders are sometimes tied to its sides.

Despite their experience and daring the Americans are often drowned in bad weather. Sometimes the skin on the baidarkas is not strong enough to withstand a prolonged buffeting and tears, or they are too weak to defend themselves against the fury of the elements and perish.

It is extremely frightening to travel in a baidarka unless you are used to it for even in calm weather with a steady wind it seems as though the waves threaten to capsize it. But in fact in one of these boats a man is exposed to less danger than appears at first sight. In my spare time on Kad'iak I learnt how to paddle a one-man baidarka and grew so accustomed to it that I eventually went quite a distance out to sea in it.

The Aleutians mainly use one-man baidarkas but the Koniagas and other tribes prefer two-seaters. The three-seaters are used only for village chieftains and for Russians.

From the attached sketches [not published--Ed.] one can better see the shape of these boats.

In fighting the Koniagas use spears, bows and arrows. The shaft of a spear is wooden with a point of metal or sharpened bone, or even a razor-sharp stone. The islanders have large shields which give them good protection from arrows but are easily pierced by bullets.

The Koniaga bows are very simple and fragile. Those used by the Kinai and Aliaksintsy are taut and bound round with gut and are carved and skilfully decorated. Their arrows are short with stone heads and rarely metal ones. In general, though, the Koniagas are bad shots with bows. The weapons they use for hunting sea animals have been produced by them to a high degree of perfection and are very varied. The arrows used for this are longer and specially made. They are fired not from a bow but by means of a board.

XXIII

THE CLIMATE OF KAD'IAK. TOPOGRAPHY. PRODUCTS OF THE SOIL.

The coasts of Asia and America, washed by the Northern Sea and the Eastern Ocean, are subject to dampness and mist. The climate in the maritime areas is not cold, in accordance with the latitude, but rainy and unhealthy. In addition in the middle of summer the heat is not intense because, of course, of the proximity of a large expanse of sea and because of the almost constant wind. On the Alaska Peninsula, which consists of a chain of very high mountains, the winters are incomparably colder than on Kad'iak although the latter is separated from Aliaska only by straits some forty versts wide. For a more exact knowledge of the climate of Kad'iak I will describe the thermometer readings and the weather recorded in the 7½ months I spent there.

The first half of November was reasonably fine and warm but the second half was mostly overcast and rainy. The highest reading of the mercury was +6½° of warmth and the lowest +1°. When west winds blew it was always clear and cold while east and southeast winds brought mist.

From December 1st to 14th it rained almost constantly and sometimes a damp snow fell. The mercury in the thermometer varied between freezing point and +5°. The snow which fell was soon washed away by the rain, and by 18th December it remained only on the very tops of the mountains. The other half of December was clearer and the thermometer varied as before. On the 26th there were very strong winds from the northwest and on the 28th from the west. These tore the roofs from many of the houses and the Bay was covered with columns of seaspray.

Snow fell at the beginning of January, but none of it remained by the 8th. The thermometer read between 1½° and 4° of warmth. From the middle of January the days became clearer and the cold increased to 16¾° below, while the winds were from the west and northwest.

From the beginning of February until the 10th the weather was clear with occasional blizzards and the cold varied between 9° and 2° below. The wind blew more from the north and at times very strongly. On the 10th, however, the wind veered to south-southwest and with that came overcase weather which continued almost without a break until the 21st. The thermometer at that time showed between 5° and 2° of warmth. At the end of February the days were fine and at one time the cold increased to -2°. On the 28th there was an extremely violent storm from the west.

In the first days of March there was mixed rain and snow and the frost increased to -8°. On the 8th there were strong winds from the west-northwest and the Northern Lights were visible. On the 13th there was a great storm from the west and on the 16th an even more violent one. During the remainder of March the weather was stormy and changeable, the thermometer rose to +4° and only twice dropped to -2°.

The first days of April were fine and the cold increased to -5° with winds mainly from the northwest. After that the weather became changeable, but mainly fine. Just occasionally the northeast and east winds would blow up a mist and the southeast rain. The warmth varied between +9° and +3°.

In May the weather was more often overcast or rainy. The temperature rose from +3½° to +6°, and on fine days as high as +9° or +10°.

Between 3rd June and the 8th the weather was splendid and the temperature rose from 5° to 11°, but from then until the 18th it was overcast and rainy almost without a break. From the 23rd to the 27th it was fine once more and most of the time calm or with very light winds.

According to the evidence, however, of those who had been living on Kad'iak for some time, this winter had been milder than normal. In hard winters the new port, St. Paul's, is ice-blocked. From my day-to-day observations it was noticeable that the climate on Kad'iak is damp, but that over the year there are more fine days there than overcast ones. I list below the number of days in each month when there was no snow, cloud, rain, drizzle or mist:

From the middle of November to December the number of clear days was: -- 6

From the middle of November to December	6
In December	20
In January	10
In February	14
In March	12
In April	15
In May	5
From 1st June to 27th	10

The damp and mists are what prevent wheat from ripening on Kad'iak although the soil is fertile. The stalks grow tall, but because of a lack of warmth the ears never ripen. On the other hand, barley grows quite well, as do the majority of garden vegetables.

The bedrock of the soil on the Kurile and Aleutian Islands in northwest America consists of bare rock like the mountains on these islands and shores. In places the rock is covered with tundra and in others with a thin layer of earth. The same is true of Kad'iak. The earth mentioned above carries definite traces of the effects of volcanic fire--for which I have already presented proof. Even now it is all prone to earth tremors which happen every year on Kad'iak. In 1788 this island and its surroundings suffered a severe earth tremor which lasted for 17 days. At this time the fire-breathing mountains [volcanos] on Alaska beyond Kamyshatsk Bay opened a new crater which is still smoking to this day. On Kad'iak the earthquake was terrifying. After the first tremors the sea suddenly withdrew from the shore; then the Koniagas and the Russians took to the hills. Several moments later the water came back in a huge mountainous rush and crashed onto the shore. This incoming tidal wave broke the ships' hawsers (ropes used for mooring the ships) and carried them up onto one of the villager's huts. Some yurtas were washed away altogether. On the same day there were two such tidal waves. For 17 days there was a series of violent tremors which caused landslides from the mountains and shores. The capes fell away and left many pillars of rock standing.

Once on the Kurile Islands the tremors were even worse. The sea rushed away from the shore and crashed back again with such violent force that many who had not taken refuge on higher ground were drowned. A Russian merchantman moored at the shore was carried inland for three versts, where it has remained ever since.

On Kad'iak in 1792 there was another violent earthquake which lasted for 18 hours. All the native huts were destroyed and several cliff faces collapsed. A ship which was entering Three Saints Bay at the time encountered a violent storm and suffered a great deal of damage from the abnormal buffeting.

Earthquakes on Kad'iak always happen at the same

time as on Aliaska, and from the direction in which they begin there the cause of this is perhaps the smoking mountain at Kamyshatsk, north from Kad'iak.

At many places on the island I noticed that if you stamp your foot it sounds as if the earth is hollow. The same thing happens on the Aleutian Islands. One day when some promyshlenniks went to collect hot sulfur on the Island of Four Mountains one of them dropped through the earth and disappeared right before the eyes of his comrades. I was assured that on this island at low tide the large rocks which were revealed offshore moved of themselves and knocked against each other.

Kad'iak, like the other islands in this part of the world, consists of a rocky mountain ridge between the chains of which there are strips of fertile soil good for haymaking and crop-growing, so that cattle-breeding on the island could be carried on with reasonable success. The earth produces many useful plants, some of which are especially efficacious against scurvy, such as: couch grass, wild celery, wild onions, wild garlic, cucumber grass and some others. I do not know what name cucumber grass goes under in natural history, but on Kad'iak it is so called because of the smell which is just like that of cucumbers. On Kad'iak there also grow knotweed, or snake root, sarana, ferns and other plants used by the Koniagas and Russians as food. Whortleberry or shiksha, bilberry, red currant, here called the *kislitsa*, red-bilberry, raspberry, all grow in profusion and in places there are cranberries. The raspberries are notable because they grow to a remarkable size, but they are very watery and not as tasty as the normal ones. These raspberries are so large that I have seen berries the size of a groshen. The growth of grass is quite slow, at least compared with grass on Kamchatka.

The Aleutian Islands do not have any trees. Those which are nearest to Kamchatka have low bushes on them. Beginning with the Island of Umnak a sparse growth of elder is noticeable. Further north in Aliaska there are fir and birch as on Kad'iak where even wild apple trees can be found from time to time, very twisted and gnarled and no longer producing any fruit. About the trees of the mainland of America I shall say nothing, since much has already been written about them by Vancouver and several other explorers.

XXIV

ANIMALS, BIRDS, FISHES AND CRUSTACEANS OF NORTHWEST AMERICA.

It should not be expected that this description should contain anything that a scientist might say--that is, the division of the animals according to species. In the first place because much of this information is already available and in the second place because I know no natural history. Thus in my description of the animals I shall have more to say about the ways in which they are caught, as a main means of support for the savages, whose food supply always depends upon success at hunting. For this reason these tribes always respect a good hunter who often has precedence over the chief at village meetings.

I shall begin with the land animals which are to be found on the Aleutian Islands: Kad'iak, Aliaska, in Kinai and Chugatsk Bay and throughout the whole of the northwest coast of America.

The land animals are bears, wolves, foxes, polar foxes, hares, lynxes, mink, deer, elk, wild goats, wolverines, marmots, sables, wild sheep, muskrats, squirrels [evrashki], rabbits, ermine, mice and the American hedgehog.

Bears

There are no bears on the Aleutian Islands as far as Unimak; on the other hand they are to be found everywhere on the mainland of northwest America, but their fur varies in color. In Kinai and Chugatsk Bays they are black and in other places brown; the latter are known as red [*krasnyi*] bears. The skins of the latter species are not valuable and are used generally as bed covers in America, and for other domestic purposes. The black bears are not inferior in quality to those sent from Hudson's Bay--but the company cannot acquire them in large quantities as it has no establishments in the hinterland of America.

The local bears are very tame, especially the black ones; they rarely attack people, even when they are wounded and, in most cases, they try to escape. According to the savages and Russian promyshlenniks, there are bears with tails four or five *vershki* long, which are said to be very aggressive, so that the hunters try to avoid shooting them. The Russians are not much engaged in hunting these animals. For the most part when they are brought down by arrows they are finished off with guns. A small quantity of their pelts is also bartered from the savages. On the Kitovye [whale] Islands, *polar* (white) bears are occasionally to be seen, brought there by the ice.

The Milevsk Aleuts trap bears in large numbers. They strip naked and surround the bear. This is called hunting by roundup [*oblava*]. As they go round the bear they shoot at it with bows and arrows. When the bear sees so many people it dashes at some of them. Those who are in its path move to one side and the others then fire their bows and arrows. In Kinai Bay one woman kills between 10 and 12 bears a year with no other weapons but a bow and a knife, and aided only by some small dogs which are generally used for this purpose by the Kinai people. On Kad'iak sometimes two or three people in a group creep up on an animal and fire arrows at it, and if it attacks them they fight it off with spears. The Aliaskans, like the Koniagas, always send their best hunter alone against bears. He takes his bow and just two stone-tipped arrows, for the stone causes quite serious wounds. The hunter will lie in wait near the bear's habitual path and shoot at the bear at absolutely point-blank range, after which he dodges away to the side, leaving his parka. If the bear is not killed by the first shot and attacks then he falls upon the coat and tears it to pieces and this gives the hunter time to aim his other arrow.

If a bear is discovered with her cubs the mother is shot first, because it has been discovered that otherwise a wounded mother tries to escape and only save the cubs. If someone is inexperienced enough, though, to shoot one of the cubs then he will be in great danger from the mother who normally in such cases will attack the hunter with great violence. The aim of bear hunting amongst all the peoples of northwest America is in general considered to consist of creeping up on the bear as quietly as possible, which is here called bear-stalking.

In the spring the bears begin to come out of their dens, as soon as the green shoots which they live on begin to show. In the winter they lie in hollows in the ground, living on a store of roots, such as: yellow roots, fern-roots and others. In Russia I have heard that bears exist through the winter by sucking their paws. If this is the case then the bears hereabouts have more foresight and lay in a good stock of food. At the same time the animal keeps his den clean and goes outside for his other needs. In order to open a bear's den a fire is lit at the entrance. The smoke from this forces the animal to come out and face inevitable death at the hands of the people outside.

Wolves

These animals breed along the whole of the mainland coast, while on Aliaksa there are great numbers of them where they kill deer and catch them most skilfully. As the deer always run against the wind and has a well-developed sense of smell the wolves approach them in a semi-circle out of the wind. Then one of them will run out front. The deer, catching sight of it or smelling it, starts back and rarely escapes from the pack following on its heels. When this happens next to the sea the deer will go into the water and either escape to a nearby island, or be drowned.

The Aliaskans shoot wolves with bows or catch them in pits which they dig in the hillside where the wolves are most often to be found. These pits are thinly covered with grass and moss and they are often baited. The Kinai people hang nooses from the trees near the wolves' haunts and place bait in them. The tree is bent with its crown to the ground and it is so primed that when the wolf lands in the noose he shakes the tree; it then springs up, lifting the animal with it and strangling it.

Foxes

In our trade fox furs are divided into black, brownish black, *sivodushki* and red. The *sivodushki* and the brown come naturally from the black fox interbreeding with other species. One species of *sivodushka* is known as the *krestovki* [reddy-brown]; amongst the red foxes there is the *ognevki* [flame-colored], the best examples of which are caught on the Kurile Islands. Island foxes are generally better specimens than those on the mainland but their coats are coarser and they are less valuable than the others. Many of the black and brownish black foxes are caught on the Fox Islands; but the best specimens of all are to be had in the region of Kinai Bay and these are in no way inferior to the best from Kamchatka and Siberia.

These animals breed more in areas which are not wooded because, perhaps, they find more roots for themselves in these places, for fish and other sources of food are not always in supply.

No foxes are caught in the summer for at that time they are shedding their coats and their pelts are worthless. It is noticeable that at this time of year they are bolder and come right up to you, but in the winter and the autumn they are extremely cautious. It is surprising that such an intelligent animal as the fox has not learnt from its sum of experience when man should be avoided. I witnessed a similar set of circumstances on Sitka where, because food was short, we were shooting ravens. These birds had got to know a gun on sight so well that it was very difficult to stalk them, but if you had only a stick in your hand you could walk to within five paces of a raven without frightening it.

In the summer a tall coarse grass grows on Kad'iak and all the other islands. Under these conditions the foxes are forced to beat paths for themselves along which to run until the first snow comes and the grass dies off. From October onwards, when the foxes' pelts have fully recovered, the Russians begin to trap them in the following ways: primed traps [*kleptsy*] are set up on the foxes' path; they are called wooden lasts [*kolodki*]. They are made from tightly stretched sticks into which two metal teeth have been set. A thread is run from the sticks across the path so that when the fox touches it with its paw the sticks spring back and hit the animal so hard with the teeth so that it is nearly always killed on the spot. This is a very convenient way of trapping foxes but so effective that over the course of several years the fox population has already decreased. At the same time the traps can also present a danger to people, so that during the fox-trapping season it is very advisable to go inland or otherwise to be on constant guard against treading on a foxes' run. The traps are so skilfully camouflaged with earth and grass that not infrequently the hunters themselves get caught in their own traps. I have seen several men in America crippled as a result of this.

The Aliaskans catch foxes in the following fashion: they construct a circle of wattle fence and leave a narrow entrance to it facing the foxes' run. In the narrow opening is a noose. Inside the trap they place animal bones or some other kind of bait. In addition all the savages fire arrows at the foxes.

Hares

On the coast of the mainland these are to be found in reasonable quantities, but there are none on any of the islands. In Aliaska they are caught with nooses and parkas are made from their skins.

Polar Foxes

In Alaska only the white ones are to be found while on Bering, Mednyi and the Kitovye Islands there are blue and white. There were none of these animals originally on the Andreianov Islands but they have been introduced from Bering Island so that they now yield good profits to the company. When the Kitovye Islands were first discovered there were only blue polar foxes to be seen there, but after several years some white ones were carried to the island from the north on ice floes. Since then the two species have mingled and the blue ones have lost some of their quality.

The polar foxes are like dogs, not only because of their looks and bark, but in another way which distinguishes them from other animals. In summer when they are shedding they are very tame. As their new coat grows so does their sense of caution. If they are caught when young they can be trained to follow their master everywhere, like a dog. Polar foxes live in burrows in families, and are very playful, a quality which again distinguishes them from other animals. Often these foxes begin to play with people and in this way they are caught and pay dearly for being so trusting. If a man puts down a knife or some other object when he is working, the polar fox will try to sneak up and carry it off to bury it very carefully in the ground. Sometimes a polar fox will come up behind a person sitting down and nip at his coat or his boots. They seem to find pleasure in alarming people.

Lynxes

These are to be found all among the mainland coast of America. For the most part, however, the skins of these animals are obtained from Chugatsk Bay and the Copper River. Lynxes from this part of America are second to none in quality. I do not know if the savages have any special method of trapping them or whether they simply shoot them at random.

Minks

These are to be found all over America. Their pelts are very cheap and there is consequently no attempt to kill them on a large scale.

Wild Deer [*Caribou*]

The deer feed on a white lichen which grows on the rocky mountain slopes. Thus they remain over the whole of America and on some of the islands off the coast. They breed in very large numbers on Aliaksa, where the high mountains are especially favorable for this animal. The deer come every year in great herds to the south of Alaska and then go back. The inhabitants know of this and wait for the deer in narrow defiles. Opposite the island of Unga there is a headland on which there is such a place. The Aleuts go there at the right time and hide in preparation. One man goes behind the deer and frightens them. The animals rush straight at the people who are hiding who shoot them with bows and arrows. Deer hunting is very difficult, except at that time when they are crossing. In order to hunt them you have to go high up in the mountains and stalk them with the greatest of care, and out of the wind as well.

Wild Sheep

They are to be found throughout the mainland coast and they live in the mountains. There are two breeds of sheep: one has thick white wool and horns like our goats, but their meat is very tasty. The others have a thick and very smooth wool from which the Koliuzhes make their woolen clothes. The rams of this species have white horns, while the females are very fleet of foot and jump from rock to rock and across ravines which would stop any man from even thinking of crossing. They sometimes stand on overhanging cliffs which are so craggy that only their four feet can stand there.

The Koliuzhes hunt the sheep with specially trained dogs which try to drive them to the owner who stands ready with his bow and arrows.

Elk

They breed on the mainland of America but, it would seem, not in great numbers. They are killed with bows and arrows and the savages cover their breastplates with the skins, thus gaining some protection from arrows and spears.

Wild Goats

These are to be found throughout the mainland coast of America and on many of the islands offshore. Practically no use is made of their skins, but their flesh is very tasty.

Wolverines

These breed more in the interior of America than along its coasts. This animal, which is well known for its greed and slyness, is the same as here. A wolverine will often sit in a tree waiting for a deer to come along to examine a specially dropped piece of moss; then it falls on the animal's neck and bites through its throat.

Marmots [*tarbagany*]

On Aliaksa there are none, but they breed inland in America to the east of Kinai Bay. Marmots, a species of gopher [*ianatov*], usually live on hillsides or near declivities in groups in burrows which they develop into a maze with several entrances, some of them false ones. A marmot is very awkward to dig out of its burrow, for the sand in which the burrow is made constantly fills up the entrance. The little animal does not go far away from its burrow. In addition it has such a highly developed sense of smell that the wind has only to blow for it to know whether any danger threatens from that particular direction. Marmots are very playful and normally sit on their hind legs and whistle like gophers [*surôk*] and when they eat they hold the food with their front paws. Just like the squirrel they lay in no stores for the winter but lie the whole time in their burrows, as though half dead. If you shoot one marmot the others will all come running up until they see or scent the presence of a man, for living as they do on the ledges of the high cliffs they have grown used to the constant crashing noise produced by rocks tumbling down the face of the cliffs or from falls of snow.

Marmots are caught in various ways. Sometimes a noose is placed over the entrance to their burrows, and sometimes a block or wood or cages like the traps of the Vitim sable hunters which crush the animal and the marmot is caught, whether entering the burrow or coming out of it. As there are many entrances to the burrow they stuff them all up except the one next to which some kind of trap has been set to catch the animal. The latter is very cunning though; when it notices that some of the holes have been blocked up it does not go into the others but will sit inside for a week or two until the extremes of hunger drive it out. Thus once a burrow has been located all the marmots living in it are caught. This animal may easily be tamed and can with time become domesticated.

Sables [*soboli*]

The American sable is the name given to the marten [*kunitsa*] which is widespread on the mainland above latitude 60°. The martens obtained [in trade] from the Chugchi in Gizhiginsk also come from parts of America near the Bering Straits.

Squirrels [*evrashki*]

They live in burrows in ones and, more rarely, in twos, because they are so vicious that they cannot live together and bite each other spitefully. The female of this species has a pouch below her belly in which she carries her young. Like the marmot the squirrels eat sitting upright. They are caught in the same way as marmots. These animals are to be found mostly on Evrashech'ia Island, on Ukamok, many of the Aleutian Islands and in other places where the company has reserved for itself alone the right of catching squirrels and forbidden the native inhabitants to do so.

Rabbits [*kroliki*]

In Kinai Bay many of these are caught with nooses, but they are also common in other areas. In winter if you come across rabbit tracks you will find the animal itself nearby. When the rabbit hears people it leaps up and runs around. While this happens a pole with a noose is put into the ground and the people retire. When the rabbit sees that they have gone it comes back to its old place, and falls into the noose, through which it is seldom able to chew.

Muskrats [*vykhukholi*]

Are common throughout America, but there is little profit to be had from trading their pelts perhaps because they are not very expensive, or because there is not much use to which they can be put.

Ermine [*gornostai*]

This animal is found all over America, but in very small numbers and it is also not as big and well-built and is definitely much inferior to the ermine of Tomsk. The Koliuzhes place especially high store by ermine skins. The company could exchange them for sea otter skins very profitably. Baranov mentioned several times in his writing the sending of ermine, but it was not deemed necessary to carry out his request until the Americans of the United States ordered the goods from St. Petersburg and took them to the northwest coast of America, which caused the price of ermine skins to drop considerably.

Land [*Field?*] *Mice* [*myshi zemlianyia*]

These are to be found on Kad'iak and on all the Aleutian Islands; they live several together in burrows and lay in food stocks for the winter consisting of sarana, snake root and other roots. They pack this round with the buttercup-root (it is poisonous and the Koniagas used to dip their arrowheads into it) so that the other mice, when they find this store should eat the buttercup which looks very like knotwood. The natives try to find the animals' burrows every winter and they remove the whole store. The savages believe that as a result the mice will suffocate for they have found them dying from suffocation which has given rise to this fable.

The American Hedgehog [*iozh, or ëzh*]

The Aliaksintsy call it a *niunik* and it breeds on the coast of the American mainland. When another animal is chasing a niunik then it points up at it, like a porcupine, spikes from the hind part of its back where they are longest and strongest. The savages eat niunik meat.

In addition to the animals mentioned above on Kad'iak near the old harbor and on Ukamok there are wild dogs, which have bred from those escaping from the settlements, but they rarely attack people although they sometimes roam around in large packs.

Amphibious Animals

River Otters [*vydra rechnaia*]

This animal breeds all along the American coast and on the offshore islands as well as on the Aleutians. It makes its burrow near the lake or sea into which it sometimes descends to get food. If an otter sees a duck in the water it very quickly and skilfully dives under it from quite a distance away.

The animal grows accustomed to human company. During my stay on Kad'iak one otter lived in the promyshlenniks' barracks and swam along behind the baidarkas. In order to catch otters, the hunters wait on their regular run, especially when the snow has turned wet and frozen again for then the animal's tail, which it normally uses as a support with which to jump out of the way, soon gets rubbed raw and cannot aid in hastening the animal's flight so that a man may easily catch up with an otter and kill it with a stick.

Beavers [*bobr*]

In the Siberian trade this animal is known as a river beaver [otter] in order to distinguish it from the sea beaver [otter] which are also incorrectly called sea otters. Beavers are common throughout America, but the best may be caught on the River Sushitna which flows into the north end of Kinai Bay. So many amazing things have been written about the beaver's capabilities and his social life, that I consider it necessary to say something about what I have heard from the hunters of this animal and who have had the chance to find out these things.

Beavers build their nests right next to the water and if the water there is low they raise the level by building dams in the streams. For this they usually choose a spot where the stream is narrow. They bring small logs there on their backs and place them across the stream. Then they throw on some brushwood, chewing it up with their teeth. Should they need more wood they chew the trunk of a tree from one side and wait till the wind brings it down or it comes down of its own accord. Then they trim it with their teeth and float it downstream with the current if it is above the dam; if it is below then two or three beavers carry it on their backs. In fact, they do not need very big trees for their dam, and it does not contain poles upright in the river, as many writers have maintained.

When in this manner the dam has been completed, and the water begins to rise they start to hollow out their home, which normally has two entrances, one out above the water and the other below. They choose a place to build the house in a spot which is surrounded by willow, but they do not touch this except in dire need and go further off to eat. When the beavers are lying in their house they put their tail out through the hole made into the water, otherwise the hard tight skin which covers this part of their body dries out and splits. No one, it would seem, has mentioned this before.

If beavers are attacked in their home then they jump into the water, since because of this animal's short legs it is easy to catch on land. Thus the first thing that is done is to break down the dam and to let the water out. If some of the beavers escape then they repair the dam with surprising speed.

According to the account of several hunters and explorers the beavers or northeastern America always live in large colonies. In the northwest, however, no more than two or three are ever found in one burrow and often only one. This description of the life and habits of beavers is somewhat different from the others. But it may be that in various places animals of the same species differ as much as people do.

Sea Otters [*morskaia vydra*]

In Russian trading this animal is incorrectly known as the sea beaver, although it is very similar to the river otter and they can only be distinguished by the fact that the former live along the sea coasts, never stray far away from there and live on food from the sea. This animal breeds near the Kurile Islands, Kamchatka, the Aleutian Islands and all along the coast of America from the 60th parallel to the 30th parallel, and perhaps even further south.

The sea otter is deserving of a better description than I am able to give, for value of the skins of these animals has been the motivating force behind all the private undertakings in the area. It is well known how Bering lost his ship and died on the island which has been named after him, and how his companions who were saved took a large number of sea otter pelts to Kamchatka and sold them at extremely high prices. Ever since then merchants, filled with a desire for riches, have been equipping ships in Okhotsk and Kamchatka and sending them to the east. These seafarers, like the Argonauts, have the single aim of finding sea otters, for by comparison with the skins of this animal the remainder of the fur trade is worth very little.

These animals love to live in colonies, in places where man has not yet disturbed and frightened them. They spend the greater part of their time in the water and sometimes bask on sandbanks, but they never go far away from the shore. Thus if you see a sea otter in the water you can be sure that land is not far away. They have no particular time for mating since one may see suddenly females with pup, with small pups and large ones beside them. The females carry one pup each and, more rarely, two and they love them dearly. They always carry the little ones on their backs and fetch them seaweed and shellfish from the sea-bed and, in general, care for their welfare. When the hunters see a female with her pup, they try to catch the latter, for although to begin with the mother dives under the water, it normally swims up to the baidarka afterwards, looks pityingly at its pup which has been taken away, and is killed. Their tender affection for their young is further illustrated by the fact that they will carry the pups around even when the latter are dead, decomposing or even simply bones.

The Koliuzhes hunt sea otters in the following manner: they find them basking on sandbanks, quietly surround them and kill them with sticks or shoot them with guns. But the Koniagas, Aliaksintsy, Chugaches, Kinai and the Aleuts shoot them with rifles in the water. When these animals are sighted from several baidarkas they surround them and fire arrows at them. The otters take fright and dive into the water; with this first dive it can go as far as two versts. But as soon as it shows above the water, the Americans, without giving it a chance to get back its breath, fire arrows at it again and force it to dive. As a result the dives become shorter and shorter in duration. In the end the otter is incapable of going under any more and is killed by the arrows. But if it is wounded earlier in the proceedings it tires more quickly.

If one arrows hits home but the rope attached to it breaks then another arrow is fired, and when the otter is killed they measure the rope left on the arrow in order to determine to whom the pelt should belong. If several shots hit it at the same time then the skin is said to belong to the person whose arrows is nearest to the tail when the animal is wounded in the back, and nearest to the throat when the animal is wounded in the belly. No one ever protests these decisions, and they serve as laws for the hunters.

Walruses [*morzh*]

This animal is also referred to as the sea horse, and only breeds in the most northerly regions, and always lives in herds on the ice floes or on the low-lying islands. Walruses are not as fearsome as they look. The hunters are able to come right in close to them and stab them with long spears. These are specially made so that they quickly pierce this animal's very thick skin. At the same time the hunters take care always to stand to one side, for the animal always tries to get into the sea and can crush a man that they would otherwise never have attacked. It is remarkable that once a walrus was killed in Kinai Bay, where they hardly ever appear. They are only killed for their tusks for the Russian hunters do not know how to put walrus skin to good use though this is very necessary.

Sea Lion [*siuch*]

This sea lion can be distinguished from other sea lions by the fact that it has no skin on its face which can sometimes cover the eyes, as is evident from the descriptions of sea lions on the island of Juan Fernandez. There may be other ways of distinguishing between these animals, but I shall speak only about the sea lion's habits and methods of catching it.

These animals breed everywhere where man, the enemy and destroyer of everything, worries them least. They usually lie on the rocks at the edge of the sea where the big waves break. The violence of the water in no way disturbs these animals from scaling the cliff wall and even aids them in this endeavor. They will swim up to the cliff on the crest of a wave, cling on to a rock with their fore-flippers, and hang there until another wave comes which pushes them further up. The sea lions always dive head-first from the cliffs, however high these might be, having first balanced on their hind flippers. Sometimes they are killed on underwater rocks this way. They never make for a baidarka which encourages the Americans, fearing nothing, to approach them close by.

For the whole of April and half of May, the sea lions lie in one spot and only go into the sea to find food. When this animal catches a plaice, it grips it with its teeth and throws it violently into the air. Thus a piece of the fish remains in its mouth and the rest falls into the water. But the sea lion seizes this and goes on throwing it about in this way until it has eaten all of it. In the middle of May the sea lion bulls swim away and collect the unmated cows, returning in the middle of June, and they mate in the remaining days of the month. At the same time the mated cows pup and lie with their young, then drag them with their teeth into the sea and teach them to swim. Each bull lies in a separate space, surrounded by his cows, for which he has fought, quite fiercely, and not one of them has no wounds. Sometimes two bulls get hold of the same cow and tear her to pieces and throw her into the sea. For the remainder of the year the sea lion change their territory, as they are often forced to do by man.

On the Bering and Kotovye Islands the sea lions lie on the shore, for there are no craggy rocks offshore. Because of this they can there be cut off from the sea, chased further inland and the small ones killed with sticks and the older ones shot, for when the latter are annoyed they can wound a man quite seriously. Quite a lot of people are needed to herd these animals into the middle of the island. If there are not enough people then the animals will escape by throwing themselves in the sea and crushing everyone that gets in the way, although they would never intentionally attack anyone. It is not possible to drive a fierce bull sea lion into the center of the island quickly, for to begin with he will defend himself with his teeth but later he will offer no resistance. This large animal moves on land at such speed, despite the shortness and flexible nature of his flippers, that a man cannot keep up with him; but on the other hand because of the effort of carrying so much fat he soon gets tired and sometimes falls dead as a result.

The sea lions, lying on the offshore rocks, are shot by the Russians with rifles but not at the moment the animal is diving in the water for in this case the dead animal will fall into the water and sink immediately. When it is wounded this animal leaps into the sea. The hunters then try to hook the body with a sharp harpoon attached to a large inflated bladder and this is the only method the Koniagas use for catching the animal.

When a sea lion is seen sleeping in the water, the hunters row up to him very quietly and shoot him with a harpoon with an inflated sea lion bladder attached to it or an inflated sealskin. They try to get the blade into the neck, for the animal bends it every time it dives and so will soon tire from the extreme pain. During the first couple of dives, even with the harpoon in it the sea lion goes under water so quickly that the baidarka cannot catch it, but gradually drops behind; gradually it tires and then more blades are fired into it.

True, quite an effort is needed to tire this animal. To the south of Kad'iak they used to go into a little, narrow bay, and a net was then stretched across the entrance, the ends of which were taken into a large baidarka. When the sea lions got caught in the net they sometimes dragged the baidarka after them for some ten to fifteen versts although all the rowers were paddling.

All the bowmen assure me that when they kill a sea

lion on a high rock above the waterline they have to wash the blood off it or else no more of the animals will ever lie there.

Sea lion meat is used as food and the fat is prized more than that extracted from any other sea animal. Kamleikas are made from the guts, and the skins are used to cover large baidaras. Lakhtaks of the cow's skin are considered the best for baidarkas.

Seal [*tiulen'*]

In Eastern Siberia and America this animal is known as a hairseal [*nerpa*], and breeds off all the coasts washed by the Pacific Ocean and the Sea of Okhotsk. There are various species of seal. In America there has been a noticeable decrease in the numbers of this animal, for it is absolutely necessary to catch them and it goes on all the time, because the skins are used to cover baidarkas which every savage needs. In addition the meat and fat are used as food and the gut is used for making clothes.

The hairseals gather in August and have their pups in the last days of May and June; in other words they carry the pups for about nine months. In June and July they bask on the rocks, roaring all the time. When, having crept up, a hunter goes out to kill them he either throws off or shoots the young ones first, lying nearest to the water, for above the noise of the roar the others cannot hear this.

Seal-catching is a very tricky business and a good hunter is respected amongst the savages; in some places they are driven inland and killed with clubs which the hunters call a 'driving back'; but this rarely happens because large numbers of people are needed.

When the tide is in a net is stretched across in front of the rocks on which the seals are basking in such a way that the current will not carry it away. The net is about eight sazhens in length and one sazhen wide. Small stones are attached to the bottom edge and floats attached to the top so that the net stays upright in the water. When it is pulled taut the hunters sit on the rocks and shout and imitate the seals' calls and wave a decoy consisting of an inflated sealskin. When the animals see the decoy on the rocks they think that it is a seal, and the come over to it. The man waving the sealskin, in the position demanded by the placing of the net, how throws a stone into the net. The animals take fright, dash away and get tangled up in the net.

Sometimes the hunter sitting with the decoy waits till the seals reach him and then he kills them with a club or fires a harpoon with an animal bladder attached.

Seals, especially in summer, sleep deeply on the seaweed or near it. When the men in the baidarka see this they paddle very quietly and attach a hook. As they do this the hunters always shout to wake the seal, for the Americans have learnt by experience that if the animal is wounded while asleep it often escapes by diving to the bottom of the sea where it becomes entangled in the weeds. Sometimes they have to wait half an hour or an hour for it to die and come to the top of the water carried by the hook and inflated bag.

If a seal is shot in the sea they try to attach a line to it as quickly as possible, since otherwise the animal will sink quickly, especially in the winter and summer when there is no fat on it.

The Chugaches have a special method for catching seals. On a warm, stormy night a man goes out and stands on the cape by deep water and waits for the animals to come into the bay for shelter. He steers them with a long pole in which a harpoon is fixed with a rope about 15 or 20 sazhens long. When he has speared a seal he lets go all the rope, then he pulls the animal in and, having tired him in this way, finishes him off with a club.

In the spring, when ice is carried into the straits, the Chugaches will set off in a baidarka, loading it so that it is level with the water. Then when the edge of the boat is packed round with ice, the man at the front places a large chunk of ice on the prow of the boat so that he is entirely concealed and breaks a hole through it so that he can guide the others.

Paddling very quickly they come up near to the seals lying on the ice. The forward man in the baidarka shoots at them through the hole in the ice. They place the dead seals in the baidarka, throwing out a compensating number of stones. By this means in a short time they can kill between ten and twelve seals--as many, that is, as the baidarka can carry.

Seals live for the most part on fish. The hunters maintain that these animals will never go on a rock where blood has been spilt, or even where a knife has been sharpened.

Sea Cows [*korovye morskiia*]

These animals, called by the Spaniards *manatu* and by the French *Lamentine*, can also be included in the amphibians for it is always to be found by the seashore although it never goes out to sea, but they occasionally remain in the sea during the ebb tide. The sea cow is much larger than the sea lion for it is from 3 to 4 sazhens long and weighs upwards of 200 puds. Its meat is tastier than the other amphibians. At the beginning of Russian exploration of the Pacific there were large numbers of sea cows near Bering Island but they have been driven away from the area by over-hunting, since it often happens that a whole animal would be killed just for the sake of the kidneys which are considered a delicacy. Since then the Russians have seen no sign of any anywhere. The sea cows have in all probability gone to the Bering Straits where the ships of the Russian-American Company never go.

Sea Cats [*kot morskoi*]

I shall discuss this animal in my second journey in the description of my stay on the Seal Islands.

Whales [*kit*]

These animals breed off all the coasts of the Pacific, but especially off Bering Island, on Kad'iak in Kizhdetsk Bay and in the straits separating Spruce Island from Kad'iak. There are various species of whale and the blubber from the so-called *Plovuns* has the particular quality that it will not boil in the stomach, like mercury. The savages sometimes eat it in jest, and the Russians make soap of it by mixing it with shells. The *Cachelot* species brings the American Company no particular profit, although the extraction of spermaceti is already widely known about.

The whale has been described by a great many natural scientists, but I consider it necessary to say something about the way they are caught, for the perfection of the hunting and artifacts will give some idea of the level of culture of the Koniagas.

Many superstitious rituals are connected with whale hunting. These the hunters will often not reveal to outsiders. But they usually have the result that the number of people taking part in this hunting has decreased considerably. They take the bodies of outstanding people who have died and place them in remote caves where it is sometimes possible to discover upwards of ten such bodies. One of the whale hunters told Baranov: "When you die I shall try and steal your body." Before the whale hunt starts the hunters meet together in the cave and remove the bodies and place them in a stream, then they drink the water from it and commit many other wicked acts. They do the same every time they kill a large whale. When a hunter dies then the others cut pieces off his body and rub their arrows with it. They also dry the pieces and preserve them from rotting in every possible way, thinking that if the flesh rots they themselves may die. When the hunter is at home he has the skin hanging on a thread. But when he is travelling or hunting he always takes it with him.

In May and June the whales come offshore in large numbers and the hunters gather there where there are most. There are special spears for killing these animals. A short slate spear from 3½ to 4½ vershki long is tied to a short stick which is placed in a long pole, and not fastened to it.

When the weather is calm the hunter goes out in his two-seater or, more usually, one-seater baidarka; he rows out to the spot where he expects the whales to surface. Then he fires to hit them under the tail fin or the side fin, which are known as flippers. If this animal is wounded in this place it soon dies. Thus, choosing a favorable moment, he throws his spear and rows away, for the whale when it is wounded throws itself down with great force and may either crush the baidarka with its tail or capsize it with the rough water caused by the movement. The stone blade stays in the whale and the pole in the water. The hunter goes away, assured that the animal he has wounded will be dead in three or four days and will float to the surface. Then the carcass will be towed to the shore, if it is spotted. If not, the carcass will be left to the mercy of the winds and sometimes drifts so far that whales killed near Kad'iak have been found washed up on the shores of Unalashka. Sometimes a hunter will follow a whale for a whole day waiting for a chance to wound it.

Each man engaged in whale hunting has his own mark on his stone spear. This helps to show who has killed a particular whale. The signs are recorded in the company office which allows one-third of the animal to go to the person catching it and takes two-thirds for itself. The American, however, usually divides his share with his colleagues, each one of whom would do the same. When the whale is shot quite large chunks of meat are cut out near the wounded part and then thrown away, for this meat has already spoilt and is turning blue. When a whale is washed up that has not been shot but has died of natural causes the Americans only use its meat for food if the birds and animals eat it, otherwise they are afraid to touch it in case the animal has died from an infectious disease.

To carry the whale to the village they cut it into strips. They maintain that it is easier to cut it with a simple metal knife than with a sharp one which folds. In order to extract a large amount of fat from the whale the Russians and the Americans consider it best to let it lie so that it should turn sour.

The Koniagas assured me that the whales do not live on herrings, but on the same small fish on which the halibut and cod feed.

The Killer Whale [*morskaia kosatka (Dauphin de mer)*]

These animals breed off all the coasts but especially, it seems, off the Kurile Islands. Almost no attempt is made to catch them, for their flesh is considered inedible, even by the savages. Thus it is only used as food when the animal happens to be found washed up on the beach.

Killer whales are great enemies of the whale, although they often swim together. Several killer whales will attack one whale and because of their agility they manage to avoid the blows of its tail. They bite it with their sharp teeth and torture it, so that sometimes the whale lets out a fearful roar and leaps out of the water. Then when the killer whales have killed the huge animal they eat only its cheeks and tongue and the remainder is often thrown up on the beach and used by the natives. The killer whales also eat in the same way seals who on seeing them, run for the shore, although the killer whales never come close in. The hunters try to use this opportunity to catch the seals.

The Porpoise [*morskaia svinka (Marsouin)*]

This animal breeds near the shore and for some distance away; also off Kad'iak, more on the north side of the island where the Koniagas catch them for food, for the dolphin's meat is quite delicious. They kill them with arrows fired from a board; these have a spear shaft made in a special fashion so that it sticks in the thin skin and fat of this animal. When it is wounded it begins to dive under the water. The dolphin only remains on the surface of the water for a few seconds and during this time they try to shoot it. In winter this animal is so cautious that if it sights a baidarka it disappears altogether from the surface of the water. They seem to take some pleasure in swimming near a vessel and in gamboling around it, especially if the wind is fresh. But if one of them is wounded by a harpoon then all the others will disappear in an instant.

Beluga

This animal differs greatly from the fish of the same name and I am very sorry that I have never seen one, for it would seem that the beluga has not yet been precisely described. It is said to have a head like a horse, and this is perhaps why some peoples call it a sea-horse. Others confuse the beluga with the sea-cow although there is not the slightest resemblance. The beluga sometimes enter the Okhota and other rivers and breed in large numbers in Kinai Bay, where the inhabitants use their skins to make baidaras, as do the inhabitants of the north coast of Aliaksa beyond the Ugashintsy.

Land Birds

The white-headed and white-tailed eagle are to be found throughout northwestern America and the islands off the coast. The young birds have grey tails, the feathers from which are used as arrow-flights since they are the most supple. And for this reason alone the eagles are caught with traps when the fish are coming up the rivers. American eagles have not been recorded as feeding on anything but fish and shells. In winter in Sitka we have eaten birds of this species, but their meat is very sinewy, dark and of unpleasant taste.

Ravens and magpies are to be found everywhere. The magpies on Sitka differ from those which breed in Russia, for instead of having white spots they have azure ones and an attractive crest.

Partridges, especially on Kad'iak, are found in large numbers and they are extremely tasty and this is perhaps more than ever explained by the lack of good game birds, since the wild ducks are also used as food, as are fish and sea plants. In the winter there are also white partridges.

On Kad'iak I have seen larks, but in fact I do not recall any large land birds; there are some small ones, but not very noteworthy.

In the spring two species of sandpiper fly in. One is small, multi-colored and pretty. The other is completely black with white legs, a red beak and the same color round the eyes. But both species of sandpiper should really be included in the list of birds of the seashore, since the first kind always live on the shore and the second are mostly to be found near offshore rocks and cliffs. The black sandpiper, when it sees a man, keeps flying round his head and calling. Seal hunters do not like this bird for the reason that it seems to want to warn the seal with its cries of the fate that is being prepared for it, and if often succeeds in frightening the deer away. The islanders are glad when they have shot a black sandpiper. The seagulls also fly around people's heads when they go anywhere near the gull nests with eggs in. The eggs of the black sandpiper are the same size as chickens' eggs and very tasty.

On Kad'iak there is a third species of tiny piper which appears only in the winter, in great flocks, and sits along the seashore so close together that one volley will often kill forty or fifty of these birds, which are very tasty.

The Kinai people decorate their bows with the yellow feathers of a bird which is so rarely caught that few of the savages have seen one. It is said to be about the same size as a magpie.

Sometimes hummingbirds fly here. While I was there one was shot on the island of Sitka, which is at latitude 57° and separated from the mainland by two wide straits and a large island. Hummingbirds are also to be found in the Bering Straits.

Cranes arrive on Kad'iak in the spring in small numbers and they are just as cautious here as they are elsewhere.

Herons of various species breed throughout northwestern America and in Sitka they seemed very tasty to us.

Water Birds

The swans on Kad'iak are only birds of passage; they rarely stop for the summer to have their young; maybe only one or two pairs do so. In Chugatsk Bay there are many of them and this is where swans' skins come from, which are extremely warm and quite strong.

The geese in northwestern America are divided into *laida* [shore] geese and *tundra* geese, that is: one kind always sit on the beaches and the others always in the interior, and these two kinds are absolutely different. The Russians in America normally call the beaches *laidas*, and they often use the word tundra to describe the interior of the country. The eggs of the wild geese have a white shell, whiter than those of our domestic geese. This bird rarely stays to nest on Kad'iak--and then in small numbers only. They are normally migrants, in spring and autumn, and at the latter time they stay on the island longer, especially if there are south or east winds blowing, for they always fly away with the west wind. When the geese only fly a short way away from Kad'iak, and the wind is strong they come back again, and sometimes they are so tired that they fall to the ground where they can be caught by hand. The geese rarely winter, even on Kad'iak, and then only in small numbers.

In general almost all the birds fly away to lay their eggs and raise their young on the northern shores of Aliaska, in that wild and empty area where they will almost never be disturbed by man. There are said to be an unbelievable number of geese, swans and all kinds of game birds there.

On Kad'iak the geese are caught with snares, while in Chugatsk Bay, where they stay for the whole summer, the inhabitants wait until they begin to shed their coats. Then a large number of baidarkas is assembled and the geese are herded together in large numbers and driven to the shore. There the women and children wade into the water and kill them with sticks. Only a small number manage to escape.

In autumn and winter there is a large number of ducks off all the coasts of Kad'iak, but in summer they fly off to lay their eggs off the northern shore of Aliaksa, or elsewhere. Around Sitka there are far fewer ducks. There are a large number of different species in America, and they are widgeon [*savka*], rockduck [*kamenushka*], scoters [*turpan*], harlequin [*pestriak*] and others. In addition loons [*gagara*] also breed and several different species of divers [*nyrka*].

The harlequins form the largest species of sea ducks and they are always to be found off the capes which stick out into the open sea, and for some distance offshore. They are so fat that they can only rise out of the water with great effort. Rockducks are so called because they often perch on isolated rocks. A description of scoters and widgeon can be found in the writings of Steller and Krasheninnikov.

Other species of ducks like the golden eye [*gogol*], mallard [*selezen'*] and merganser [*krokhal*] breed on Kad'iak and can be included as river ducks; they also taste better than sea ducks. Birds of this species are generally so plentiful on Kad'iak that they form a considerable percentage of the food supply, especially for anyone who has a gun and likes shooting.

The ducks are caught in various ways. When several baidarkas sight a flock of these birds they paddle up to them, suddenly fire several arrows and shout for all they are worth. At this some of the ducks take fright, but before they can fly out of the water they have to dive. Thus they surely fall into the hands of the Americans, who give them no chance to draw breath, firing a constant barrage of arrows at them. In the end the ducks become so tired that they pass out, and are killed with paddles, or they escape ashore where they are caught by hand.

Ducks are also caught with nets or counterweights. For this method a narrow strait is chosen, or a narrow river mouth, across which a net is stretched in the following manner: one end of a rope attached to the top side of the net is tied to the bank and a man sitting on the opposite shore holds the other end of this rope. The net is then in such a position that its lower edge is almost touching the water. This method of hunting is only employed in the mornings at sunrise, and in the evenings at sunset. For at the first time the ducks are flying from the sea into the bays and sounds, and at the latter time of day they are flying off to spend the night on the shore. Ducks usually fly very quickly, and some species fly so low over the water that in the twilight some always get caught in the net, which is then immediately lowered into the water, thus trapping the birds. When this catch has been removed the net is raised again in expectation of another flight.

Shooting ducks is not difficult, especially in the mornings and in frosty weather for then the birds are very unwilling to come up from the water and can be approached quite near. It is best to try and come downwind for the ducks always take off into the wind. The gun should be loaded with the heaviest kind of shot, for sea birds are in general very tough and it will be difficult to kill unless you hit them in the neck or head.

The *ara* [guillemot] is a species of diver which flies very clumsily and lays eggs on the cliff-face in little burrows. They can be caught with snares, but more often with nets which will trap perhaps fifty or even a hundred at one time. The net is about three square sazhens in size. The upper edge of the net is attached to a pole by means of knots which will come undone of their own accord when this is necessary. At the sides are attached several rings made from whalebone with which the net is looped to the pole at the top, and these ropes are tied firmly to the bottom corners. With this net a man will walk along the top of the cliff where the guillemots are sitting. He lets out enough rope to allow the net to reach to where the birds are sitting below, takes the ends in his hands and casts out the net. The birds fly up from their perches at the noise and become entangled in the net. The weight of the birds pulls the rope through the rings and the net forms a sack from which the birds cannot escape.

This method of bird catching is quite dangerous; for it can happen that a man may be pulled over the cliff by the falling of the net, and the sudden weight of the birds in it, and dashed to his death below. In places where this has happened the Americans stick a pole in the ground and do not hunt there again.

Starichok is a smaller species of diver with a sharp bill, a black beak and a lighter-colored underbelly. These birds are caught with traps which are placed at the entrance to their nesting holes. They may sometimes also be taken out of these holes by hand. Sometimes nets are hung over the area where *starichoks* breed and they are caught in this way.

The *uril* [shag] is a species of cormorant, and is completely black. Sometimes small numbers of them grow long white feathers or, to be more precise, hairs, on their breasts. These birds always perch on craggy rocks, and steep cliff-faces, and never further than five or ten versts away from the seashore. Urils are very inquisitive birds and always circle five or six times round a vessel as it approaches the shore. They are caught by using the same kind of nets as for the aras, but only at night. Otherwise on quiet, clear days a man will don clothes the same color as the rocks on which he sits, take a sack and place in front of him several decoy urils. The birds are attracted to the latter and the man then throws the sack over them. It has been noticed that urils do not see very well in bright sunlight.

At night when the urils have stopped calling and are asleep a man may creep up to them and pick off the one on the edge and take it some way down so that it does not frighten the others when it is taken. The urils will move up thinking they are yielding place to their comrades; then the man will try to grasp them quickly by the head and place them in a sack and then start on the next in line.

Uril eggs have white shells, taste very unpleasant and they have the peculiar characteristic that they cannot be hard-boiled.

Toporka and *ipatka* are two species of sea parrot, which are very similar. They nest in holes in the tundra and they are caught with traps or removed from their holes by hand. Thick gloves have to be worn for these birds can give nasty pecks. Their eggs are very tasty.

Toporkas and ipatkas sometimes fly several hundred miles out to sea so that they can never serve as a sign that land is near.

The seagulls [*chaika*] which breed in northwestern America are of different species. They usually lay their eggs on inaccessible cliff ledges to keep them safe from foxes, but it does not keep them safe from people who manage to climb up with the aid of poles and ropes to get them, although it costs many their life.

Seagulls' eggs have a white shell with green speckles. They can be used fresh until the middle of June; from then on they are usually hatched but they may be stored in fat.

Seagulls feed on fish and dead whales over which, together with many other birds, they wheel and call. Thus they show men the spot where the whale is floating. The Russians and the Americans do not use those dead whales as food which the birds will not peck at--this serves as the surest proof that the meat is harmful.

Albatrosses, which the Russians in America call "seven-sazhen seagulls", never appear in closed-in bays, but only fly in the open sea and sometimes for long distances. Their young are light black [*sic*] in color but may later become white. To this very day not one American knows where the albatrosses lay their eggs and raise their young.

Fulmars [*glupysh*] (*Petres*) are always to be found on the coast and for a great distance offshore. Near Unalashka they breed in great numbers. There are several different species, but white ones are rare.

In the Eastern Pacific so-called *sea robbers* [*mor-skie razboiniki*] (skuas) are often sighted. They chase the fulmars and take away the fish the latter have caught.

Near the shore breeds a small waterbird called the sea sparrow or *tugurushka*, which produces a very strange call at night time.

On Aliaska according to some accounts there is a small, extremely pretty bird with long legs and webbed feet (between its claws) which enables it to run along in the water in calm weather.

I shall not proceed to mention several other American birds in the expectation that Dr. Langsdorff, who has been there, will bring them to the notice of the world in his natural history of the region.

Fish

The main source of food for the inhabitants of the northern and northeastern coasts of Siberia, Kamchatka, the Aleutian Islands and northwestern America consists of fish, which does not always breed in the rivers flowing past the places in which they live, but come up-river from the sea in great shoals at certain times of the year. Unfavorable weather, which produces in the above-mentioned places very little in the way of edible crops, too few to feed people, has nevertheless rewarded them with another more reliable, if not more easily accessible source of food. The time when the fish will appear is so well known by the inhabitants that they place as much, if not more, reliance in it than others do in the ripening of a crop. Nearly all the fish coming up the river are of the salmon species, but not every species comes up every river, and in some rivers the fish go up early and in some late.

It has been noted that when the fish get near the mouth of the river they will not enter it until it rains, and afterwards they go up it very quickly. The inhabitants, in anticipation of this, block the river with a dam or fish weirs (*zapor*, as they are called in those parts). The fish cannot pass beyond these and are caught there. The preparation of these weirs beforehand has already been described elsewhere. The savages do not spend a great deal of time drying iukola. During rainy weather, however, the Russians gather it into specially made barns so that it does not rot and decompose from the damp. In hot weather flies land on the iukola, and produce a great number of larvae which harm the food. But just as a harvest of corn is not always successful, so the catch of fish is not always sufficient. This happens for various reasons: a heavy snowfall, or heavy rains in the springtime which cause the water in the rivers to rise to a great height and the speed of the current carries away the weirs and all the fish go right upstream.

When the fish are cleaned the men make sure not to leave any rubbish on the river banks, or they put it out at low tide, so that it will be washed away by the currents in the sea, otherwise the fish will cease coming up this river, or at least so I was assured.

The various species of salmon are called by the following names:

(1) *Chavycha* (Eastern salmon) -- the most tasty and fatty species, but it goes up the rivers less often and is more difficult to catch.

(2) *Gorbusha* (humpback salmon) -- this is rather similar to the *pal'ia* which can be caught in Lake Ladoga. The gorbusha is the smallest species and it always arrives in great numbers.

(3) *Krasnaia ryba* (lit. red fish, i.e. red salmon) -- (known) in Okhotsk as *niarka*). This appears first in almost all the rivers.

(4) *Khaiko*, which is like *lokh* (lake salmon).

(5) *Kizhuch* -- this comes up the rivers with the tide and goes down again with the outgoing tide and then remains in the bay in between. In Okhotsk this fish is known as the *keta* and goes well upstream on the Okhota.

All these fishes, when they go upstream against the rapid current, constantly lose weight, and when they reach calm water or a lake they remain there and die, so that many will never return to the sea again. A more lengthy description of this may be found in the writings of Mr. Krasheninnikov.

Salmon and trout come up some rivers to spend the winter in the lakes and in spring return to the sea.

Amongst the salt-water fish providing food for the inhabitants, the most important are the halibut (*paltus*) and cod (*treska*). In former times near Kad'iak there were many halibut, but now very few appear, but there are a great many cod which arrive off the shore in great shoals at springtime. Even in winter they can be caught in the sea not far from the island if the weather is calm enough to let the baidarkas go out to fish. Even though there are so many cod no stocks of them are laid in against the future. They are simply a temporary source of food until the reappearance of the salmon. In the region of Afognak fair quantities of halibut may be caught (a large species of flounder [*kambala*]. These are usually following smaller fish and are sometimes thrown onto the shore by the violence of the waves. Sometimes the men stick sharpened sticks into them and drag them out of the water in that way. Normally, however, they catch them with lines cast from the land.

Near Sitka there are many cod and halibut can be caught in certain places, even the whole winter through, when all there is for baiting the hooks is cuttlefish, of which these fish are extremely fond. Between Sitka and Jakobi Island in the spring there is such a large quantity of halibut that the whole bay, which is in places as much as five versts wide, seems fully of this fish. Near Sitka and Yakutat the halibut are very strong and Baranov used to say that he had seen one more than two sazhens long and its head weighed one pud and thirty pounds. Fish of this species are strong in relation to their size. When an American hooks a big halibut he never gives the line a sudden jerk in case the wood splits or the baidarka is capsized, so he draws it in and lets it out again until the halibut is exhausted; after this the fish can be killed with a blow on the head from a stick.

Herring [*sel'di*] only appear in one bay near the old port which is in consequence called Sel'dianyi proliv [Herring Bay]. In Sitka they arrive in March in great shoals, right under the fort itself, and remain there for about two weeks. During this period it would be a good idea to lay in stocks of them if only there were salt, but since there is none the local hunters are deprived of this source of food also.

Vakhnia, which in the town of Arkhangel'sk are called *navaga*, come in autumn and winter to the new harbor on Kad'iak--but not every year.

Kalaga and *kaiura* (in Kamchatka *riamzhi*) may be caught from time to time off the rocks. The wily ways of the latter fish has caused people to call it *kaiur* as workers in Kamchatka and America are called.

Near the rocks a fish with quite a large head in relation to its round body is sometimes caught. It has no bones and has an opening on its underbelly with the help of which it clings so fast to the rocks that it seems as though it grows there, and it is very difficult to prise it away.

The *ter'puga* [razor-fish] is a small fish so called because of the roughness of its skin--they are occasionally caught near the rocks.

Morskie byki [sea-bulls] enter the bays together with other fish in rough weather. Both they and the *kaiurs* make excellent fish soup.

Near the island of Atkha, at a depth of 80 sazhens, it is possible to catch a very beautiful fish, the name of which I could not discover.

On Kad'iak there are occasionally sea perch [*okun'*] which are in looks and taste very much like river ones.

It may be that I have omitted several species of fish but I hope that it will be easy to forgive me for this. Though I could make no detailed description this will naturally not be omitted by Doctor Langsdorff. At one time on Kad'iak they caught a fish which, according to Dr. Langsdorff, belonged to a tropical species which had of course strayed so far by accident.

VOCABULARY OF DIALECTS OF THE KOLIUZH PEOPLES, BETWEEN CHUGACH AND YAKUTAT BAYS

English	*Russian*	*Koliuzh*
Be well	Zdorovo zhivesh'	Veekhaskivzhet
Reply	Otvet	A-khateiat
This is bad	Eto khudo	Na ute
Let us trade	Davai torgovat'sia	Agun' ate.
Girl	Devka	Siaavit
Young girl	Molodaia devka	Chagyeiu kuchety siaavit
Dear one	Milen'kaia	Siakt
Man	Mushchina	Ka
Young man	Molodoi chelovek	Khva
Old man	Starik	Utysen-ka
Lad	Otrok	Gettuk
Old woman	Starukha	Sian
Beavers	Bobry	Iukhchi
Beaver tails	Khvosty bobrovye	Iukhsity
Many beavers	Mnogo bobrov	Siagytiin iukhchi
Go/come	Podi	Aku
Come here	Podi siuda	Aku-te
Farewell	Proshchai	Te-kuski
Go, farewell	Podi, proshchai	A te te
I	Ia	Khat
Thou	Ty	Vee
I want to eat	Est' khochu	Khagyanu vaga
I want to drink	Pit' khochu	In khitu vaga
Water	Voda	In
Fish	Ryba	Khat
Silver salmon	Kizhuch	Tliuk
Halibut	Paltus	Chatl'
Red salmon	Krasnaia	Kat
Humpback salmon	Gorbusha	Kvask
Dog salmon	Khaiko	Tyll'
King salmon	Chavycha	Tia
Cod	Treska	Chak
Hair seal	Ner'pa	Tsa
Sea lion	Siuch'	Taan
Sea lion whiskers	Usy siuch'i	Taan kitatsiagi
Sea lion pup	Siuchonok	Taan-etty
Fur seal	Kotik	Kon
Porpoise	Svinka	Chich'
Whale	Kit	Iagg
Whale bone	Usy kitovy	Iagy-khen
Bear	Medved'	Khuch'
Ermine	Gornostai	Ta
Marmot	Tarbagan	Tsakh
Ground squirrel	Evrashka	Tsetl'k
Hare	Zaets	Kakh
Sable	Sobol'	Kukh
Wild sheep	Dikoi baran	Chansiua
Deer	Olen'	Vottsikh

English	*Russian*	*Koliuzh*
(Elk) Moose	(Los') Sokhatoi	Tsysku
Wolf	Volk	Kouch
Squirrel	Belka	Tselkhan
Otter	Vydra	Kusta
Mussel, small black	Rakushka malaia chernaia	Kusta
White	Belaia	Ultlitlet
Turnips	Repki	Nits
Crawfish	Rak	Naaku
River beaver	Bobr rechnoi	Spyity
Tree	Derevo voobshche	Tliugu
Fir	El'	As
Larch	Listvenitsa	Gen
Yellow cedar	Dushnoe	Khagg
Sitka spruce	Chaga	Tliakh
(Driftwood) Redwood	(Vykidnoe) krasnoe derevo	Nykh
Alder	Ol'kha	Kiisis
Poplar	Topol	Tok
Stone	Kamen'	Te
Iron	Zhelezo	Kaets
Copper	Med'	Ik
Green copper	Zelenaia med'	Iknach
Tin	Olovo	Kouk
Lead bullets	Svintsovyia puli	Unatutytli
Powder	Porokh	Una-tukenny
Gun	Ruzh'e	Una
Spear on a handle	Kop'ë na ratovishche	Uakatl
Hand spear	Kop'ë ruchnoe	Kotlia
Big arrow	Bol'shaia strela	Ata
Small [arrow]	Malaia luchnaia	Chuinit
Bow	Luk	Siaks'
Ax	Topor	Senkhvavy
Knife	Nozh	Tlitta
Koniaga hatchet	Koniagskoi toporik	Khutta
Needle	Igla	Ta-aketl
Fire	Ogon'	Kan
Smoke	Dym	Chik
Firewood	Drova	Ken
Give	Podai	Ashei
Quick	Skoro	Chaiuk
Go	Poezzhai	Negekokh
Come	Priezzhai	Atekon' naekokh
Lay down	Lozhis'	Natta
To sleep	Spat'	Natapov
Get up	Vstavai	Sianyu
Get down	Sadis'	Kanyu
No	Net	Tlek
It is	Est'	Agu
Inhale (take snuff)	Niukhai	Isnykh
Vessel	Sudno	An
Skin baidara	Baidara lakhtashnaia	Tsiakokh
Wooden baidara	Baidara dereviannaia	Iakou
Wooden boat	Bot dereviannoi	Chat
Row	Grebi	Akha
Faster	Sil'nee	Tliaakuiakh
Mast	Machta	Kitliagas

English	*Russian*	*Koliuzh*
Day	Den'	Keiuvaia
Night	Noch'	Kha anna
Sun	Solntse	Kakan
Sky	Nebo	Kiiva
Month	Mesiats	Tys
Stars	Zvezdy	Kutkhanaga
Cloud	Oblako	Kuknats
Snow	Sneg	Tlet
Rain	Dozhd'	Siu
Ice	Led	Tyk
Wind	Vetr	Kilcha
Good weather	Dobraia pogoda	Eke kilcha
Bad weather	Khudaia pogoda	Tlek'kliushki kilcha
All night	Khorosho	Ek
Bad	Khudo	Tlek kliushki
Dark	Tomno	Kauchiket
Light	Svetlo	Kivaa
Hot	Zharko	Getta
Cold	Kholodno	Seat
Parka	Parka	Kuttets
Kamleika[?]	Kamleika ragduzhnaia	Atkhest
Nankeen shirt and kamleika	Rub. i kaml. kitaichataia	Tlikutets
Kerchief	Platok	Nakhlia
Mantle	Plashch	Kuu
Cloth mantle	Plashch sukonnoi	Kaets kuu
Moosehide mantle	Losinnoi plashch	Tsisk kuu
Squirrelskin parka	Parka evrashich'ia	Tselke kutes
Marmotskin parka	Parka tarbagan'ia	Tsiakh kutes
Marmotskin mantle	Plashch tarbaganii	Tsiakh ku-u
Beads	Biser	Kagut
White beads	Beloi biser	Nek Kagut
Blue beads	Goluboi biser	Tollo kagut
Red beads	Krasnoi biser	Kan kagut
Scissors	Nozhnitsy	Kasekhese
Comb	Greben'	Klyto
Ring	Persten' ili kol'tso	Tliak kanys
Hat	Shliapa	Shchakhu
Deerskin boots	Torbasy	Kan
Tobacco	Tabak	Kanch'
Snuff tobacco	Niukhai tabak	Akhlituch'
Frock coat (surtout) or stormcoat with buttons	Sertuk ili kapot s pugovitsami	Kanaamia
Mirror	Zerkalo	Tunakh-kaettin
	1	Tlek
	2	Tekh
	3	Netsk
	4	Taakun
	5	Keechin
	6	Takhatuusiu
	7	Tletuusiu
	8	Netskytyusiu
	9	Kuusiuk
	10	Chinkat

English	*Russian*	*Koliuzh*
	20	Tleeka
	30	Takhka
Sea	More	Etl'
Lake	Ozero	A
River	Reka	In-tak
Small river	Malen'kaia rechka	In-naku-u
Few	Malo	Kuvach'
Many	Mnogo	Siagetegin
Wave	Burun	Tyt
Died	Umer	Nanna
	Utit	Utogechok
Sick	Bolen	Ganniuk
He is dying	Umiraet	Tanannan
Health	Zdorov	Tlekotli gaianiak
Angry	Serdit	Tlekotl'-pushchku
To be angry	Serditsia	Kantu-gannuk
Bad man	Khudoi chelovek	Tlekotl' kykaoty tlinkit
Good man	Dobroi chelovek	Kykzotyiut tlinkit
Good girl	Khoroshaia devka	Iukke siavyt
Bad girl	Khudaia devka	Tlek-kliuske siavyt
Beauty	Krasavitsa	Tlekh-tlekh eke siavyt
I love you	Liubliu Ia tebia	Akhty-vaseku khet veo
I want to urinate	Mochit'sia khochu	Atliukh khatuvaga
I want to defecate	Isprazh. khochu	Kinty khatuava
I want to vomit	Blevat' khochu	Ashts khatuava
Let us sleep together	So mnoi liazhem spat'	I in nakkakheik kuski
Give	Darite	Akhchit'
I give	Dariu	Ichity-takhany
Give	Podari	Tuchitty
An able seamstress	Devka provor. shit' umeiushchaia	Sekuk oia vyt
Hut	Zhilo	An
Barabara (dwelling)	Bara bara	Ite
Cannon	Pushka	Unatlin
Spoon	Lozhka	Seltl'
Cup	Chashka	Tsik
Kettle	Kotel	Kontl'
People around Sitka	Narod okolo Sitki	Sitka-kogan
Chilkat people	Chilkhatskie	Chilkhat kogan
Strong man	Sil'noi chelovek	L'tli-chinka
Promyshlennik	Promyshlennik	Tsatyka
Warrior	Voin	Kva-aka
We want to live peacefully	My khotim mirno zhit'	L'tmo konkan ugan
Live at peace with us and nothing will happen	Vy s nami zhivite mirno i nikogo ne obizhaite	Ikhvan kun akhtugu-khet kakket cha-ekhkh nakaty
Friend	Drug	Akhekavu
Acquaintance	Znakomyi	Chitliok khasiaisu-ka
White	Beloe	Tleete-khety
Red	Krasnoe	Kaake-kety
Black	Chernoe	Tuche-khety
Green	Zelenoe	Nekhentok-ekhety

English	*Russian*	*Koliuzh*
Winter	Zima	Taaku
Summer	Leto	Kutaan
North	Sever	Khun
East	Vostok	Siaalakhet
South	Polden'	Gendy
West	Zapad	Ghan
Eagle	Orel	Chaak
Gull	Chaika	Kitliaty
Raven	Voron	Elyltl'
Duck	Utka	Kaakhu
Goose	Gus'	Taagok
Swan	Lebed'	Koktl'
Owl	Filin	Tsieko
Meat	Miaso	Tligi
Fat (or blubber)	Zhir	Iikh
Eggs	Iaitsa	Kot
Box	Iashchik	Kouk
Sarana lily	Sarana	Kukh
Bracken fern	Paporotnik	Kotlkh
Yellow sweet(?)	Zheltoe sladkoe	Kantok
Larch sap (gum?)	Sok'listvennichnyi	Siok
Raspberry	Malina	Tleko
Blackberry	Chernitsa	Kanata
Currant	Smorodina	Sshiakh
Strawberry	Klubnika	Ssioku
Cloudberry	Moroshka	Neikon
Grass	Trava	Chuukon
Father	Otets	Is
Mother	Mat'	Akhtlia
Brother	Brat	Akhonokh
Sister	Sestra	Akhtliak
Son	Syn	Akhgit
Daughter	Doch'	Akhsyi
Grandfather	Ded	Iltliko
Children	Deti	Togotki
Wife	Zhena	Akhlkhset
Head	Golova	Akhsian
Face	Litso	Igga
Eye	Glaza	Khavak
Hair	Volosy	Akhsiakhau
Animal wool	Sherst' na zvere	Akha
Teeth	Zuby	Akh'iu
Mouth	Rot	Akhke
Tongue	Iazyk	Tutliut
Ears	Ushi	Akhkuk
Hands	Ruki	Akhchin
Fingers	Pal'tsy	Akhkusy
Finger (toe) nails	Nogti	
Shoulders	Plecha	
Legs	Nogi	Ikus
Abdomen	Briukho	Akhik
Spine	Spina	Tushek
Buttock	Zhopa	Akhtuk
Male reproductive organ	Tainoi ud muzhskoi	Tliml'
Female reproductive organ	Tainoi ud zhenskoi	Kus

English	*Russian*	*Koliuzh*
A Russian	Ruskoi chelovek	Kuskekhan
Kad'iak islanders and Aliaksintsy	Kad'iakskie i Aliaks.	Kankoan
Chugaches	Chugachi	Kushek
Kinaitsy	Kinaets	Tisnakozn
Fox Islanders	Lis'evskie	Tiakha-koan
Yakutat people	Iakutatskie	Tliakhaikh-koan
Akoi people	Akoiskie	Akai-koan
Say	Skazhi	Kenennyk
Speak	Govori	Iukaten
Listen	Slushai	Keetsaakh
Fire (shoot)	Pali, streliai	Atuun
Chop	Koli	Okoltl
Cut	Rezh	Nekas
Sew	Shei	Kaka
Beat	Bei	Chak
Look	Smotri	Tleshyn
Cut	Rubi	Atkhut
Tear (imp.)	Deri	Nasetl
Dress	Odevaisia	Atuku
Put on shoes	Obuvaisia	Atykun
Undress	Razdevaisia	Agekh-kozyk
Cry	Krichi	Naik
Dance	Pliashi	Negetlekh
Sing	Poi pesni	Atkasi
Hush	Molchi	Iteketl
Fool	Durak	Tliakuski
Thief	Vor	Tautsaty
He stole	Ukral	Utautau
Hunt	Promyshliai	Kanaekokh
Call	Zovi	Kikhokh
Call	Klich'	Naip
Bring	Privezi	Aty-kakhtokha
Cook	Vari	Kaseta
Heat	Zhar'	Natsik
Bird down	Pukh ptichei	Kotl
Feather	Per'e	Tako
Land	Zemlia	Llin-kitaanny
Island	Ostrov	Kaat
Bay	Bukhta	Kseikh
Strait	Proliv	Sit
Sand bar	Mel'	Llin
Shallow	Melko	Ltle kaatmin
Deep	Gluboko	In-tlin
Far	Daleko	Naatle
Near	Blizko	Tleka-tliuunatli
Nauseating	Toshno	Khatukhletis
Too bad	Zhal'	Gak-sikee
To weep	Plakat'	Kak
To smile	Smeiat'sia	Atoiok
To laugh at	Nasmekhaet'sia	Katleius
Don't laugh	Ne nasmekhaisia	Iltlil' katleus
Chief	Toion	Ankau
Slave	Rab, nevol'nik	Kookh
Female slave	Nevol'nitsa	Siavyt kookh

English	*Russian*	*Koliuzh*
Dog	Sobaka	Ketl' (in Yakutat khauva)
Are there many?	Mnogo li?	Kunsa?
Is it far?	Daleko li?	Uvase ekunatli?
It is far	Daleko	Uvasekiizhe nalleka
Is it?	Est' li?	Agoke?
Funeral equipment	Na pominkakh igrushka	Kutetl'
Simple dance	Prostaia pliaska	Tleekh

VOCABULARY OF DIALECTS OF THE PEOPLES LIVING AROUND KINAI BAY

English	*Russian*	*Kinai*
Go/come	Podi	Uga
How did he walk?	Kakovo khodil?	Ukh?
Healthily	Zdorovo	Painzilia
I shall go	Poidu	Kkhyio
Girl	Devka	Kisna
Wife	Zhena	Sioo
Daughter	Doch'	Setsaa
Son	Syn	Siia
Relative	Rodnoi	Sitni
Give	Podai	Yiada
Bring	Prinesi	Siuilkat
Water	Voda	Piltni
Fire	Ogon'	Tazi
Sea	More	Tykaa roio nuty
River	Reka	Kytnu
Lake	Ozero	Bon
Many/much	Mnogo	Tynalatosa
Little/few	Malo	Maalchak
None	Netu	Kykol'
All	Vse	Tantskho
I want to eat	Est' khochu	Taschin
I want to drink	Pit' khochu	Pitli ktatliu
He went	Poekhal	Tazno
He arrived	Priekhal	Toaznik
Sun	Solntse	Nii
Month	Mesiats	Tliakaannu
Stars	Zvezdy	Sin
Weather	Pogoda	Talkotsit kanitsy
Spirit called up by sorcery	Dukh v koldovstve prizyvaemyi	Nustat-tlia
God (The old people think that if he loves someone he gives that person luck, but who created everything and where he is they do not know.)	Bog (Stariki dumaiut, chto on kogo liubit, tomu daet shchastie, a kto vse sozdal i gde on obitaet, togo ne znaiut.)	Nakkhtyltane

English	*Russian*	*Kinai*
	1	Tselkei
	2	Tykha
	3	Tokkhke
	4	Tenki
	5	Tsielialo
	6	Kozheini
	7	Kantseogi
	8	Ltakolli
	9	Lkhetsetkho
	10	Koliuzhun
	11	Tselkoikty
	12	Tykhaokty
	13	Tokaiukty
	14	Tinkeokhsty
	15	Tseliookty
	16	Kultsynokty
	17	Kantsaiolty
	18	Ltakaliokty
	19	Lkatsekhtokty
	20	Tseliootna
	30	Tatkhuliuzhun
	40	Tet-kuliazhun
	50	Tskelio-kuliazhun
	60	Kus-kuliuzhun
	70	Kantsioo-kuliazhun
	80	Ltakol-kuliazhun
	90	Etsitko-kuliazhun
	100	Otaoslian
Father	Otets	Stukta
Mother	Mat'	Anna
Uncle	Diadia	Azia ili zialia
Nephew	Plemiannik	Uzia
Son-in-law and brother-in-law	Ziat' i shurin	Slin
Father-in-law	Test'	Tsiastun
Brother	Brat	Kylia
Sister	Sestra	Tacha
Child	Rebenok	Tskaniken
Big brother	Bol'shoi brat	Agalia
Big sister	Bol'shaia sestra	Utalia
Old man	Starik	Usinta
Young	Molodoi	Kitl
Old woman	Starukha	Kisinta
Young girl	Molodaia devka	Kisenkoia
Good girl	Khoroshaia devka	Tygagaitlia
Bad girl	Khudaia devka	Tsiogolta
Good man	Dobroi chelovek	Tygagytlia
Bad man	Khudoi chelovek	Tsiogykhta
Angry	Serditoi	Kytsnanikhia
I love you	Ia tebia liubliu	Nanaaetsiut
To sleep	Spat'	Nogagostani
I	Ia	Sii
Thou	Ty	Nan
Give me	Dai mne	Ikhonda
To me	Ko mne	Sinta

English	*Russian*	*Kinai*
Hut	Zhilo	Kaiakh
What sort of hut?	Kakogo zhila?	Ntatu kaiakhtana?
What is it called?	Kak zovut?	Nchatu izhykilia?
Russian	Ruskoi	Kaziakhtan
Priest	Pop	Takinlias (koi krestit)
Day	Den'	Chan
Night	Noch'	Tliak
It dawns	Razsvetaet	Kogol tsiolia
Light	Svetlo	Talkon
Dark	Temno	Ilkhatl
Stone	Kamen'	Kalkhniki
Sea beaver (otter)	Bobr morskoi	Tupys
River beaver	Bobr rechnoi	Knuia
Black bear	Chornoi medved'	Altasi
Red bear	Krasnoi medved'	Anikhta
Lynx	Rys'	Kazno
Sable	Sobol'	Ktsiaosia
Otter	Vydra	Takhten
Mink	Norka	Tashicha
Muskrat	Vykhukhol'	Tuchiuta
Ermine	Gornostai	Kaoltsina
Wolf	Volk	Tekin
Dog	Sobaka	Tlika; skogolo
Glutton (wolverine)	Rossomakha	Tstukumytli
Deer (caribou)	Olen'	Pyttsikh
Wool, fleece, hair	Sherst'	Kgygo
Fox	Lisitsa	Kagvyiak, kaniultsa
Sheep	Baran	Niochi
Squirrel	Belka	Leka
Whale	Kit	Tashlin
Hair seal	Ner'pa	Kutsiatli
Porpoise	Svinka	Tsilvi
Beluga	Beluga	Koiusi
Killer whale (orca)	Kosatka	Tsykinka
Bird	Ptitsa	Kakasli
Swan	Lebed'	Kokys
Goose	Gus'	Nutake
Duck	Utka	Agaslia
Gull	Chaika	Bach' chichakoia
Crane	Zhuravl'	Untatlia
Eagle	Orel	Datlika
Sandpiper, snipe	Kulichok	Tsekatukalkesa
Eggs	Iaitsa	Kgazia
Feather	Per'e	Kitsia
Down	Pukh	Ktuk kaetken'
(Type of porcupine) niunik	(Rod. dikob.) niunik	Nini
Iron	Zhelezo	Ikot'e tain
Copper	Med'	Chuchuna
Tin and lead	Olovo i svinets	Tain toga
Iron (adj.)	Zheleznoi	Soos
Mica	Sliuda	Kutsiakty
Fish	Ryba	Tlioka
Meat	Miaso	Kychonna, kytsyn
King salmon	Chavycha	Tliokhakz

English	*Russian*	*Kinai*
Red salmon	Krasnaia	Tykkh'khoia
Silver salmon	Kizhuch'	Nutliagy
Humpbacked salmon	Gorbusha	Kogona
	Gol'tsy	Ustliagy, siakylia
	Seiga	Tliaga
Parka	Parka	Togaa, stgianka
Shirt	Rubakha	Sisyona
Gut kamleika	Kishoshnaia kamleika	Makez'e
Leather (chamois) kamleika	Ragdushnaia kamleika	Kystoga
	Torbasy kamleika	Siolstlia
Marmot parka	Tarbagan'ia parka	Kygytoga
Ground squirrel parka	Evrashech'ia parka	Kumia toga
Marmot	Tabagan	Kykhy
Ground squirrel	Evrashka	Kuisia
	Rogduga	Kyes
	Ishkat	Khaki
Beads	Biser	Naaltchetkoia, siaskoskoia
Coral beads	Korol'ki	Tynzikeika
Halibut	Paltusina	Siagik
Cod	Treska	Atkiiak
Iukola	Iukola	Vava
	Nakhoi	L'lioanizha
Herring	Sel'di	Kutsnakokha
Haddock	Vakhnia	Tliozntita
Forest	Les	Tsvalia
Fir	El'	Tsiatlia
Larch	Listven'	Kalkty
Birch	Bereza	Chukkhuia
Mountain Ash	Riabina	Dkonia
Alder	Ol'kha	Kankyia
Poplar	Topol'	Asni
Willow	Tal'nik	Tundelkii
Berries	Iagody	Kenka
Cloudberry	Moroshka	Kytlia
Raspberry	Malina	Kolkaa
Crowberry	Shoksha [Shiksha]	Tkylinkyka
Cranberry	Brusnitsa	Khykka
	Kniazhenitsa	Nauiankytlia
Blueberry	Golubika	Tsykika
Currant	Smorodina	Nuutgyn'
Blackberry	Chernika	Kantsia
Red current	Krasnaia smorodina	Tsioluntlia
Berries on sweet-briar	Iagody na shipovnike	Kis
White hazel	Kalina	Chun'tsia
Strawberry tree(?)	Toloknianka	Tyntsizi
	Koren'ia	
Bracken fern	Paporotnik	Okh
Sarana lily	Sarana	Kynastli
	Kutagarnoe	Oltsnakutsia
Yellow sweet (A particular plant which is suitable for kissel [jelly], kasha and in flour.)	Zheltoe sladkoe (Rastenie osobago roda, koe goditsia v kisele, kashe i v muku.)	Kyndiaskitsi ktlilia

English	*Russian*	*Kinai*
I want	Khochu	Tsetasiu
I do not want	Ne khochu	Kuchu utstasia
Give	Podai	Anta
Bring	Prinesi	Siatunkkheilkit
Send him	Poshli ego	Ktaas dats nyn dinia
Sooner	Skoree	Ugasta
Go/come	Podi	Un
Run fast	Begi skoro	Uga tylkus
Hot water	Goriachaia voda	Nagolykhsi vyltni
Cold water	Kholodnaia voda	Nagol kytsy
Firewood	Drova	Tsika
Grass	Trava	Kichen
Earth	Zemlia	Altnen
Clay	Glina	Takeitline
Thunder	Grom	Ktytni
Lightning	Molniia	Siobylia
Bow	Luk	Tsylten
Arrow	Strelka	Izin
Spear	Kop'e	Tagin
Attack	Napadenie	Ulinant nal'liok
Killed	Ubit	Chitnakh
He killed	Ubil	Chitlion
They killed	Ubili	Chekitliok
Sit	Sadis'	Nitsiut
Get up	Vstavai	Ktaniltsit
He fled	Ubezhal	Enishaaltan
They fled	Ubezhali	Tynata enita altatl
Parsley	Petrushka	Kyntyntli
	Makarsha	Tanaliona
Fat	Zhir	Tsinty, tliogy
Sheep	Baranii	Nutsitsinty
Deer	Olenii	Pytsikhtsinty
Hair seal	Nerpichii	Kutsiaaltsinty
Moose, elk	Los', ili sokhatoi	Tanakia
Wild goat	Iaman	Spa
Wood-sorrel	Kislitsa	Kshi
Sky	Nebo	Kuian
Smoke	Dym	Taskyty
Clouds	Oblaka	Kkhas
Fog	Tuman	Nianiki
Snow	Sneg	Azzakh
Rain	Dozhd'	Alkun
Cold	Kholodno	Ktekkhuts
Warm	Teplo	Tkynagalgys
Frost	Moroz	Ktekkhots
Hot	Zharko	Nagolgos'
Ice	Led	Ten
Hail	Grad	
Weather	Pogodia	Kanitsi
Wind	Vetr	Iutalnon
East	Vostok	Ktultlia
West	Zapad	Sudutsini
North	Sever	Tsiniani
South	Polden'	Kykhkats
Bold	Udaloi	Tagyltyen

English	*Russian*	*Kinai*
Russian fur hunter	Promyshlennik	Tkogoilten
Warrior	Voin	Tarylchaakyn
Archer	Strelok	Tkosin-kteltesen
Thief	Vor	Kheteisin
Lazy awkward person	Lenivoi-neprovornoi	Tseket niken
Commandant	Nachal'nik	Kysska
Worker	Rabotnik	Ten'a
Slave	Nevol'nik	Ulchana
Yurta	Iurta	Kania
Kitchen	Povarnia	Katlist
Bath	Bania	Nli
Communal sleeping room	Zhupan	Nlekoia
Handicraft woman	Rukodel'naia devka	Kots kogain kon'kelki
To go on campaign	Pokhodom itti	Tuchkiliana
Young man	Chelovek	Kokhtaana
Head	Golova	Aisiagge
Forehead	Lob	Siantukh
Hair	Volosy	Stsygo
Bald	Pleshivoi	Kotsynulkaten
Ears	Ushi	Stsoga
Brows	Brovi	Skazytli
Eyes	Glaza	Snaga
Eyelashes	Resnitsy	Snootutlia
Mouth	Rot	Syziak
Tongue	Iazyk	Stsylio
Teeth	Zuby	Szakoistli
Throat	Gorlo	Szaka
Neck	Sheia	Skhkazh
Chest	Grud'	Sita
Shoulders	Plecha	Sasyk
Arm	Ruka }	Skona
Arms	Ruki	
Leg	Noga }	Skaetlna
Legs	Nogi	
Belly	Briukho	Stsiutlia
Spine	Spina	Sinikh
Ribs and bones	Rebra i kosti	Tsintsiu
Body	Telo	Sigis
Meat	Miaso	Tsyn
Guts	Kishki	Sintsika
Rump	Zadnitsa	Skkhy
Male reproductive organ	Tainoi ud muzhskoi	Stskosa
Female reproductive organ	Tainoi ud zhenskoi	Stsina
To suck	Sosat'	Lech'
To defecate	Isprazhniat'sia	Styikkhat
To vomit	Blevat'	Niantvakh
To fornicate	Bludit'	Stunaetsiu
Look	Smotri	Niitliant
See	Vidish'	Niiytliantu
I do not see	Ne vizhu	Kuchiu znashliaakie
Hear	Slyshu	Kydykntiasnis
I do not hear	Ne slyshu	Kudu kuchiu kidukysnik
Freely	Vol'no	Geichuten

English	*Russian*	*Kinai*
To smile	Smeiat'sia	Chaaglekh
To cry	Plakat'	
To joke	Shutit'	Chichuuli
I joke	Shuchu	Isu
Speak	Govori	Kyinas
I speak	Govoriu	Kansiasia
Say	Skazyvai	Nukheilnyk
You lie	Lzhosh'	Gyichit
True	Pravda	Kludets
False	Nepravda	Khenchit
He drowned	Utonul	Nudalkat
Killed	Ubit	Tikeitliok
He died	Pomer	Chichok
I cannot	Ne mogu	Chinakh
Sick	Bolen	Chitazny
Healthy	Zdorov	Chtatnuchok
Strong	Silen	Chageisty
Wet	Mokro	Nokeitliak
Dry	Sukho	Atnaalkan
Baidara	Baidara	Baaty
Baidarka	Baidarka	Kankhvan
Birchbark boat	Berestenaia lodka	Bakaa
Oar	Veslo	Kaniity
Go	Poezzhai	Ogotynias
Bring (not in own hands)	Privezi	Tungamlchitl
Bring (in own hands)	Prinesi	Sinukailkit
Carry away	Otvezi	Nugatiailnis
Carry away	Otnesi	Bytsiaa
Give back	Otdai	Liokaityiltsit
Tie	Viazhi	Nulkhalia
Cut	Rubi	Yntsiatl
Burn	Zhgi	Bokanaiktyyltliut
Row	Grebi	Takeitsykh
Strongly	Sil'no	Uga
Put	Kladi	Nyniltatlia
Trade	Torgui	Kenkat
Sell	Prodai	Kkhoniltatlia
What are you asking?	Chto prosish'	Etakoninzen
Pour	Lei	Mankeitlesh
Beat	Bei	Badeino
Untie	Razviazhi	Kodyltiud
Shoot	Streliai	Kteiltesia
Mosquitoes	Komary	Tsykh
Midges	Moshka	Kyl'ytse
Spittle	Plevok	Tomm
Mouse	Mysh'	Tlinaa
Frog	Liagushka	Nogoia
A smith or someone who knows how to work iron and copper	Kuznets ili kto kovat' umeet zhelezo i med'	Nukatsten
Leaf tobacco	Tabak lištovoi	Kytgon
Ground (e.g. flour)	Molotoi	
Birch bark	Beresta	Chokkhoia
(Vessels of birchbark)	(Posuda iz beresty) Tuiakh	Nuzziakoe

English	*Russian*	*Kinai*
Tree sulphur (pine gum?)	Sera drevesnaia	Chakh
Burning sulphur	Sera goriuchaia	Chiltykkhos
Sea water;salt	(Tozhe chto morskaia voda) sol'	Nuty
Salty	Solono	Nuteenys
Sweet	Sladko	Toolnes
Bitter	Gork'o	Chogolnek
Sorcerer	Koldun	Yleken
Ax	Topor	Kytliasi
Knife	Nozh	Kiziaki
Spear	Kop'e	Tachim
White	Belo	Talkei
Black	Cherno	Taltan
Red	Krasno	Tigaltil
Yellow	Zhelto	Titltsiagi
Blue	Sine	Okyn-ilkei
Clean	Chist	Badkaialtsel'
Sweep (imp.)	Meti	Iiunkanitlis
Scrape (imp.)	Skrebi	Kizziokh
Dig	Kopai	Kekat
Cook	Vari	Liach'
Fry	Zhar'	Kiltis
Cut (imp.)	Rezh'	Kodyltsiut
Eat	Esh'	Nlylkat
Take snuff	Niukhai	Naktut niltus
Drink	Pei	Nytnun
Sleep	Spi	Nylteiltak
Where did he go?	Kuda poshol?	Untaltutaik?
I want to sleep	Spat' khochu	Nultsistaitny
Spoon	Lozhka	Taga
Labret	(Choshka) kaluga	Nuzgi
Trough	Koryto	Mokali
Bed	Postelia	Stiilia
Blanket	Odeialo	Tsta
Poor man	Bedniazhka	Ukh
Do not be angry	Ne obizhai	Chabatyl' uku
I am sorry for you	Zhal' mne tebia	Nogyistat
Let us go	Poshli	Untyni
Call	Klich'	Mukhonzil
Shut	Zatvori	Kaiuknelkat
Open	Otvori	Chaknelkat
Do not steal	Ne vorui	Tseiaknet iiski
Do not lie, do not deceive	Ne lgi, ne obmanyvai	Ynchada geinchitku
Live well	Zhivi khoroshen'ko	Kovastezi tu
Tea	Chai	Ynda
Do not be afraid	Ne boisia	Chedychel chiku
Coward	Trus	Chagichek
Brave	Smelyi	Kochucheistik
He is a good talker	Govorit' master	Kits kanagi chudytnisen
I do not know how	Ne umeiu	Katsikateitysny
Don't you know?	Ne znaesh'?	Siun?
Nothing	Nichego	Kykkholia
All	Vse	Taen'tsko

English	*Russian*	*Kinai*
No	Net	Kocho
Kad'iak person	Kad'iakskoi	Ultsch'na
Chugach person	Chugacha	Tatliakhtana
Copper River person	Mednovskoi	Otnokhtana
Kolosh (Tlingit)	Kolosha	Tosh kolioshokh
Fox Islander	Lis'evskoi	Takheiuna
Aliaksa person	Aliaksinskoi	Nieskhakh-itina
Tundra people, beyond the Sushitna and Knyk	Tundrennye, za Sushitnoi i Knykami	Galtsiani
Tundra people, beyond Lake Iliamna	Tundrennye za Iliamnoi	Ktsialtana
People closer to the sea, who have long arrows	K moriu blizhe, u koikh dolgiia strely	Tutna
Those who go with dog teams still further into the tundra	Eshche koi esdiat na sobakakh dale sikh v tundre	Tundysiukh-tana
Vessel	Sudno	Aliutak
Sail	Parus	Tugis
Take a sniff of tobacco	Niukhai tabak	Tsnykh tyk tyltys
Pray (imp.)	Molisia	Gok nuiltli

INDEX

Afognak I., 89, 112, 114, 120, 122, 147, 192.
Agattu I., 93, 94.
Aglagomiuts, 197.
Aleksandrovsk artel, Kinai Bay, 192, 195.
Aleutian Islands, 207.
Aleuts, 86, 96, 170, 202, 208, 209, 212; clothing of, 101.
Alexander I, Emperor (1801-1825), 2, 9, 10, 14.
Aliagnagomiuts, 197.
Aliaksintsy, 86, 118, 148, 161, 193, 196, 197, 202, 210, 211, 218.
Aliaska (Aliaksa) (Alaska Peninsula), 98, 115, 225.
Alitok, Cape, 191-192.
Americans (natives of Russian America). See under ethnic name.
Americans, of U.S.A., 127, 215; alleged participants in Koliuzh attack on Sitka, 189; shipmasters rescue victims, 190.
Amlia I., 126, 127.
Animals, land:
  bears, 208-209;
  wolves, 209-210;
  foxes, 93, 210-211;
  hares, 211;
  polar foxes,
  lynxes,
  minks,
  wild deer (caribou), 212;
  wild sheep,
  elk,
  wild goats,
  wolverines, 213;
  marmots, 213-214;
  sables,
  squirrels, 214;
  rabbits,
  muskrats,
  ermine,
  mice, 215;
  hedgehog (porcupine), 215-216;
  dogs, 213, 216.
Animals, amphibious:
  otters, 105, 216;
  beavers, 216;
  sea otters, 217-218;
  walrus, 219;
  sea lion, 93, 117, 120-121, 219-221;
  seal, 221;
  sea cows, 222-223;
  sea cats (fur seals), 223;
  whales, 122, 128, 131, 175, 176, 223-224;
  killer whale (orca), 131, 225;

porpoise, 129, 174, 225;
beluga, 225.
Angara R., 28, 29.
Aniva Bay, Sakhalin I., 9, 11.
Anson, George, Baron (1697-1762), English navigator, 121.
Atkha I., 105, 126, 127, 192, 233.
Attu I., 93, 94, 129, 146.

Baidara, 86, 87, 95, 99.
Baidarka, 112, 114-115, 117, 122, 125, 133, 168, 178, 194, 196, 202-204, 218, 222, 224, 228.
Barabinsk Steppes, 26, 142.
Baranov, Aleksandr Andreevich (1746-1819), chief manager, R.A.Co. colonies, 89, 102, 104-105, 122, 123, 171, 172, 223, 233.
Baranov Island, 192.
Barents, Wilhelm (d. 1597), Dutch navigator, 99.
Beads, 149.
Bering Bay (Iakutat), 106, 192.
Bering I., 192, 211, 220.
Bird hunting, 195, 229.
Birds, land:
eagles, 226;
ravens, 210, 226;
magpies,
partridges,
larks, 226;
sandpipers, 117, 226,
humming birds,
cranes,
herons, 227.
Birds, water:
swans,
geese, 227;
ducks, 228-229;
divers, 229;
seaparrots, 108, 230;
seagulls, 230;
albatross, 130, 230;
fulmars, 128, 130, 230;
skuas, 128, 231.
Bobrovaia (Sea Otter) Bay, 194.
Bol'Sheretsk, Kamchatka, 90.
Bristol Bay, 197.
Brusenin, Vasilii (?), R.A.Co. employee, Kad'iak, 117.
Bukharin, Capt. 2nd Rank, commandant, port of Okhotsk, arrests Khvostov and Davydov, 1806, 12.
Buksgevden, Fedor Fedorovich (1750-1811), Count, Commander-in-chief of Russian army in Finland, 14, 16.
Buriat Steppe, 20.
Buriats (Bratskie), 29-30; shamans of, 32.
Bystry Strait, Uganak I., 117.

Chin'iatsk (Chiniak) Bay, Kodiak I., 101, 113, 117.
Chin'iatsk, Cape, Kodiak I., 101, 120, 124.
Chugaches, 149 n., 176, 193, 195, 197, 202, 218;

resistance to Russians, 170; exchanging of names, 170; seal hunting methods, 222.
Chugatsk Bay (Prince William Sound), 118, 192, 197, 227.
Copper R., 192; exploration by Russians, 200, 212; rumored to be cannibals, 174.
Copper R. people, 149 n.; resistance to Russians, 189; metal trade of, 199.

Davydov, Gavriil Ivanovich (1784-1809), Lieutenant. character, 19; early career, 22; enters R.A.Co. service, 3, 22; 1806-1807: raid on Japan, arrest in Okhotsk, 12; escape, 13; death, 16; publication of book, 17.
Dubenskii, Andrei, cossack staman, founder of Krasnoiarsk (1628), 28.
D'Wolf, John (1779-1872), American shipmaster. 1805: sells *Juno* at Sitka, 9, 16.

Earthquakes, 130.
Elovoi (Spruce) I., 122.
Evrashech'ia (Marmot) I., 147, 192.
Exiles, at Angara R. salt works, 28-29.

Fish, methods of catching, 123, 231;
salmon, types of, 232;
halibut, 232-233;
cod, 172, 232-233;
herring, 233;
see also Iukola.
Four Mountains, Island of, 207.
Fur trade, 29.

Hemekerk (Heemskerck), Jakob, Dutch navigator who, in 1596, with Barents, sought Northwest Passage, 99.

Iakuts, boats, 46; Tatar origin of, 76-77; habitations, 77; clothing, 77; character, 77; diet, 71, 72, 77-78; kumiss, 78; marriage, 78; keeping cattle in yurtas, 79; shamans, 79; religious beliefs, 80-81; caravan drivers, 54-55; tobacco use, 62; iron knives, 141; mental illness, 139; songs, 184.
Iakutsk, 40, 140.
Iakutsk-Okhotsk route, stations on, 48-54; Aldan R. to Allakh-Iun R. stretch, 54-63; Belaia R., 55, 62; varnaks (robbers), 55-56, 57, 67; Allakh-Iun R., Maia trib., 63, 64, 65, 135; Aiamiakon (Oimiakan), 64, 135; use of horses and reindeer on, 65; Ken-chai glacier, 69-70; "drunken grass", 70; Iudoma Cross, 72, 73, 74, 135; Iudoma R., Maia trib., 74, 135; Maia R., Aldan trib., 74; Urak R., 75, 135; Meta, Iakut settlement, 76, 135.
Iakolitsk Cape, Kad'iak I., 150.
Iasak (fur tax) collected in Kurile Islands, 92.
Igak (Ugak) Bay, 191.

Igvetsk (Afognak) artel, Afognak I., 192.
Iliamna L., 197.
Ioasaf, Archimandrite, 119, 180.
Irkutsk, 27, 28, 29, 45-46, 142.
Irkutsk gubernia, settlers in, 31.
Iukola (dried fish), 83, 119, 120, 123, 174, 176, 193, 201, 202, 231.
Ivanov, Aleksei, Lebedev Company hunter, leads expedition to interior, 1790's, 200-202.

Japanese, 6, 7.

Kad'iak Cape, 115.
Kad'iak (Kykhtakh) I., 6, 89; climate, 204-206; position, 147; vegetation, 207.
Kaiurs (native workers), 107, 114, 118, 122, 159, 178, 191, 192-193, 196.
Kakmaisk (Katmai), on Aliaska Pen., 192.
Kamchatka, 130.
Kamyshatsk Bay, 199, 206; volcano near, 206-207.
Khanokov, Petr Ivanovich (1743-1813), Admiral, commander of the port of Kronshtadt, 1.
Khvostov, Alexsandr Ivanovich, State Councillor, 1, 2.
Khvostov, Nikolai Aleksandrovich (1776-1809), early career, 1; enters Russian-American Company service. 1803: sails *Sv. Elizaveta* from Okhotsk to America; 1805: sails *Sv. Mariia* from Okhotsk to America, 5; raids Japanese ports, 12; escape from Okhotsk, 13; bravery in battle, 1808, 14-16, 133; character, 18-19; death, 16.
Kiakhta, Russo-Chinese trading center, 29.
Kinai (Kenai) Bay (Cook Inlet), 146, 192.
Kinai people, 149 n., 194, 195, 196; customs and beliefs, 197-200, 202, 218.
Kitovye (whale) Islands, 192, 208, 210, 211, 226.
Kizhuetsk (Kizhuyak) Bay, 112.
Koliuzhes (Kolosh, Tlingit), 106-107; treatment of slaves, 180; 1802: destruction of Russian settlement at Sitka, 189; attacks on American trading vessels, 197; status of women, 165; sheep hunting with dogs, 213; value of ermine, 215; sea-otter hunting, 218.
Koniagas, 101, 113-114; appearance, 148; adornment, 148-150; amusements, 116; arithmetic, 185; astronomy, 185-186; baidaras, baidarkas, 202-204; burial rites, 179-180; calendar, 186; character, 155-163, child upbringing, 163-165; clothing, 150-153; dances, 184; diet, 173-177; distaste for flogging, 116, 163; dwelling, 154-155; festivals, 107-111, 183-184; fortifications, 173; games, 182-183; geography, 185; government, 190-191; slaves, 190-191; handicrafts, 186; hunting implements, 204, 215; illness and treatment, 177-179; hostages (*amanaty*), 106; kasiats (wise men), 109, 184; kazhims (festival huts), 107-154; marriage customs, 182; concept of origins, 185; the poor, 168; population, 147, 194; religion, 170-172, 181; resistance to Russians, 105, 168-170, 188-190; slaves, 159, 162, 190-191;

songs, 184; tobacco, use of, 172, 176; warfare, 187-190; status of women, 165-167.
Korovye (Seal) Islands (the Pribylovs), 220.
Krasheninnikov, Stepan Petrovich (1711-1755), investigator of Kamchatka, 232.
Kruzenshtern, Ivan Fedorovich (1770-1846), Admiral, 5.
Ktsialtans, interior tribe beyond L. Iliamna, 197.
Kuchok I. (Nuchek?), 197.
Kuikhpagomiuts, 197.
Kukhtui R., common outlet with Okhota R., 84, 134.
Kuliugum (from Kuliugmiut? now Kuliuk) Cape, 115.
Kurile Islanders, 92-93.
Kurluk (Karluk) R., 192.
Kurile Islands:
  Alait (Alaid) I., 87, 91, 131;
  Makaronshi I., 131;
  Matmai I., 9;
  Annekotan (Onnekotan) I., 92, 131;
  Poramushir (Paramushiro) I., 91, 92, 130, 131;
  Shirinka I., 131;
  prevalence of earthquakes, 206.

Langsdorff, Georg Heinrich von (1774-1852), German naturalist with Rezanov in Russian America (1805-1806), 16, 234.
La-Pérouse, Jean François de Galaup, comte de (1741-1788), French navigator, in North Pacific in 1786 and 1787, 150.
Lebedev, Iakutsk merchant, 74.
Lebedev Company, and interior expedition of Ivanov, 200-202.
Lena R., 29; barges, 46; gorge below Boiarsk, 34; "Shchoki" (cheeks) formation, 37; red sandstone mountain, at mouth of Molva R., 41; "Stolby" (columns) formation, 44; settlements, Kachuga Landing to Iakutsk, 30-45; settlers, poverty of, 46, 140; tributaries, Irkutsk to Iakutsk, 32-45.

Malinovskii artel, Afognak I., 192.
Mednyi (Copper) I., 211.
Miasoedov, Vice-Admiral, 16.
Milevsk Aleuts, 208.
Mordvinov, Nikolai Semenovich (1754-1845), Count, statesman, 90.
Moscow, 24.
Musk, of wild goat (kaparga), 137.

Nikolaevsk artel, Kinai Bay, 192.
Novo-Arkhangel'sk (Sitka), 6.
Nuchek (Hinchinbrook) I., artel, 192.

Odinochka, definition, 115, 191.
Okhota R., 84, 132, 134, 135.
Okhotsk, description of, 82; dogs of, 83; fish, a staple food, 83; clothing of inhabitants, 83; difficulties as port, 84, 132-134.

Opal'sk Mt., Kamchatka, 91.

Partovshchink, definition, 194.
Paul's Harbor (Pavlovskii gavan'), Kad'iak, 102-103.
Peregrebnye Islands (Note: the Barren Islands, not to be confused with Peregrebnyi I. in Pavlof Bay), 147.
Petropavlovsk, Kamchatka, 6.
Polevoi, Aleksei Evseevich, R.A.Co. agent in Okhotsk, 82; partner of Shelikhov, 137, 140, 143.
Pillar (*stolb*), new island northwest of Unalashka (probably the island of Sv. Ioann Bogoslov, which rose from the sea 18 May 1796), 96.

Reindeer, as steeds, 72.
Rezanov, Nikolai Petrovich (1764-1807), Chamberlain, R.A.Co. official, 3, 22; mission to Japan with *Nadezhda* and *Neva*, 5; to America on *Mariia* from Petropavlovsk, 6; letter to Khvostov and Davydov, 29 August 1805, 7-8; codicil, 24 September 1806, 10-11.
Rhubarb, 28.
Rubtsov odinochka, Afognak I., 114, 120, 122, 123.
Rumiantsev, Nikolai Petrovich (1754-1826), Count, Minister of Commerce, 5, 8.
Russian-American Company, 3, 4; administration of native peoples: hostages, 106; settlements, 191-192; hunting expeditions, 194-195; payment of hunters, 195.
Russian language, variations of in Irkutsk gubernia, 32.

St. Paul I. (Pribylov Islands), 6.
St. Paul (New Harbor, Kad'iak). See Paul's Harbor.
St. Petersburg, 143.
Sakhalin I., 6, 7.
Salt works, on Angara R., 28-29; on Kuta R., 34.
Sandwich Islands, 119.
Sapozhnikov (Bisar?), promyshlennik, 113.
Sarana lilies, 196.
Sarychev, Gavriil Andreevich (1763-1831), Admiral, 129, 146, 194 n.
School, failure of at Kad'iak, 1805, 181.
Scurvy, 123.
Seamen, incompetence of, 87, 88, 89, 90.
Seguak (Seguam) I., 125, 126.
Selifanov (Selifontov), Ivan Osipovich (d. 1822). 1796: Governor-General of Irkutsk and Kolyvan, Senator; 1802-03: Governor-General of Siberia, 14, 143.
Semchin, bosun on *Elisaveta*, 1802, Okhotsk to Kad'iak, 82.
Semidi I., 195.
Shelikhov, Grigorii Ivanovich (1747-1795), merchant, 89; estimate of population, 194.
Shelikhov, Sidor, manager of R.A.Co. office in Okhotsk, 92.
Shields, James, 1794: builder of the *Phoenix*, 119.
Shilkap Cape, near Okhotsk, 132.
Shipbuilding at Okhotsk, faults of, 82, 87-88, 98, 127.

Ships:
Aleksandr Nevskii, galiot. 1801: left Okhotsk, brought epidemic to Atkha I.; October 1802: arrived Kad'iak, 105; 3 May 1803: left Kad'iak for Yakutat, 120.
Avos' (Davydov), 9.
Dobroe namerenie, built at Okhotsk for Billings expedition. 1789: wrecked at launching, 85.
Juno. 1804: (D'Wolf), arrival Sitka, sold to R.A.Co.;
Mariia (Khvostov), Aug. 1805: Okhotsk to America, 5. 1805: (Khvostov), Sitka to California, 9.
Nadezhda, sloop. 1803-1806: (Kruzenshtern), round-the-world voyage, 5; May 1805: Japan to Petropavlovsk, 6.
Neva, sloop. 1803-1806: Lisianskii, round-the-world voyage, 5.
Ol'ga, built on Kad'iak. 3 May, left for Unalashka, 120.
Orel (Note: probably the *Severo-vostochnyi orel*, or *Severnyi orel*; 1791: sent to Unalashka I. by Shelikhov and Golikov; 1792: Okhotsk to Andreianov Islands; 1799: wrecked on Chugach coast), 90.
Phoenix, R.A.Co. vessel. 1794: built by James Shields at Voskresenskaia gavan'; 1798: (Shields), Kad'iak to Okhotsk; 1799: lost on return voyage, 119.
Sv. Ekaterina. 30 May 1803: left Kad'iak for Yakutat, 122.
Sv. Elisaveta, R.A.Co. vessel, built in Okhotsk. 1802: (Khvostov), Okhotsk to Kad'iak I., 82, 105, 106; 1803: Kad'iak to Okhotsk, 4, 134.
Zosima i Savvatii. 1792: voyage of misadventure, 89.
Shipwrecks, 118-119.
Shishkov, Admiral, befriends Davydov, gets him to compile book, 17ff.
Shteingeil, Ivan Fedorovich, Baron, Governor at Tobol'sk, 82, 143.
Shteingeil, Vladimir Ivanovich (1783-1862), Baron, in service at Okhotsk from 1802; Decembrist, 82.
Shuekh (Shuyak) I., 119, 147.
Siberian route, Kazan to Irkutsk:
Kazan, 24, 143;
Okhansk (on Kama R.),
Perm,
Kungur,
Ekaterinburg, 25;
Tobol'sk, 25, 29, 142;
Ishim, 25;
Shadrynsk,
Ural Mts.,
Barabinsk Steppes, 26;
Tomsk, 27, 142;
Tom R.,
Achinsk, former town, 27;
Krasnoiarsk, 27-28, 142;
Kacha Tatars, 27;
Dubenskii, Ataman, founder of Krasnoiarsk (1628), 28;
Nizhneudinsk, 28, 31;
Saltworks, Angara R., 28.
Sitka Bay (Norfolk Sound), 190.
Sitka (Baranof) I., 6.

Sitkha (Novo-Arkhangel'sk), destroyed by Koliuzh (Tlingit), 1802, 105.
Sitkhinak I., 119, 147.
Slobodchikov, Sysoi, hunter, Kad'iak I., 102.
Sushitna R., 216-217.
Sutkhum I., 192, 195, 196.
Sv. Iona, near Okhotsk, 132.
Solov'ev, Ivan, Russian peredovshchik, atrocities against Aleuts, 188.

Tanaga I., 94, 95.
Three Saints Bay, 191, 206, 216.
Tide effect (whirlpools (suloi) or riptides), 98-98.
Tobacco, use of, 172, 176, 181, 182.
Traps, 211.
Tropin, Iakutsk merchant, contest with bear, 74.
Tsukli (Montague) I., 118.
Tugidak I., 147; hunting party, 194.
Tungus nomads, 64-65; yurtas, 65, 72; traders, 141-142.
Tungus shore, 134.

Ugak I., 101, 124.
Uganak (Uganik) Bay, 116, 117.
Uganak (Uganik) I., 115, 116.
Ugaliagomiuts, 197.
Ugashik R., 197.
Ugashintsy, 196.
Uiatsk (Uyak) Bay, Kad'iak I., 188.
Ukamok (Chirikof) I., 118-119, 125, 147, 171, 192, 194, 195, 216.
Umnak I., plants, 207.
Unalashka I., 6, 97, 119, 124, 192.
Unalga I., 125.
Unimak I., 96, 98.

Viliui R., wealth of, 141.
Vitim R., Lena trib., headwaters, 38-39, 141.
Volcanic action, and new island (Bogoslof I., 1796), 96-97; earthquakes (1792), tidal waves, 206.
Volkova, Anna Alekseevna (1781-1834), poetess, "Ode to Khvostov and Davydov", 20-21.
Voskresensk (Resurrection Bay) artel, 192.

Whales, 122; hunting of, 195-196.
Wolf. See D'Wolf.
Women, work of, 196.
"Wooded island" (Lesnoi, now Woody I.), 102, 109, 112.

Yakutat (Bering Bay), 106.
Yurta, winter, construction of, on Lena, 41-42.

Zakharov, Iakutsk merchant, 72, 73.

KODIAK ISLAND
WITH ITS ENVIRONS 1805
(from Lisianskii)
Shuiak I.
AFOGNAK I.
Co. Settlement
Co. Settlement
Evreshec
(Marmot)
North I.
Uganik I.
Elovoi
(Spruce) I.
Pavlovsk (Kodiak)
Lesnoi (Woo
Barren I.
Uganik
Uiatsk
West Point
Co. Settlement
Chiniatsk Bay
K A D I A K
Karluk
Igak
Uiak Bay
Igak Bay
S.W.
Point
Alitak
Kiliuden Bay
Co.
Settlement
Saltkhidak I.
Three Saints Bay
South Point